IMAGES
of America

NAUGATUCK REVISITED

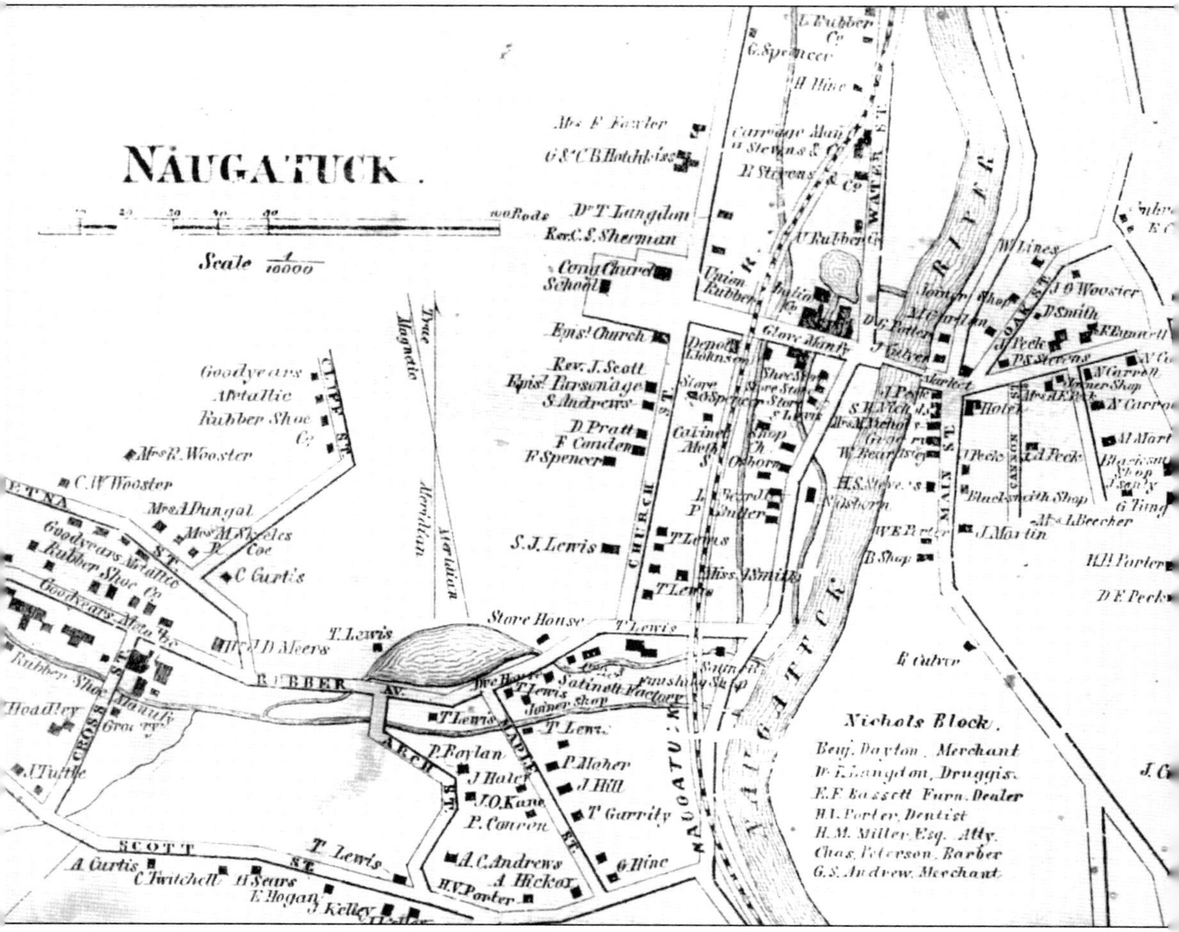

A Map of Naugatuck. This map fragment, cut from a larger map, features the center area of the borough, including some schools, churches, and factories, as well as the names of some individual property owners and local businessmen. The map is undated, but judging by some of the names, it appears to have been produced after 1850.

IMAGES *of America*

NAUGATUCK REVISITED

Ron Gagliardi

ARCADIA PUBLISHING

ISBN 978-0-7385-3603-3

Published by Arcadia Publishing
Charleston, South Carolina

Printed in the United States of America

Library of Congress Catalog Card Number: 2004103407

For all general information, contact Arcadia Publishing:
Telephone 843-853-2070
Fax 843-853-0044
E-mail sales@arcadiapublishing.com
For customer service and orders:
Toll-free 1-888-313-2665

Visit us on the Internet at www.arcadiapublishing.com

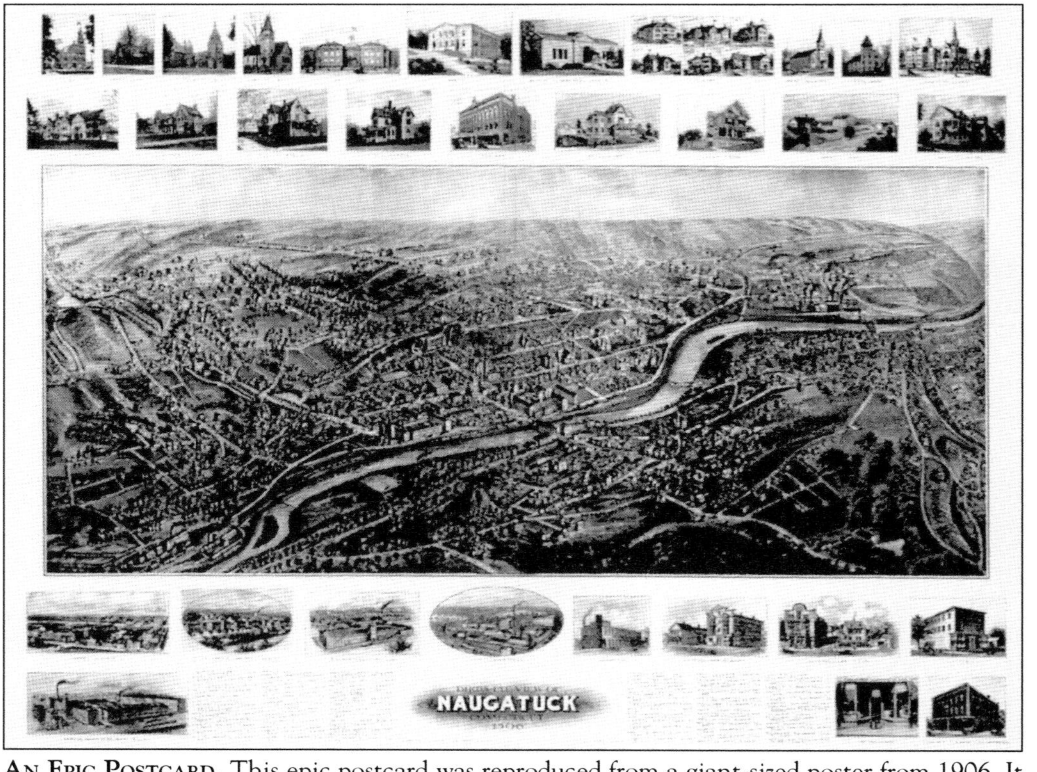

AN EPIC POSTCARD. This epic postcard was reproduced from a giant-sized poster from 1906. It presents an aerial view of the borough and features the architectural gems of Naugatuck. Shown is the U.S. Rubber (Uniroyal) complex, which now consists of only one building, No. 25. The postcards are available for purchase in the Naugatuck Historical Society Museum's gift shop.

Contents

Acknowledgments

I would like to thank my wife and children for putting up with my pain and anguish regarding approaching deadlines (again) and my parents for their continuing interest in my endeavors. I would also like to thank the three presidents of the Naugatuck Historical Society whose terms overlapped this project: Val Jablonowski, Tom Jablonowski, and especially Bridget Mariano, who, along with Sandra Clark and Marcha Cave, made up my main support team up at "the Naugazeum." Special thanks to my editor at Arcadia, Shannan Goff, who understood my approach-avoidance conflict and the contractions (and some conjunctions as well) during the birthing process of this book.

Thanks are also due to Dr. Nick Belantoni, Dana and Verna Blackwell, Kendra Bobowick, Frances Branco, Ove Braskerud, Carol Brousseau, Lucille Cannon, Shari and David Carda, Anita Carreiro, Kathleen Connolly, Tom Corcoran, Mary and Andy Doback, Ginny Donnelly, Duane Ellingson, Tony Esposito, Tom Fillius, Marge Findlay, Jeff Gagliardi, Ron Guerrera, Raechel Guest, Ken Hanks, Jacqui Hawes, Neil Hogan, Doreen Hurlburt, Mary Hyson, Frances Jackson, Joan Lamb, Earl Lindgrin, Cathy Mazotto, John McKee, Jim Miller, Jack Moffat, Alice Moss, Marilyn Nichols, Grace Nolan, Jack Pasquale (of the firm Ware, Fressola, Van Der Sluys and Adolphson), Howard Pincus, Jane Pronovost, Marshall Robinson, Jose Rodriguez, Ray Rossi, Lillian Schiller, Cliff Scofield, Frank Shea Jr., Jim and Ann Simons, Ed Spagnolo, Howard Thurston, Jim Trzaski, Sis Vanasse, John White, Helen Wilmot, Jennifer Wilmot, John Wiehn, and Ralph Zingarella.

This book is dedicated to the tireless members of the Naugatuck Historical Society and all of the "unsung heroes" who serve as docents and volunteers at the Naugatuck Historical Society Museum. They have managed to establish and run a top-flight museum in a gem of a historic building. The book is also dedicated to Dana Blackwell and the team of researchers who produced the first Arcadia book about Naugatuck. Finally, I would especially like to dedicate it to local baseball legend Frank "Spec" Shea, the Naugatuck Nugget, one of Naugatuck's brightest luminaries. Spec died on July 19, 2002. He made it big on the national baseball stage with the New York Yankees and the Washington Senators in the 1940s and 1950s. Despite his fame, he returned to his hometown, where he and his wife, Genevieve, raised their children and where he served his community as superintendent of parks and recreation.

INTRODUCTION

"Vhyfore Don't You Show Your Face In Naugatuck?" This question, put forth in Dutch and English on a post-1907 postcard, asks the receiver to come to Naugatuck for a visit. The title of the book you are holding, *Naugatuck Revisited,* asks you the same question.

About a decade ago, the members of the Naugatuck Historical Society were approached by Arcadia Publishing to produce a book about the history of their hometown. An intrepid band of historians met, divided the borough's past into chapters, and *Naugatuck* was born. That pioneering effort was very successful, and the team at Arcadia has requested a second peek into our historical closet to see what we have Naugatuckedaway. This book, *Naugatuck Revisited,* is my attempt to follow in the footsteps of town historian Dana Blackwell and his team, to continue their exploration and expand on Naugatuck's narrative. Without a doubt, theirs are big shoes to fill.

I became fascinated with the borough of Naugatuck during my tenure as the first executive director of the Naugatuck Historical Society Museum. Beginning in May 2002, I had the thrill of discovery that only comes when one is invited into a community's attic. I urge you to share the same sense of discovery I enjoyed "surfing through the centuries" every day at the office. Hunt down your trusty magnifying glass and take a close look at the images contained in this book. Most of them have been culled from the extensive collection archived at the Naugatuck Historical Society Museum, located in the imposing architectural treasure known as the former railroad station. But beyond viewing the images, I hope you will take the time to really read this book. You will learn the answers to questions about our corner of the world that you never knew you had.

Tucked away in this book's pages are answers to these fascinating questions: Which famous chimpanzee associated with which groundbreaking morning television show used to visit Naugatuck to buy sneakers? Which four exotic tropical plants are responsible for Naugatuck's success? Which famous cartoon featured a prominent local building? Does Naugatuck have something in common with the Lincoln Memorial? Did a roving band of pirates ever bury treasure in Naugatuck? Does Salem School have a major connection to the *Wizard of Oz* movie? Which famous U.S. senator visited here while campaigning for president? Which famous star of *Gone with the Wind* once got off the train in Naugatuck and found out it was the wrong stop? Which MVP pitcher for the New York Yankees was born and raised here? Is it illegal to use your mouth in a certain way on Naugatuck's streets?

Treat this book with care; it is a time machine! If you are not careful, you will find yourself transported back in time. Should you give in to this impulse, sit back, close your eyes, and relax for a few seconds before turning the page. Picture years melting, decades and centuries dropping away. Prepare to imagine yourself as an American Indian in a pristine forest or an inventor tinkering and toiling at your new company, a pieceworker on an assembly line or a pitcher in the World Series in Yankee Stadium. You will see and be these people, at least for the time you spend between the covers of this book.

I hope I have convinced you to "walk the walk" while I "talk the talk" about Naugatuck in the following pages. Take off your sneakers, wade into this river of research, and wiggle your toes. I assure you, Naugatuck's historical waters are warm and the pebbles of its past are smooth.

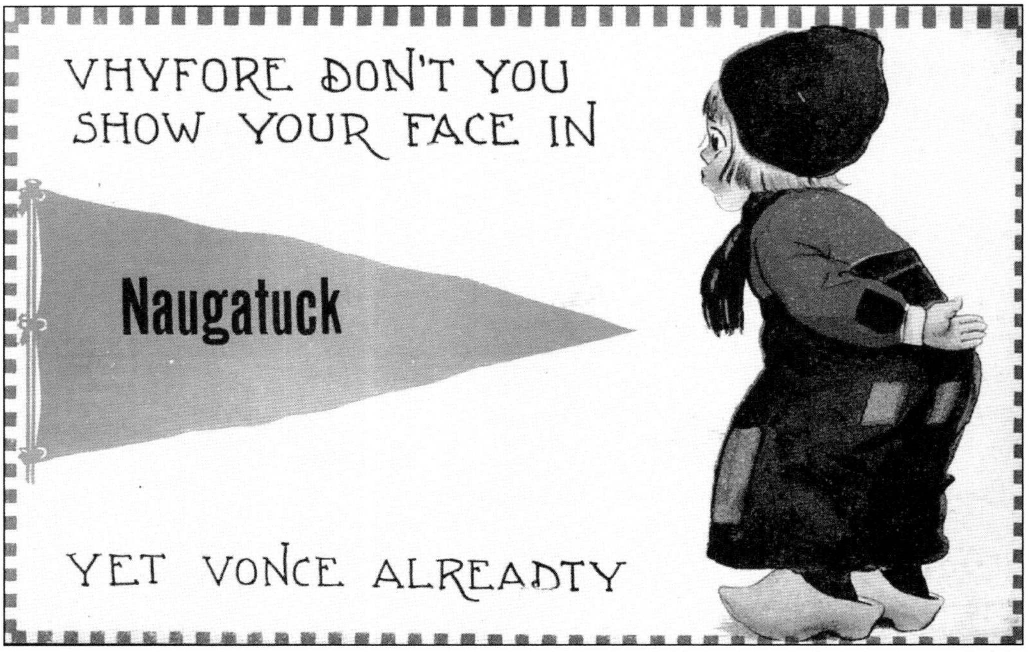

The Dutch Kids Series. Connecticut artist Bernhardt Wall produced this series, probably for the Barton and Spooner Company. The cards featured Dutch kids and phrases in Dutch-accented English. A municipality's name was printed into a space on the card, thus "personalizing" it for that place.

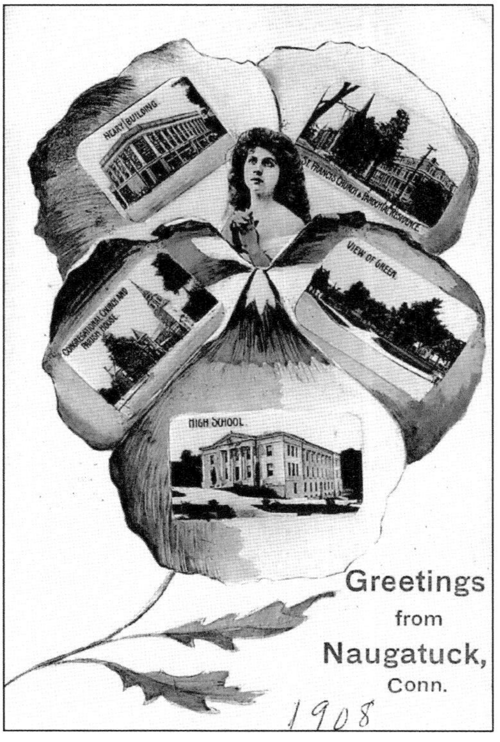

A Pansy Princess. This postcard introduced its recipient to a bouquet of Naugatuck's beauty among the petals of a pansy. The four buildings are the Neary Building, the St. Francis Church and parochial residence, the Congregational church and parish house, and the high school. A view of the green is also included. The woman in the center appears to be praying or giving thanks. This type of group shot was common in the early 20th century.

One

The Early Days and Beyond

The river that flows through the borough of Naugatuck has attracted people for as long as humans have inhabited the area. The first residents were American Indians; they were followed by white men, who started settling here between 1675 and 1680. The river has borne the name Naugatuck on documents since the first deed was given to Thomas Wheeler in 1657. There are various stories behind the origin of the name. One is that it comes from the Algonquin *nau-ka-tungh*, meaning "one tree," which could refer to a tree that may have acted as a beacon or landmark for the tribes in the area. It may also have originated from the Paugasset *nequettukh*, translated as "place of one lone tree." Another possible meaning, "bend-in-the-river place," comes from *wnogque tookoke*, a name that had been applied to Stockbridge, Massachusetts. The American Indian name was not the town's name of choice until after 1800. According to Helen Earle Sanders in her *Connecticut Town Origins*, the name was transferred to the river from some locality on or near it and from river to valley and town." At one time, in an American Indian deed from 1868, the river was called the "Nawcatuck River."

Regardless of how it came to be known by its current name, the area now called Naugatuck has had other names as well. It was part of *Matetacoke* or *Mattatuck* until that community became known as Waterbury in 1686. The first settler, Samuel Hickox Jr., built his house here in 1702. At that time, parts of the area were known as South Farms (as it is south of Waterbury) and Judd's Meadows; the former name, given in honor of landowner William Judd, was bestowed sometime before 1679. Part of the town was called Deacon's Meadow for 100 years. In 1773, the town was granted its own ministry, called the Salem Society, and the name Salem Bridge replaced Judd's Meadows. The first town meeting, in mid-June 1844, resulted in Naugatuck being separated from Waterbury.

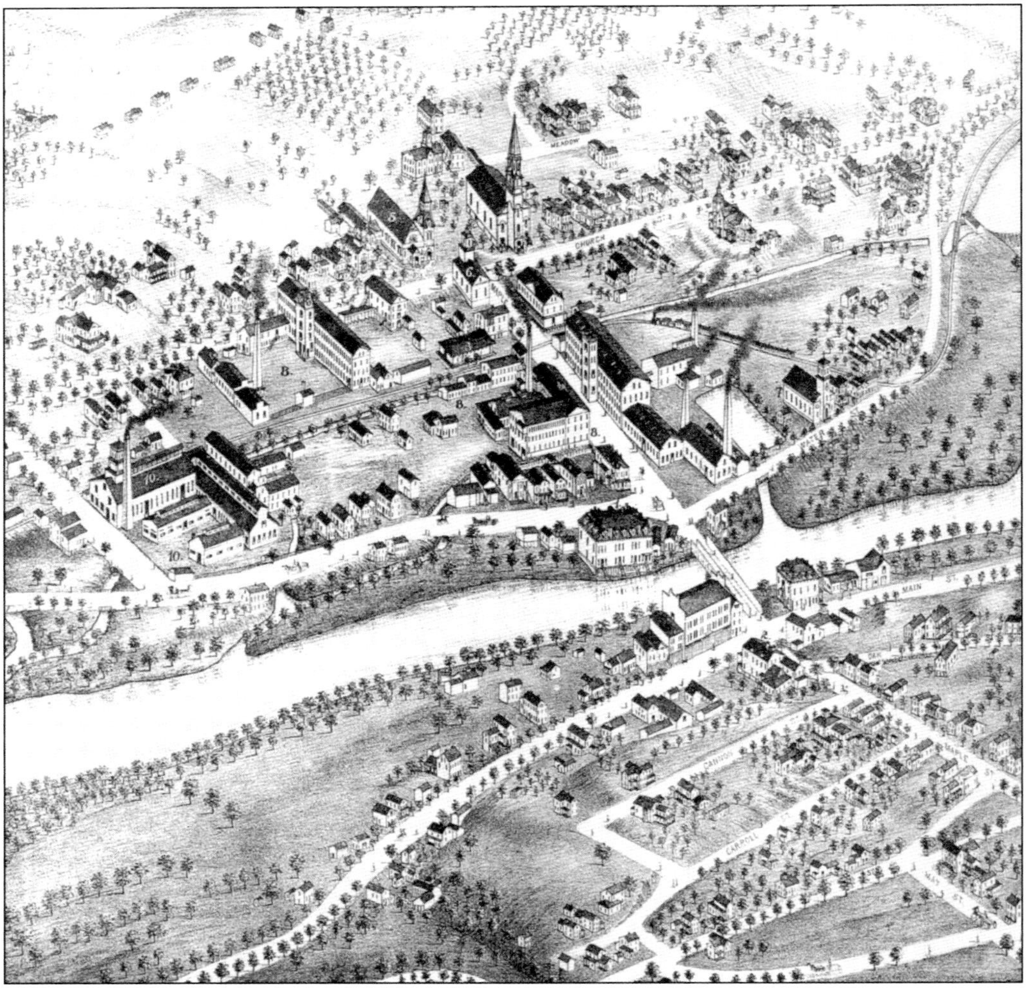

A MAP OF NAUGATUCK, 1877. O. H. Bailey and Company of Boston was the consummate mapmaker. The company's maps were aerial views of cities and towns made without the use of hot-air balloons, airplanes, or helicopters. The artist had the uncanny ability to view a municipality from ground level and draw it is if seen from the air. Naugatuck was one of the lucky towns to have had this unique portrait done in 1877.

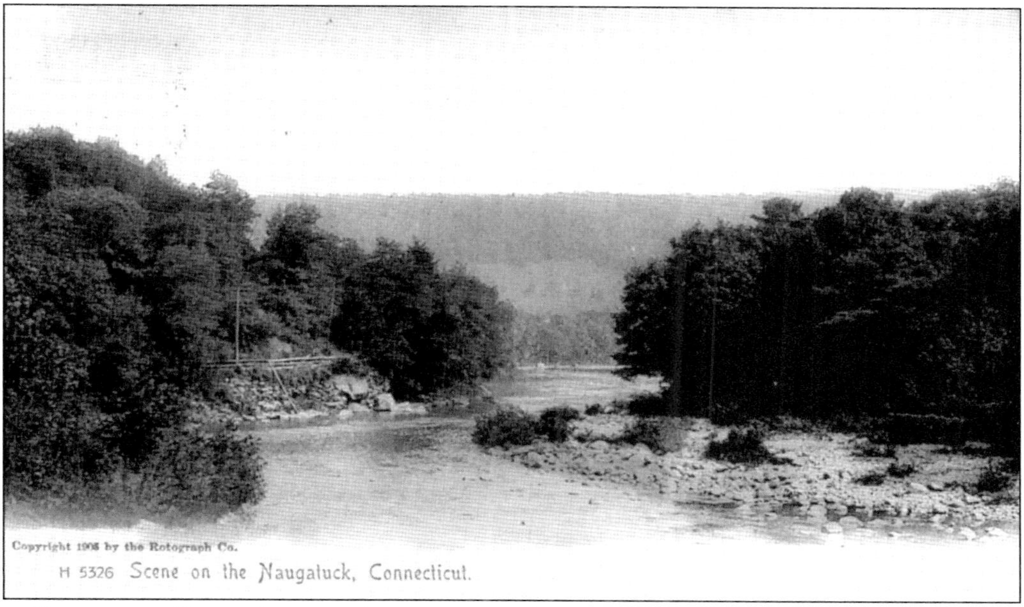

A Bend in the River. Imagine that you are an American Indian and you have come down to the Naugatuck River to drink, hunt, or fish. This is the pristine scene that would have greeted hundreds of generations of your people. Then, visitors arrived—not neighboring tribes, but a new "tribe" of fair-skinned people. There were only a few at first, beginning *c.* 1674. We can only wonder what those initial encounters must have been like.

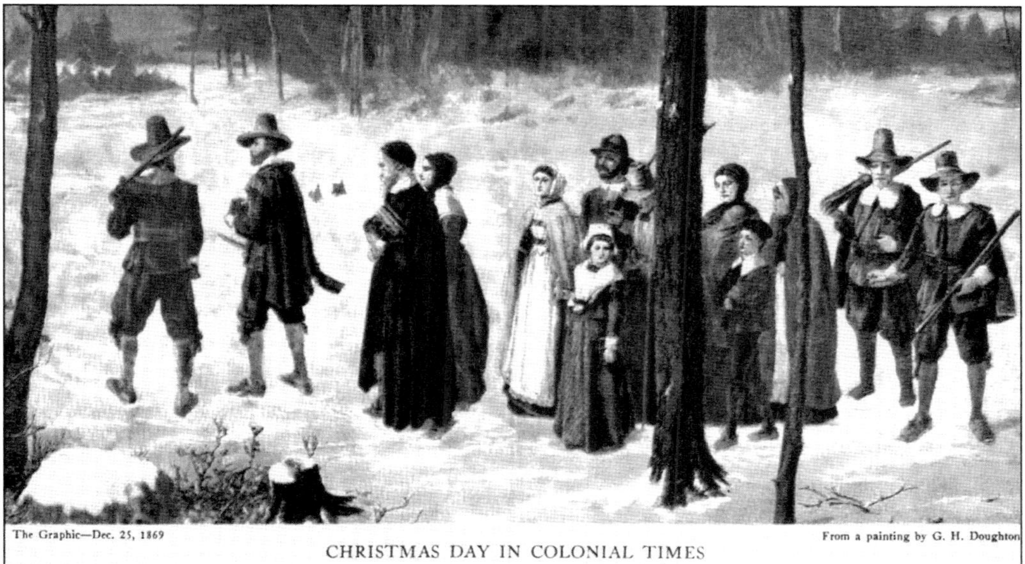

Intrepid Settlers. G. H. Doughton painted this rendition of a band of early settlers. They are walking through wintry woods, possibly on the way to Sunday services. The granting of a "winter privilege," the right for settlers to worship in their own community in order to avoid a long trek in harsh conditions, was one of the events that led to the formation of the Salem Society in what was then known as Judd's Meadows. Eventually, the name of the town was changed to Salem Bridge.

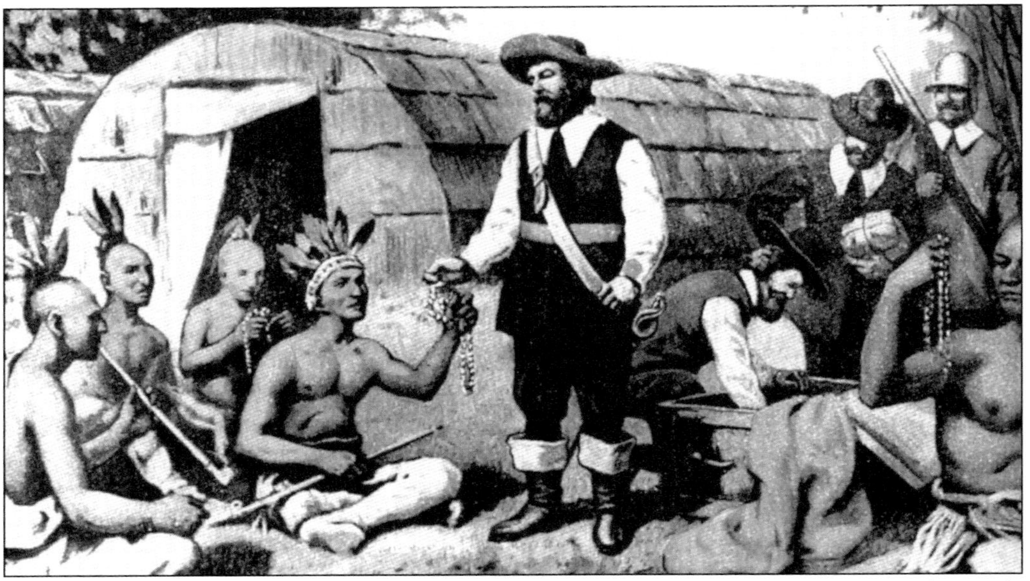

Buying Land from the American Indians. Pictured above is an artist's impression of an early land transaction between the newly arrived white man and the American Indian owners of the land. White men began visiting this area in the 1650s. Land was purchased from the Tunxis, Algonquin, and Paugasset tribes. Sometimes, land was purchased more than once from different tribes who had conflicting claims.

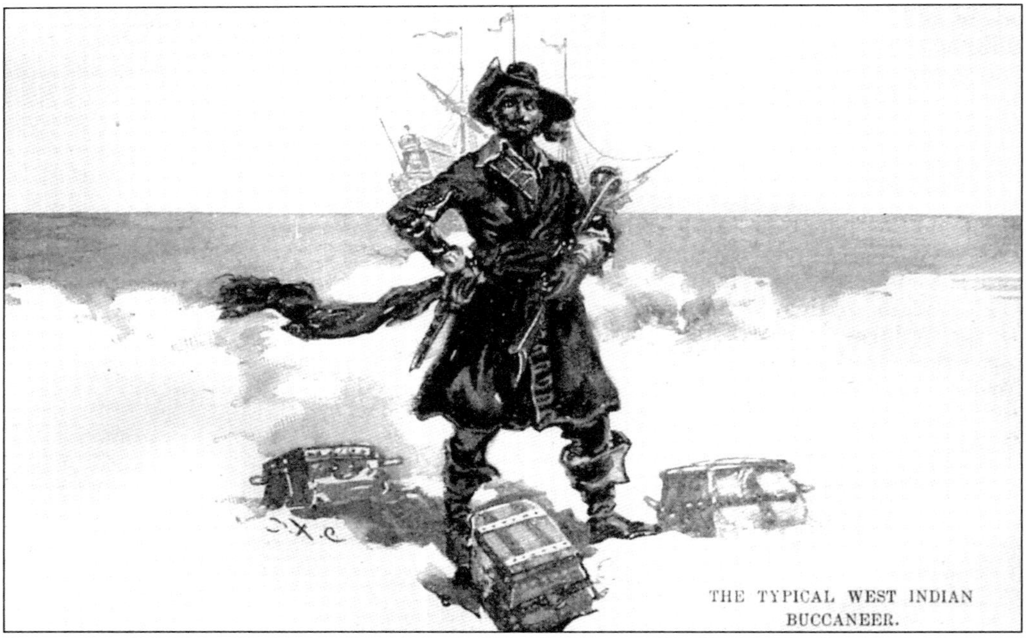

THE TYPICAL WEST INDIAN BUCCANEER.

Shiver Me Timbers. A pirate named Scarrett prowled Long Island Sound in the days prior to the Revolutionary War. Allegedly, a British man-of-war chased the pirate ship up the Housatonic River and into the Naugatuck River, where Scarrett deliberately beached and burned his ship. The story goes that the pirates fought off the British and buried their booty someplace in the High Rock area.

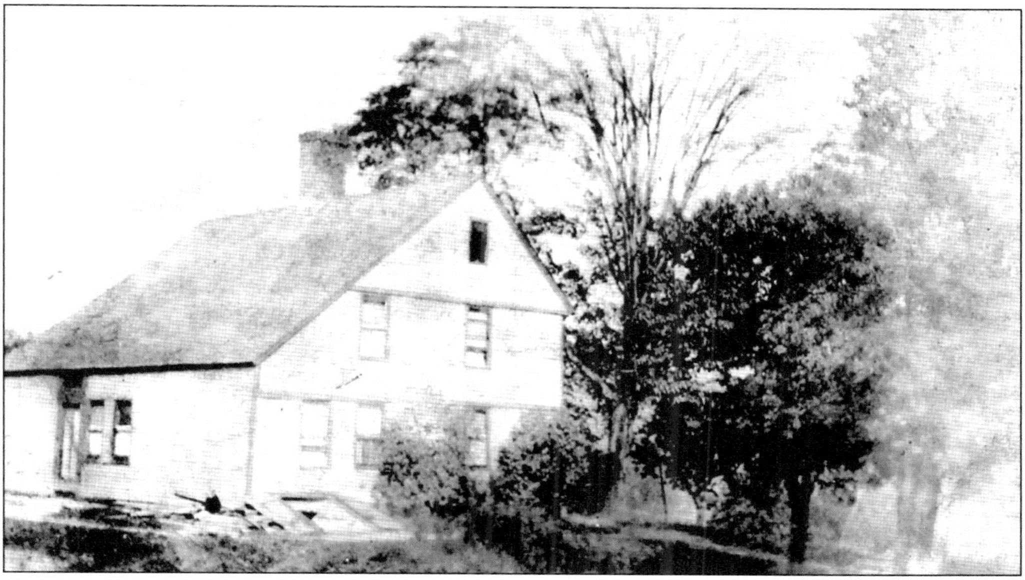

The Newly Discovered Oldest House in Naugatuck, Before. The John Lewis House was believed to be the oldest house in Naugatuck, dating from c. 1734. However, this house, the Scott House, at 67 Spencer Street, may date to before 1720. Research by Virginia Howard reveals that it was built by Edmund Scott, and, because of a stipulation in the original 1716 land grant, it would have to have been constructed c. 1720.

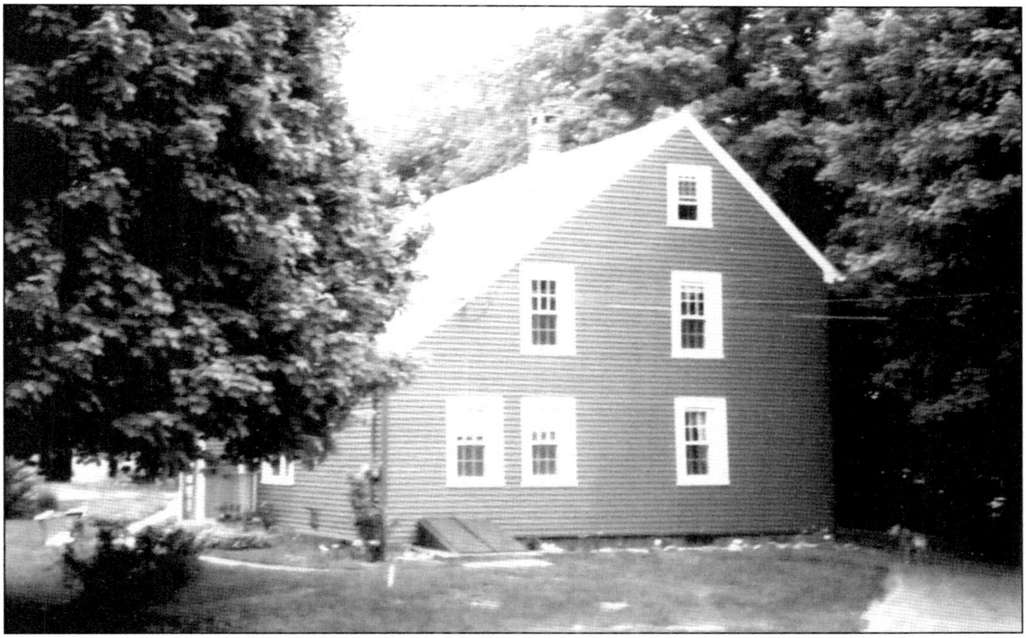

The Newly Discovered Oldest House in Naugatuck, After. The present owners of this house have been renovating the home since they purchased it in 2002. It is a classic saltbox, named after its resemblance to salt containers of Colonial times. The owners have saved nails, shingles, and part of the original floor, which will become the core of a traveling exhibit to be called "Anatomy of a Saltbox."

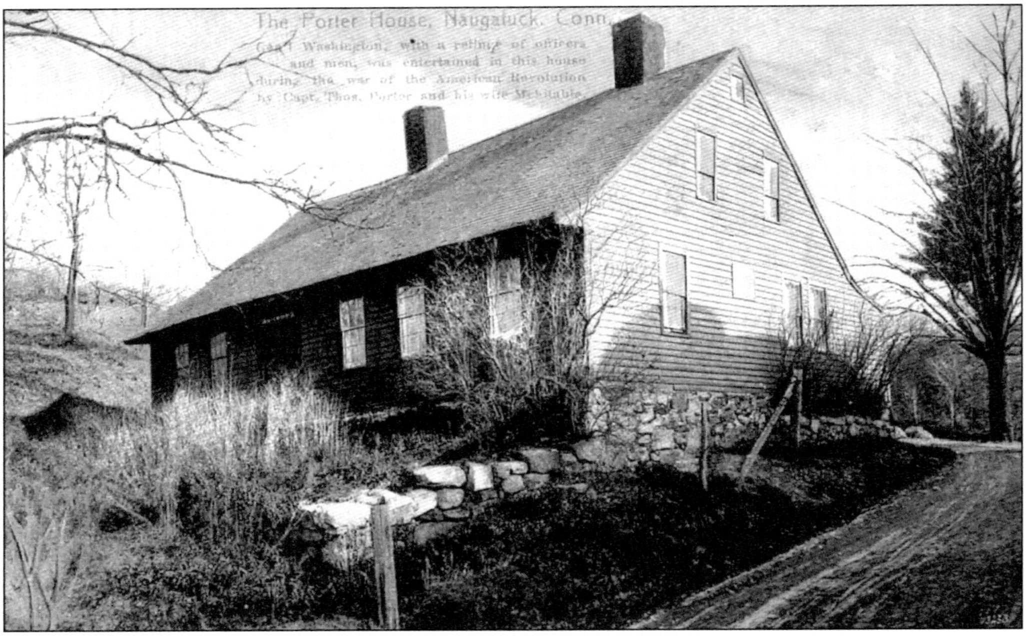

THE PORTER HOUSE: GEORGE WASHINGTON NEVER SLEPT HERE. Built by David Porter *c.* 1752, the house was an inn on the New Haven–Waterbury turnpike. In the summer of 1779, during the Revolutionary War, soldiers stayed here on their way to face the British in New Haven and West Haven. The story eventually included George Washington among those guests, but historians say that this was just a legend.

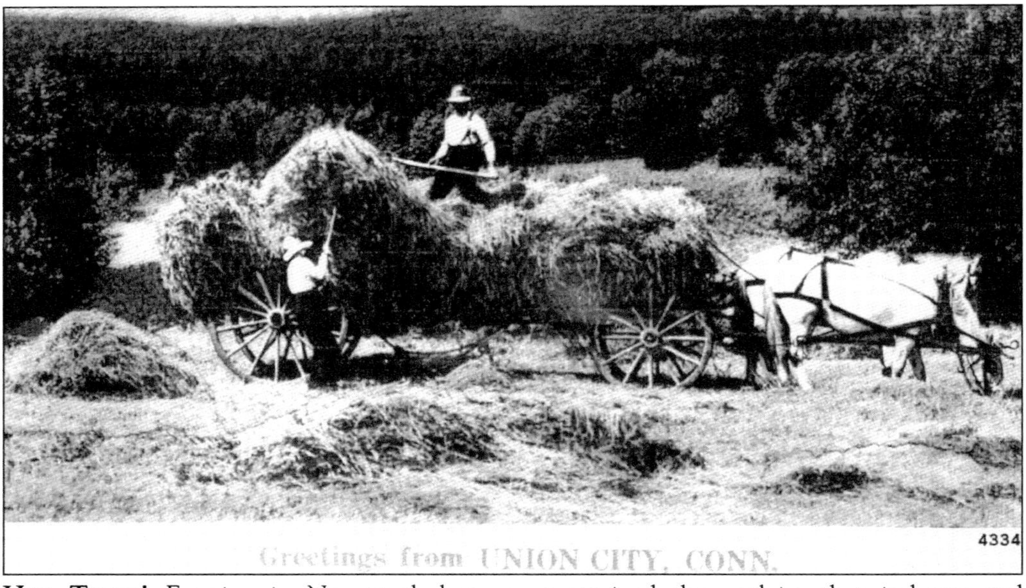

HAY THERE! Farming in Naugatuck has never received the acclaim that industry and manufacturing have. Brothers Dick, Louis, and Dave Wilmot own the last remaining major agricultural parcel in the borough, in Gunntown. It consists of 200 acres, 50 of which are still used for haying. They have formed a partnership that includes their Fox Cliff Farm and an Agway store they have operated there for almost 50 years.

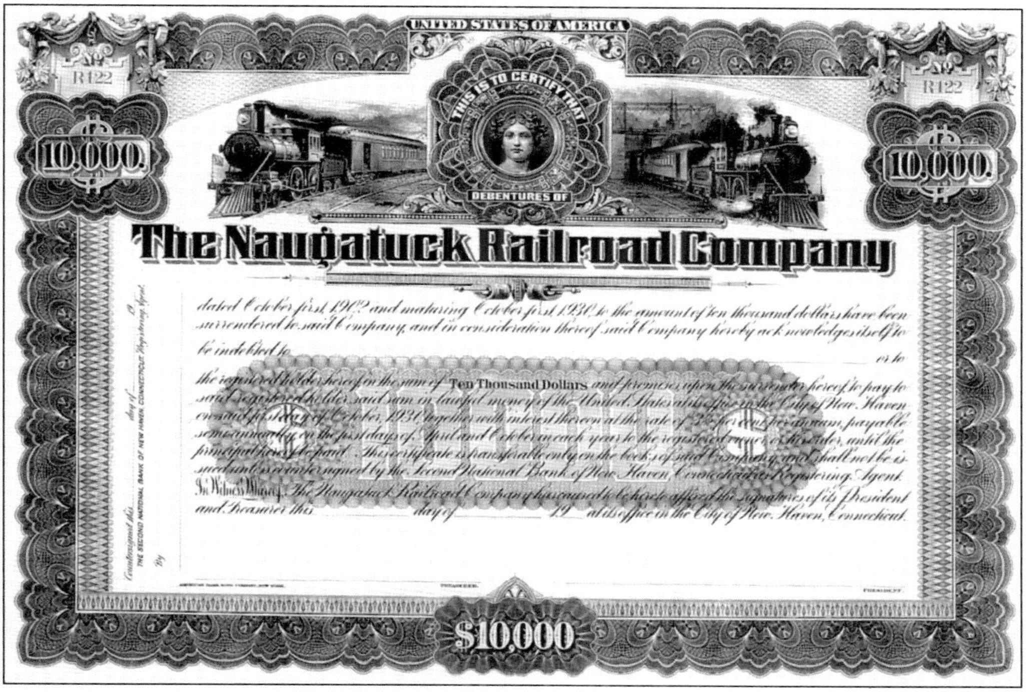

Keeping the Railroad on Track. This $10,000 bond was intended to raise capital for the Naugatuck Railroad. It was never issued and was obtained recently in an on-line auction on eBay for about $15.00. The money raised from the sale of these bonds in 1902 was used to move the railroad tracks to their current location. At the time the railroad was established, in 1845, many local investors supported Alfred Bishop in his successful endeavor.

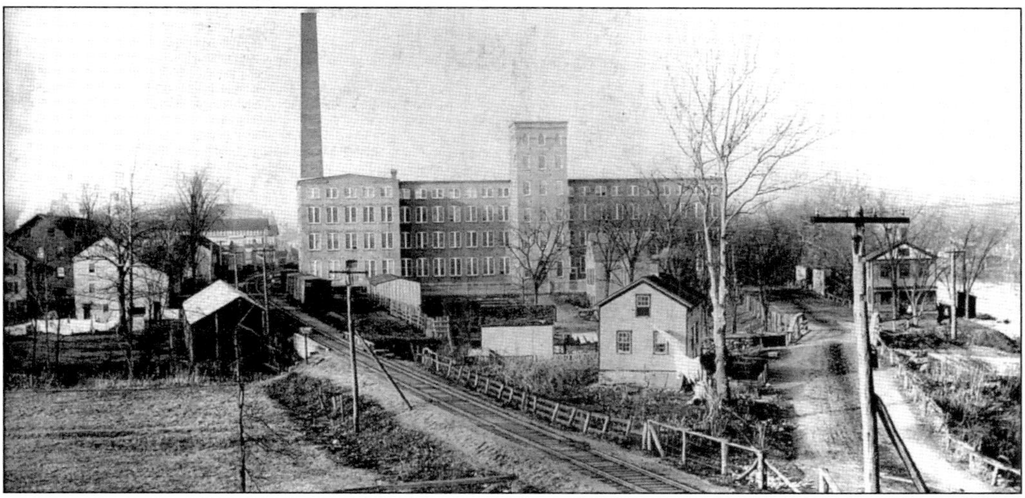

A Moving Experience. From 1906 to 1909, the railroad tracks were shifted from their previous location, which ran through the site of the original depot (where the fire department is now), to their present location. This removed some dangerous grade crossings. The bed of the Naugatuck River had to be moved to the east for almost two miles in order to accomplish the rerouting of the tracks. This view looks north toward the rubber shop on Rubber Avenue at Water Street.

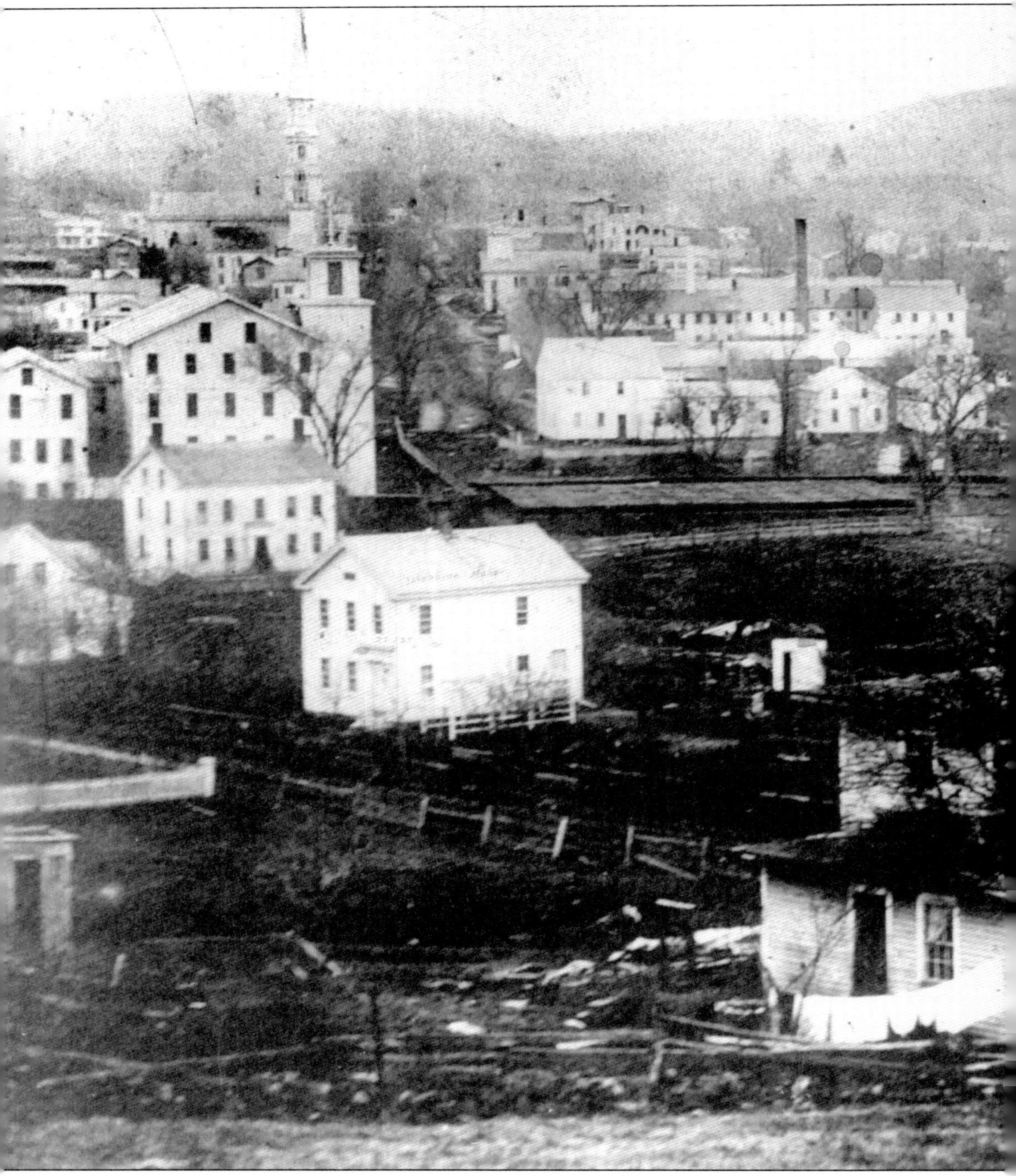

One of Naugatuck's Earliest Photographs. This is what Naugatuck looked like during the Civil War. During this era, Naugatuck companies were providing ponchos, blankets, rubber clothing, and carriage wheel hub replacements to the war effort. Of the approximately 2,400 citizens of Naugatuck at the time, 236 of them, nearly 10 percent of the population, left the borough and served in the Union army. Many joined Company H of the Connecticut 15th

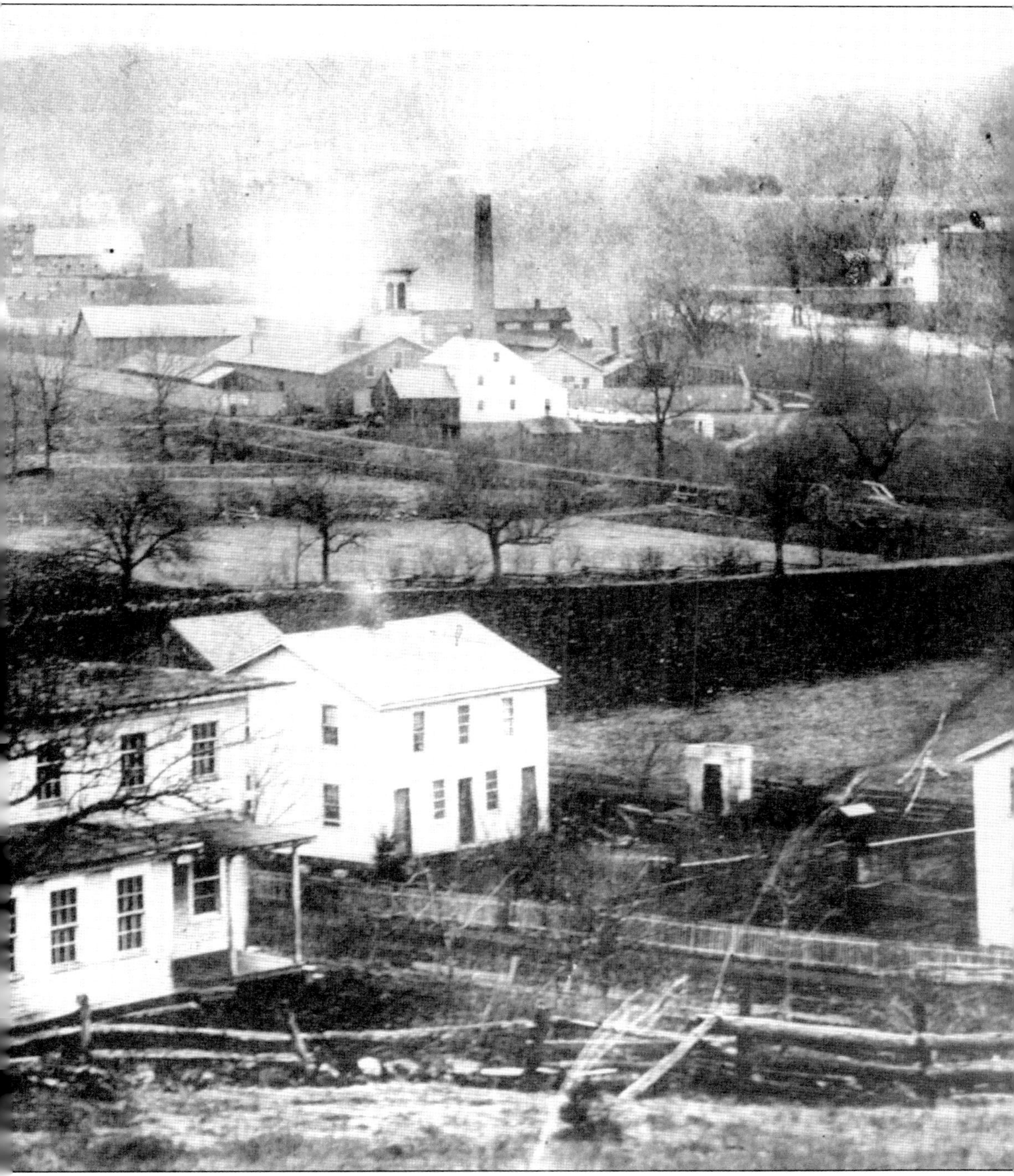

Regiment. This view, dating from 1865, looks north from Gorman Street. It was found tucked away in a crowded closet in the basement of the Naugatuck Historical Society Museum. The spire of the Congregational church is visible on the left side of the photograph; the Union Center District School is just in front of it. The building with the tall smokestack on the right is the Goodyear India Rubber Glove Company on Maple Street.

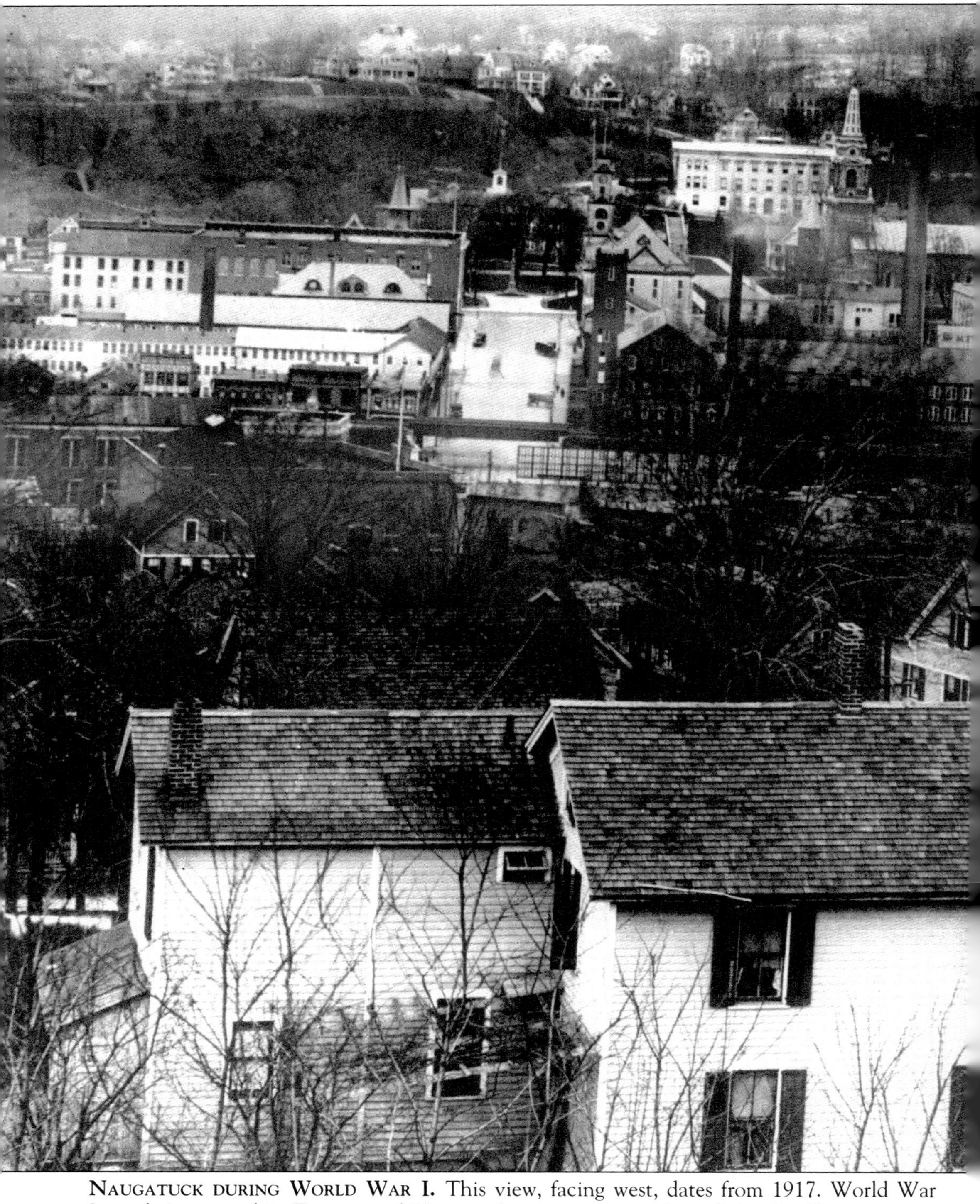

Naugatuck during World War I. This view, facing west, dates from 1917. World War I was being waged in Europe, and Naugatuck sent many people to fight the German army; 836 never returned. Local companies experienced a shortage of manpower and encouraged

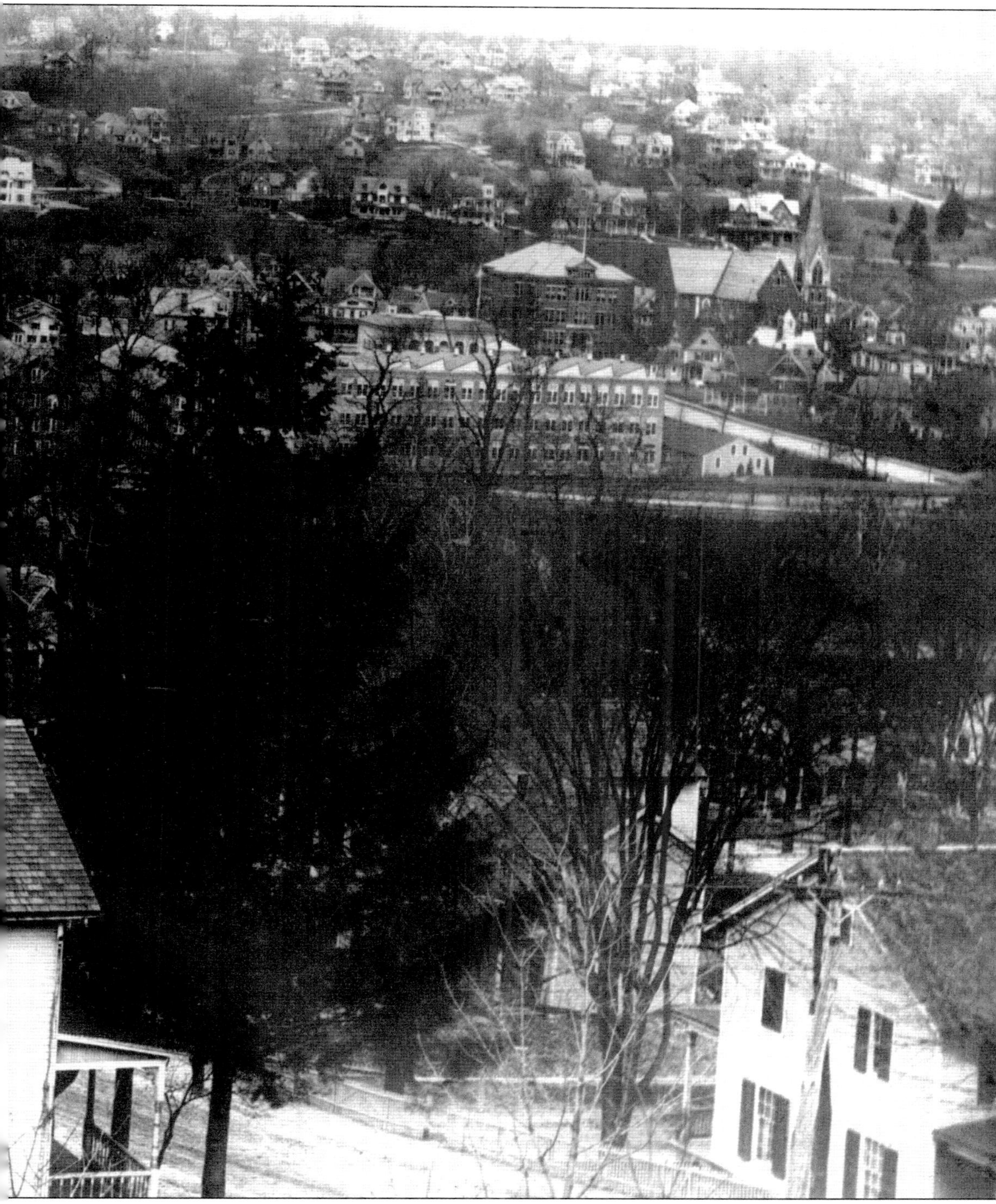

women to work in the factories. The town hall is visible in the center of the photograph. The St. Francis Roman Catholic Church is the building with the spire on the right.

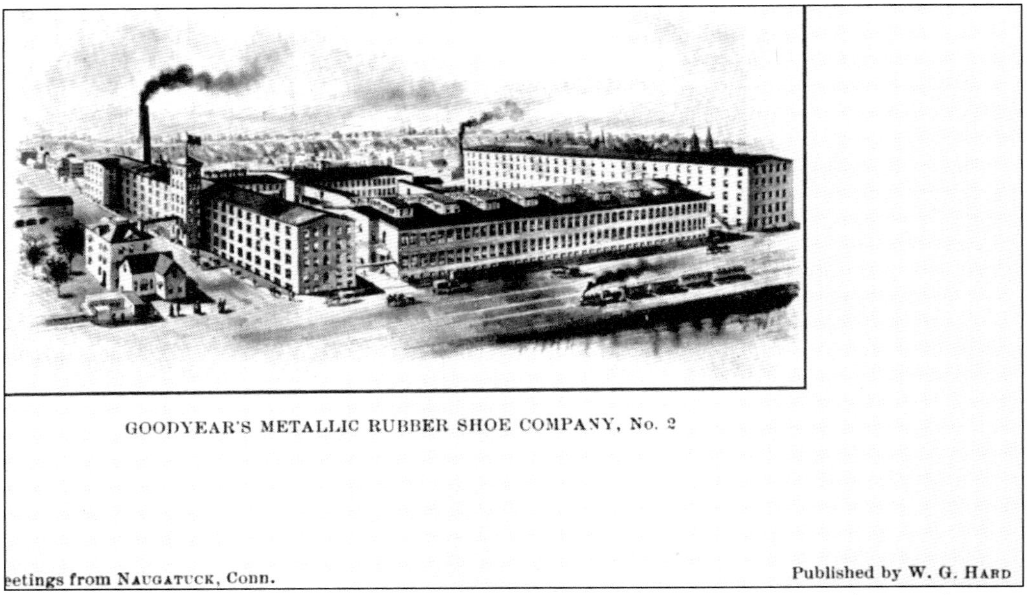

AERIAL ARTWORKS. These views of the prominent Goodyear companies provide an indication of the amount of acreage covered by local manufacturing complexes. They were cities unto themselves.

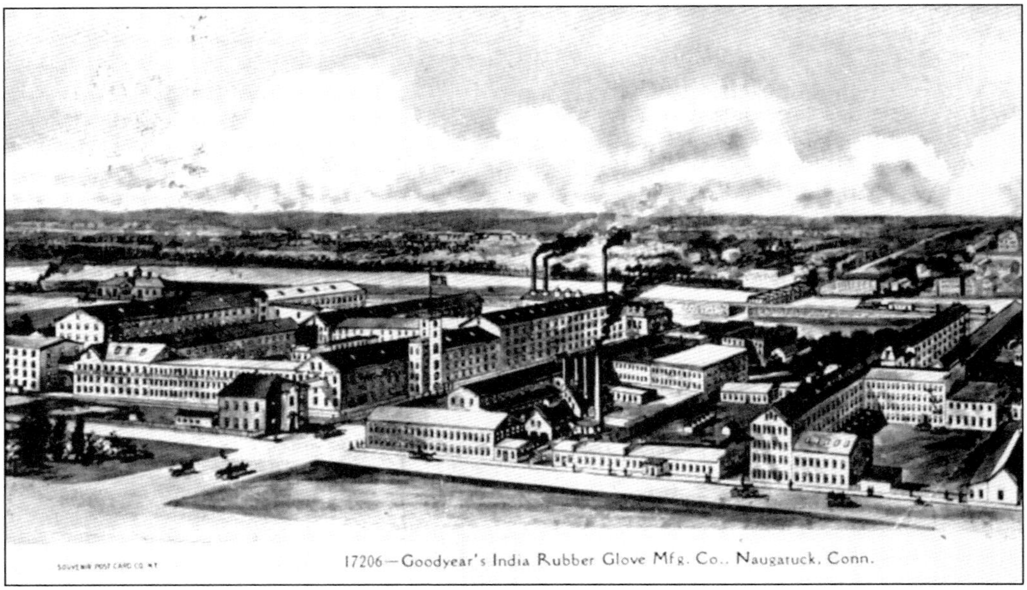

Two

LOCAL LUMINARIES, RESIDENTS, AND VISITORS

Naugatuck has had its share of local luminaries. Some are known only within its borders: businessmen, sports figures, politicians, and authors. The reader may recognize names like J. H. Whittemore, Milo Lewis, English Channel swimmer Peter Jurszinsky, Ray Legenza, William Rado, author William Leuchars, and Dr. Gerald Labriola. Many others have made a name for themselves and Naugatuck nationwide and even worldwide. Millions of people know the names of Charles Goodyear, discoverer of the vulcanization process for rubber; Peter Paul Halajian, founder of the Peter Paul Candy Company; Frank "Spec" Shea of the New York Yankees; internationally known herbalist Chief Two Moon Meridas; and Gilbert Adrian, the Hollywood costume designer of *Wizard of Oz* fame. This chapter will introduce you to or reacquaint you with many of these individuals. You will also meet other local characters, such as Johnny of the Woods and Civil War veteran Sheldon Payne.

Look carefully, for some of the photographs contain hundreds of people, frozen in time. You may want to utilize a magnifying glass for an even closer examination than the unaided eye would permit.

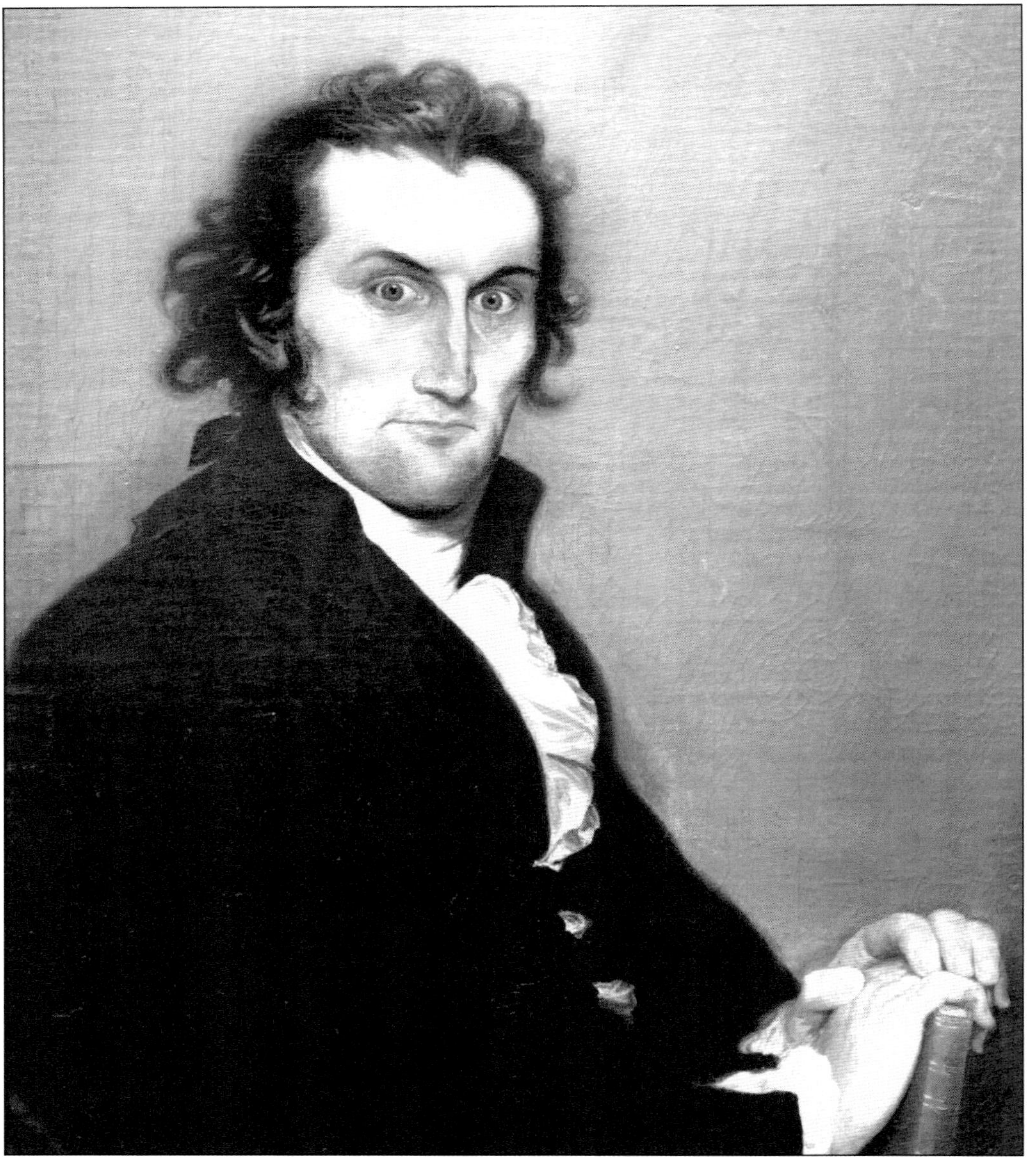

The Doctor is In. This portrait of Naugatuck-born Dr. Lemuel Hopkins has a stare that can freeze the casual art lover whose gaze happens upon those hypnotic orbs. The original oil painting was done by copyist Otis Hovey from a Copley portrait. This eye-catching artwork commands patrons' attention from the wall of the 19th Century Gallery of the Mattatuck Museum in Waterbury. Dr. Hopkins (1750–1801) offered medical attention to residents of Hartford and Litchfield and was also a founder of the Connecticut Medical Society. He was a member of the Hartford Wits, a group of *bon vivants* and *raconteurs*. One of his poetic pearls, entitled "Epitaph to a Patient Killed by a Cancer Quack," survives to balance the severity of his canvas glare: "Here lies a fool flat on his back, / The victim of a cancer quack, / Who lost his money and his life, / By plaster, caustic and by knife. / The cause is this—a pimple rose, / Southeast a little of his nose, / Which daily reddened and grew bigger / As too much drinking gave it vigor."

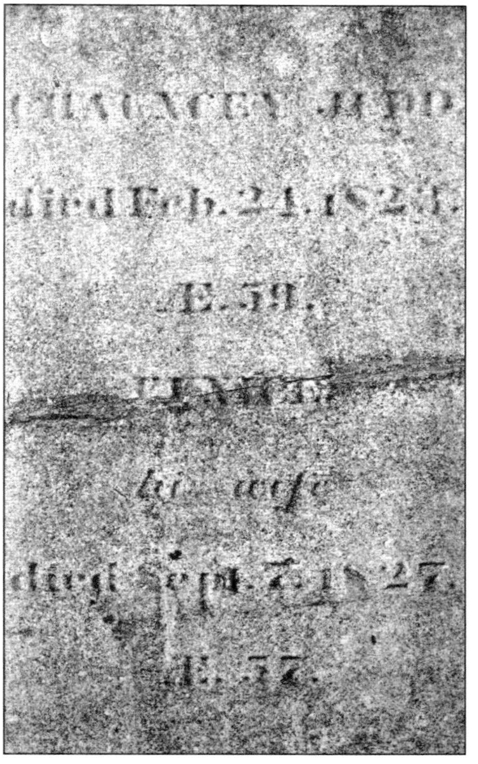

CHANUCEY JUDD: KIDNAPPED BY TORIES! The legend of Chauncey Judd is one that actually happened. Late one night in 1776, a band of young Tories was returning to Gunntown with loot from a raid in Bethany. They encountered 16-year-old Chauncey Judd on the road. He recognized some of their number, and they felt he could implicate them in the theft, so they kidnapped him. He was rescued five days later. This is a closeup of his tombstone.

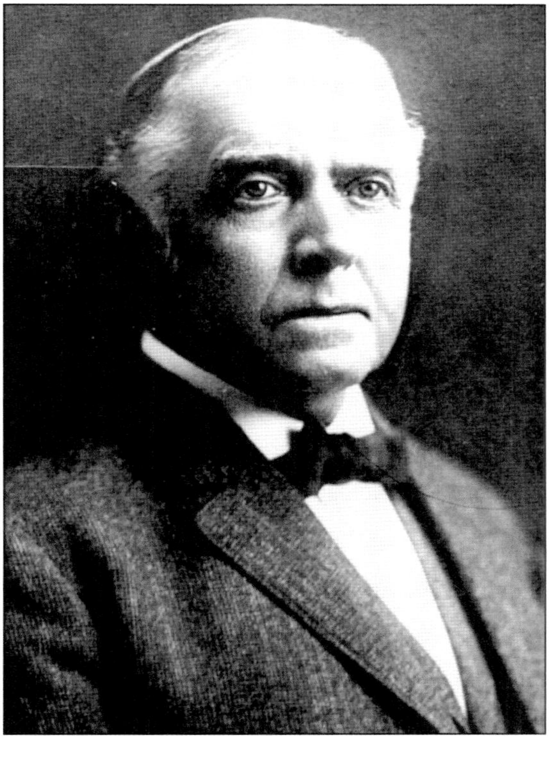

NAUGATUCK'S GREAT BENEFACTOR. John Howard Whittemore (1837–1910) arrived in Naugatuck in the spring of 1858 as a 21-year-old entrepreneur. He parlayed a $1,000 loan from a bank into an investment with Bronson Tuttle. They formed a partnership that eventually became the Naugatuck Malleable Iron Company, which was the foundation of Whittemore's immense fortune and philanthropic endeavors.

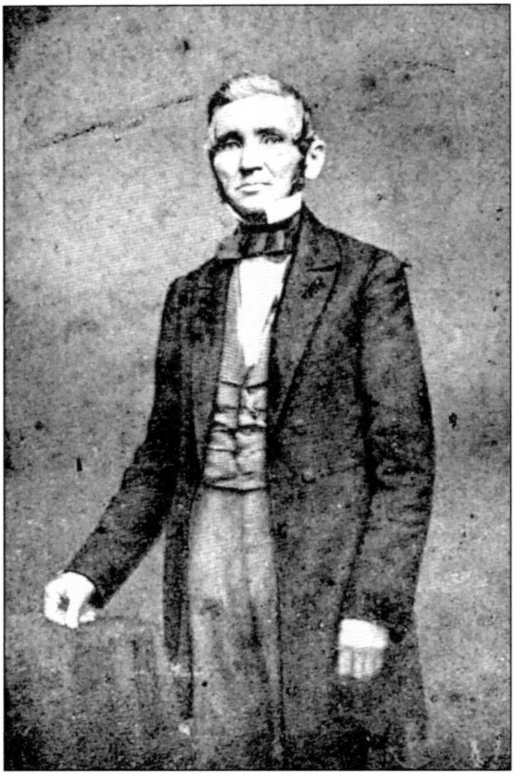

GOODYEARVILLE? The name Charles Goodyear shouts "rubber!" This man put Naugatuck on the map. If the town had not been named Naugatuck, it could have been called Goodyearville. Goodyear's story is a book waiting to be written; in fact, at least two books have been written about him: *Noble Obsession*, by Charles Slack, and *The Goodyear Story*, by Richard Korman. This photograph has "Brady" and "New York" printed on it and may have been taken by the famed Civil War photographer.

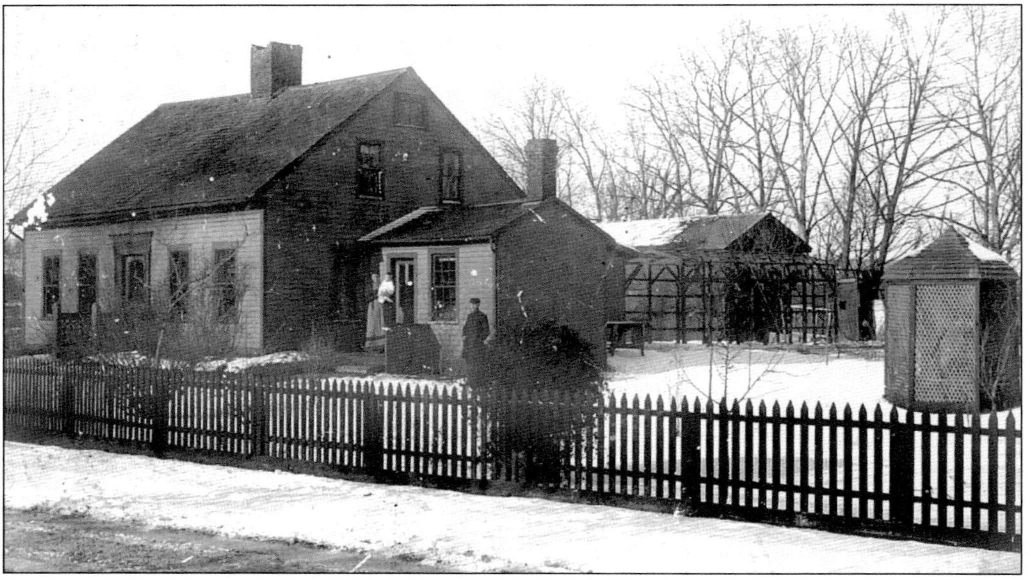

THE HOUSE THAT RUBBER BUILT. Legend has it that the spill that mixed sulfur with molten rubber occurred on the stove of the Goodyear home in Union City. It was an accident, but Goodyear's discovery of vulcanization, named after Vulcan, the Roman god of fire and volcanoes, actually happened in 1839, when he lived in Woburn, Massachusetts. Despite the fact that he earned a considerable fortune from his invention, he died $200,000 in debt.

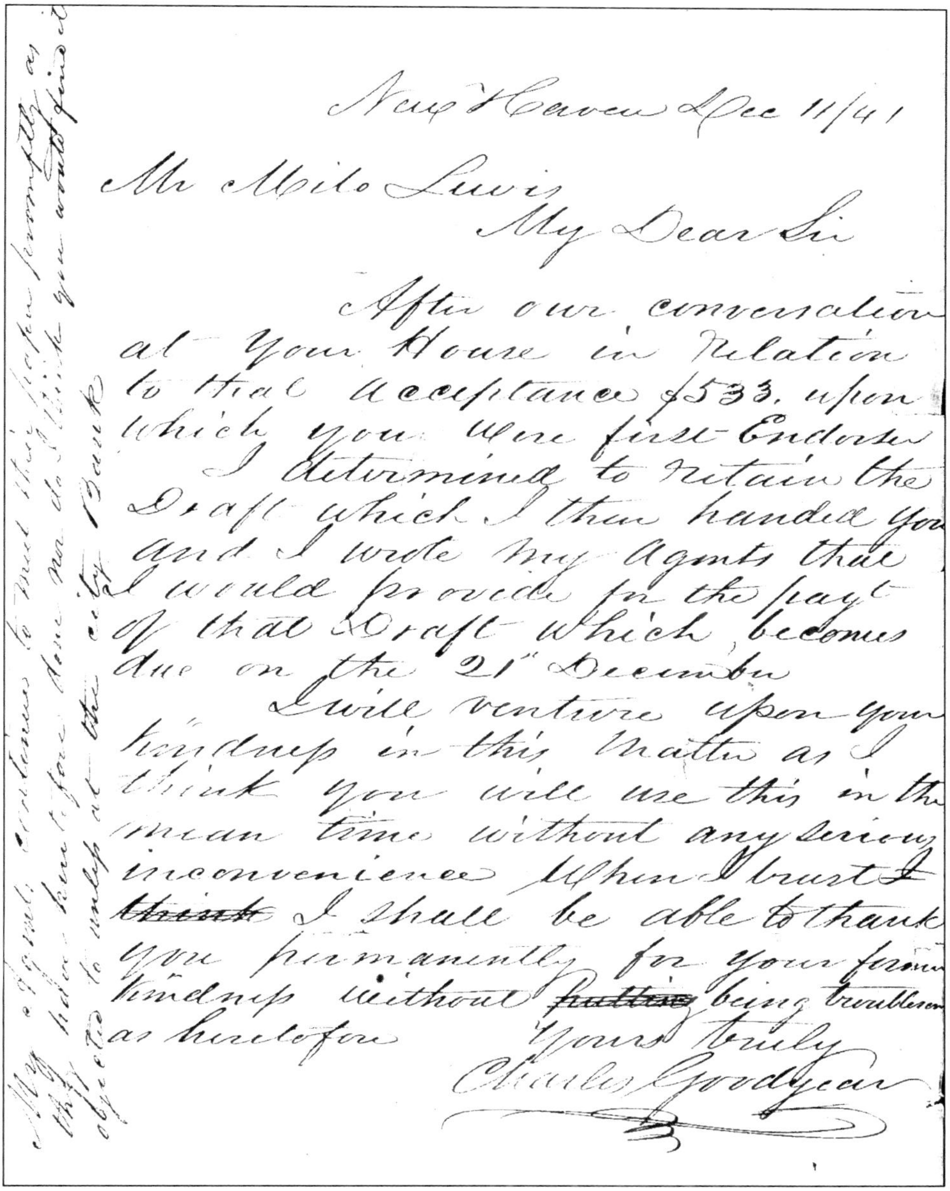

New Haven Dec 11/41

Mr Milo Lewis

My Dear Sir

After our conversation at your House in Relation to that acceptance $533. upon which you were first Endorser I determined to retain the Draft which I then handed you and I wrote my Agents that I would provide for the payt of that Draft which becomes due on the 21st December

I will venture upon your kindness in this matter as I think you will use this in the mean time without any serious inconvenience When I trust ~~think~~ I shall be able to thank you permanently for your former kindness without ~~putting~~ being troublesome as heretofore

Yours truly
Charles Goodyear

My Agent continues to meet this paper promptly as they have heretofore done nor do I think you would find it [illegible] to [illegible] at the city Bank

A Historic Letter to a Goodyear Partner. This letter's appearance in this book is a lucky accident. It was acquired by the author from an area collector who was selling a collection of letters from a Naugatuck resident and historian named Conrad Ham. Among the letters was this one to Goodyear's eventual partner, Milo Lewis. This letter was written less than two years before the fateful meeting in the summer of 1843, when Goodyear impressed Milo Lewis, William Deforest, Samuel J. Lewis (all three from Naugatuck) and Thomas Elliot (of New Haven) with his vulcanized rubber. That meeting led to Naugatuck's rubber industry. As far as can be determined, this letter was previously unknown, and its existence is being revealed for the first time in this book. According to Charles Slack, author of *Noble Obsession*, "Charles Goodyear was rather disorganized and did not keep adequate records, so any find like this letter is important for filling in the pieces of his puzzle."

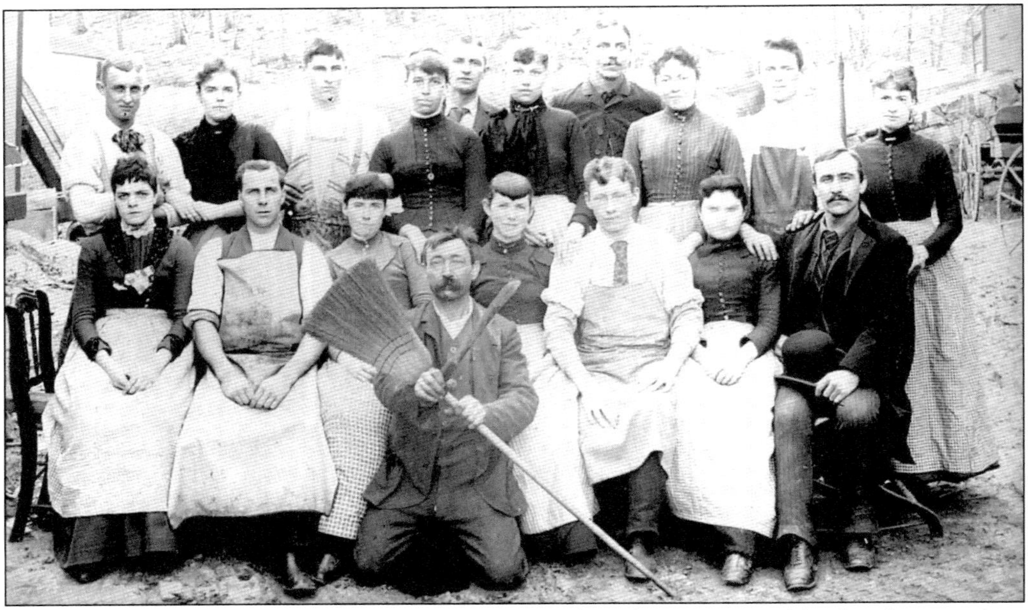

More Than Meets the Eye. It was December 1869 when this group posed for the photographer. Perhaps the crossed implements symbolize something, or maybe the photographer was feeling playful. Some of the members of the group may have enjoyed a closer relationship than that of coworkers. If you look carefully, you may discern some individuals' hands on others' shoulders and wrists. Dating in the workplace is nothing new.

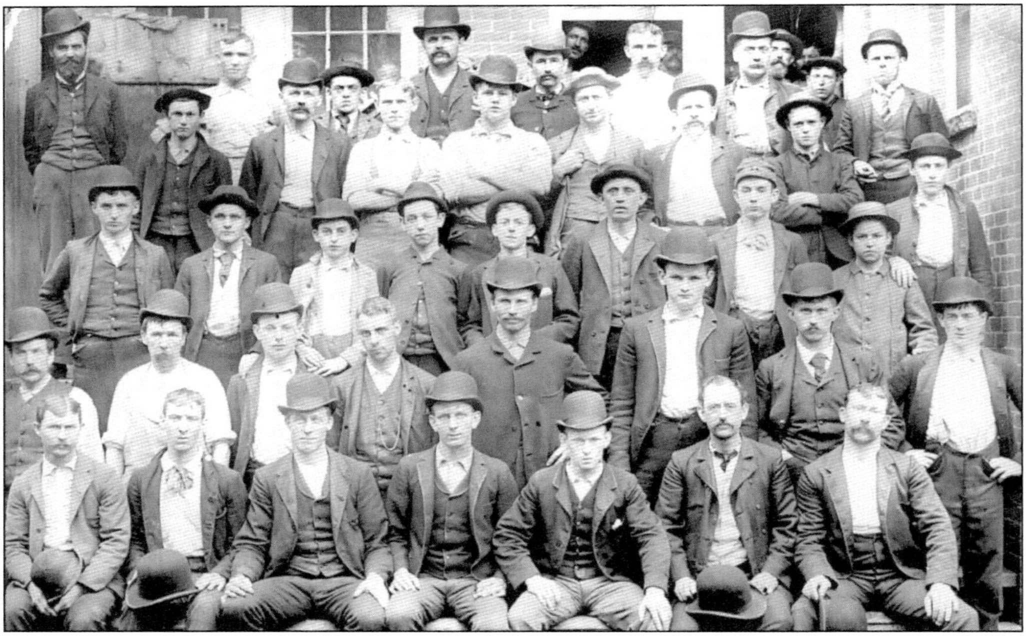

A Group in Bowlers. These men and boys were all employees of the U.S. Rubber Company. The photograph was taken sometime before 1892. Hats, mostly of the style known as the bowler, were as popular then as the baseball cap is now. There is a wide variety of ages represented here. Some of the boys would probably be banned from factory work in today's workplace.

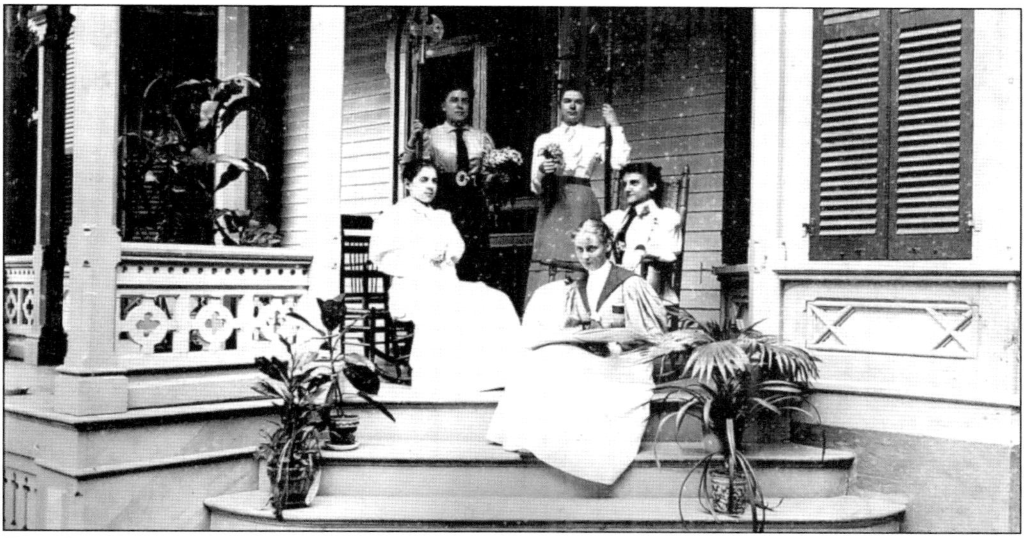

The Chocolate Cake Eaters of Glennwood Avenue. Such is the title written on the back of this photograph. The women seem more interested in plants than in chocolate cake, but the person who wrote the inscription must have known something more than is revealed in the image. The names of the women are also given on the back of the image: Beatrice Goodsell, Elizabeth Jackson, Mabel Goodsell, Beth ?, and Katherine Jackson.

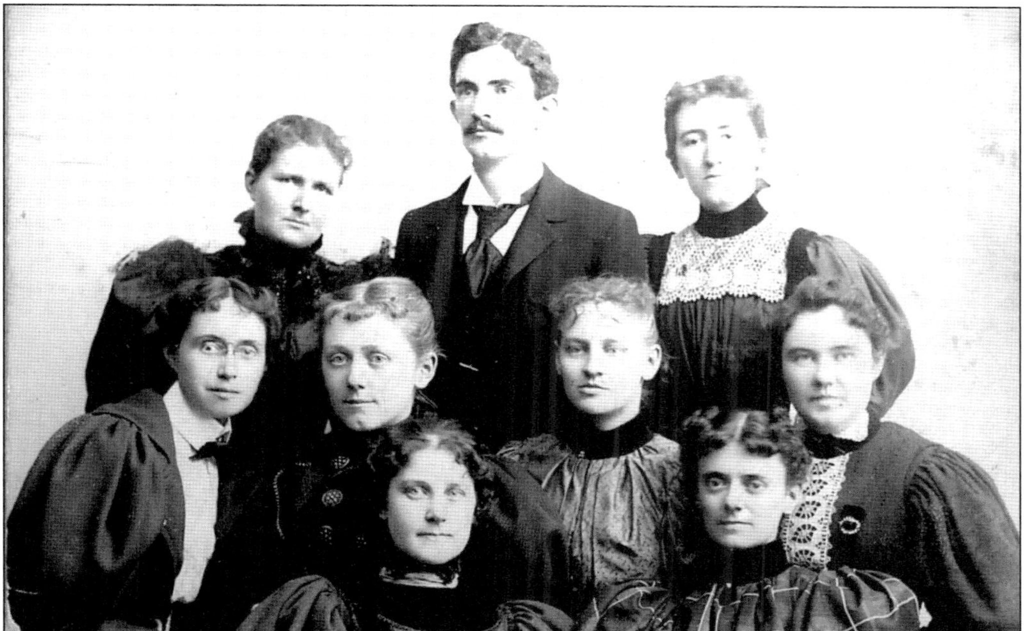

Members of the Faculty. This photograph of the Union City School faculty was taken by Naugatuck's Shepard Studio between 1893 and 1897. Pictured are, from left to right, the following: (first row) Clara Wood and Belle Meramble; (second row) Iva Callender, Anna Abell, Jane Twitchell, and Nellie Brennan; (third row) Helen Prindle, John Fitzpatrick, and unidentified. In this era, men's ties were very wide, and the shoulders of women's blouses and dresses were quite puffy.

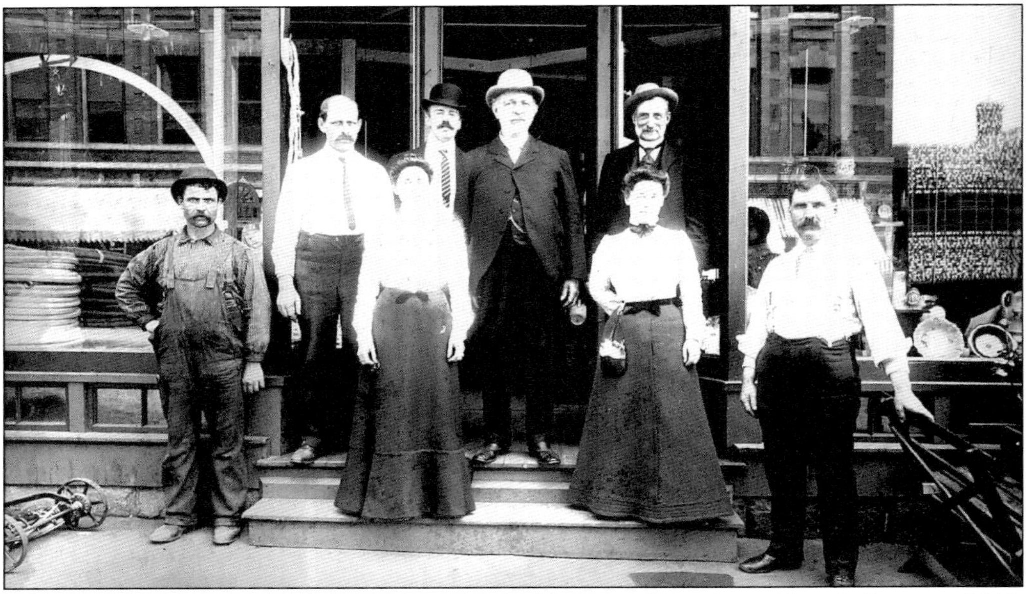

A Proud Proprietor and His Staff. If you had been strolling down Church Street *c.* 1910, you might have passed the new John M. Page store, at No. 179. John Page was fairly successful in selling household goods for many years. Page is seen here with his employees. Pictured are, from left to right, the following: (first row) ? Mancini, Fannie Williams, Jessie Twitchell, and Joe Hollibagh; (second row) H. Hawley, unidentified, John Page, and George D. Buck.

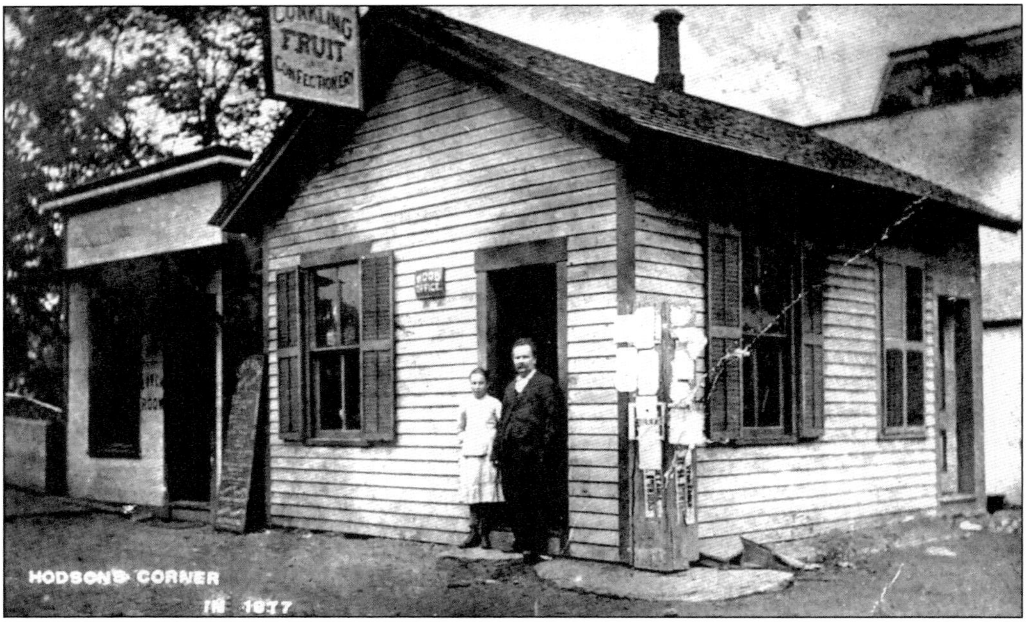

The Conkling Fruit and Confectionery Store. This image features a mom-and-pop store—an endangered species nowadays. They were small stores, often owned and operated by a couple who put in long hours six or seven days a week. These people, possibly the Conklings, are shown in 1877. They are standing proudly in front of their produce and candy store, once located at Hodson's Corner.

A Baby in a Gown. This youthful resident was brought to Naugatuck's Sabin Studio to pose for this photograph. No doubt a proud parent was positioned near the camera to coax a smile from this propped-up baby. Both boys and girls wore dresses in formal portraits through the early decades of the 20th century. Unfortunately, the photograph was not labeled, so this child's identity and gender are unknown.

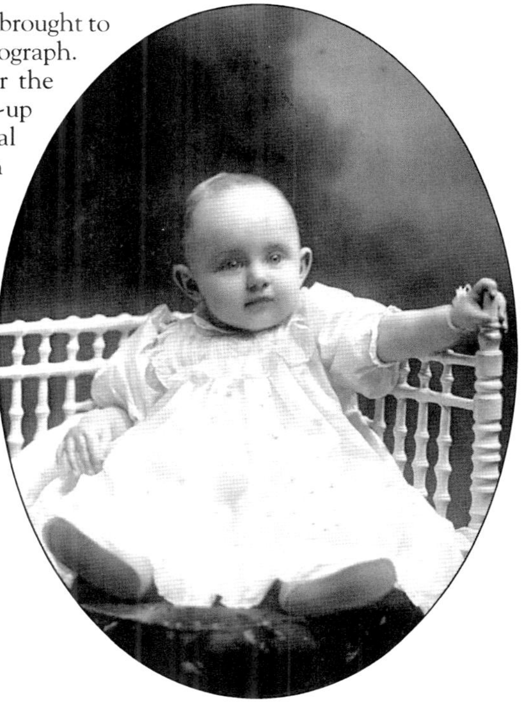

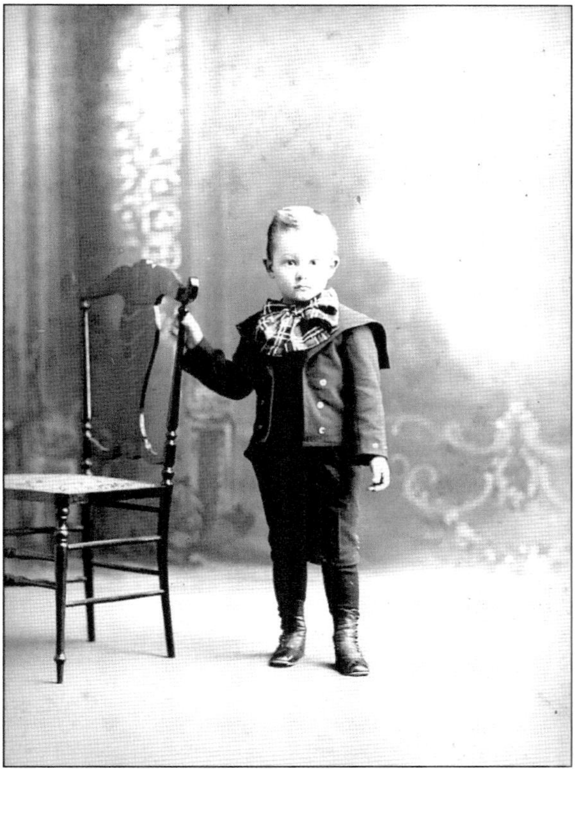

A Boy with a Chair. This dapper youngster posed by a lone chair in the Shepard Studio of Naugatuck. "Cabinet photographs" like this one were common during the early decades of studio photography, but the empty chair was not a usual prop; perhaps it was a symbol of a lost or deceased family member. The child's attire suggests he comes from a wealthy family, perhaps one of Naugatuck's industrialist families.

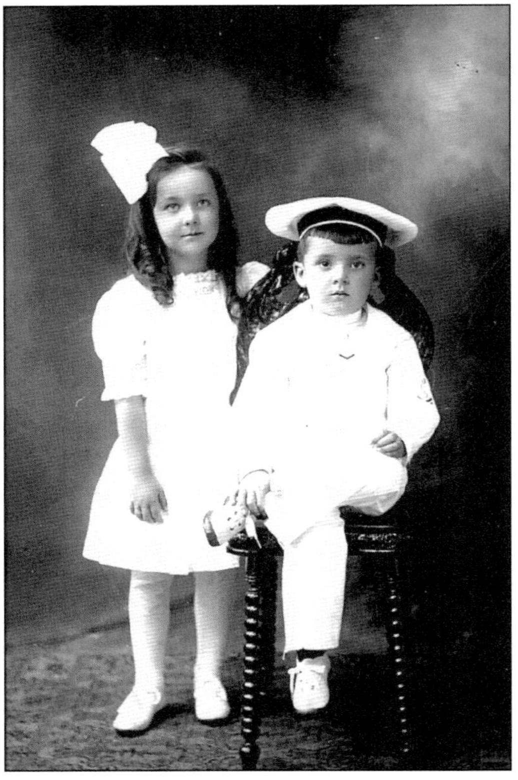

THE RUMNEY SIBLINGS. In this 1908 portrait, Isabel and Ted Rumney (the children of Sarah Culver and George Rumney) are dressed all in white. Isabel's bow and Ted's hat certainly add to the spiffiness of their attire.

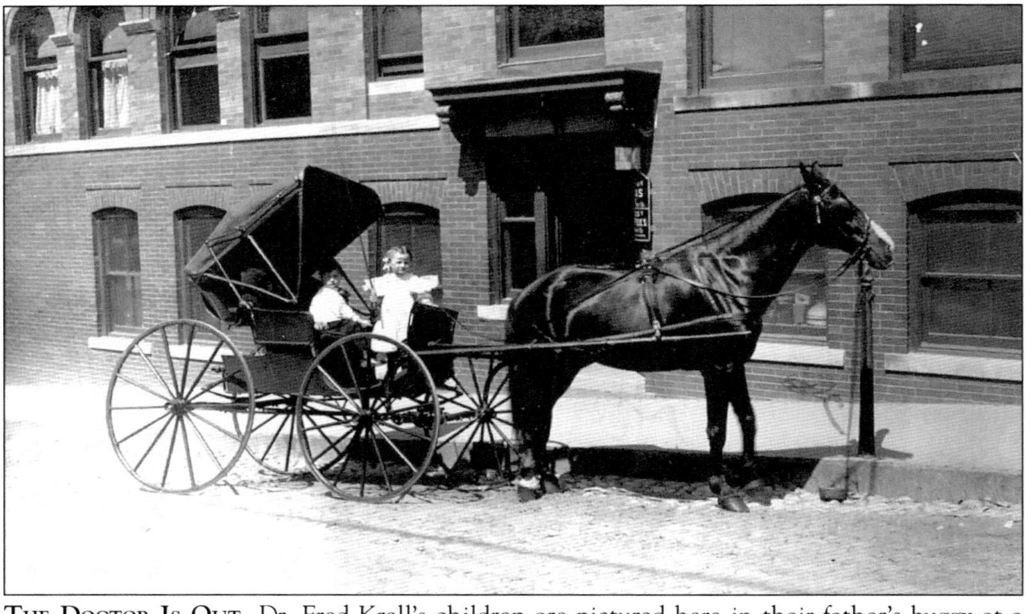

THE DOCTOR IS OUT. Dr. Fred Krell's children are pictured here in their father's buggy at a hitching post on Oak Street near the telephone company's office entrance on the east side of the Webster Block. The building was damaged in the 1955 flood and was taken down to make way for Route 8.

In the "Old Days," They Called Him a Hermit. "Johnny of the Woods" was a local character who probably would have been called homeless if he had lived today. Little is known about him, but he was one of Naugatuck's eccentric characters. He left his forest refuge long enough to pose for this portrait, in which he holds his walking stick in his right hand and his pipe in his left.

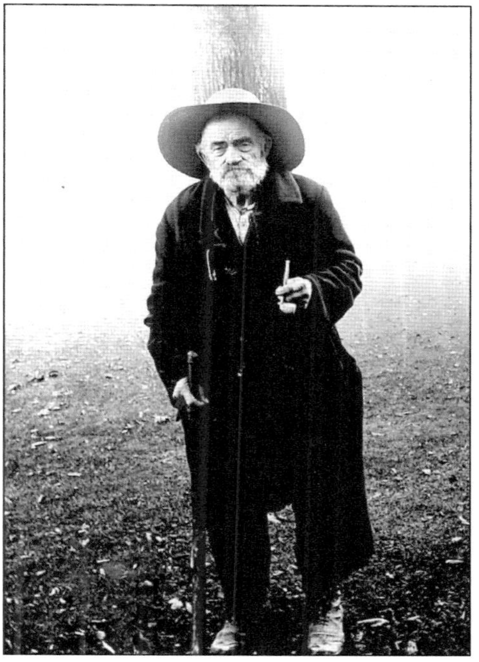

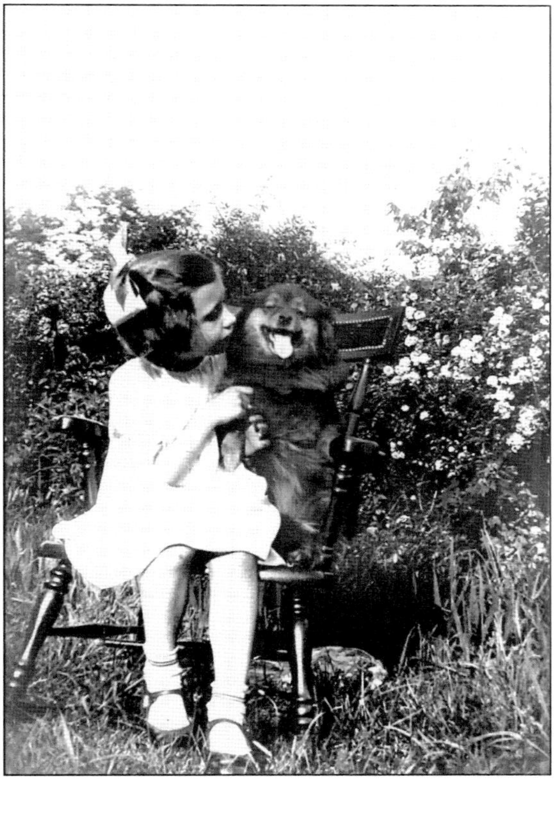

A Girl and Her Dog. It was a warm day in 1929 when Frances Burke posed with Tiny, the family Pekinese, at 112 Field Street. It was a peaceful moment during a year in which turmoil and upheaval in the economy would cause financial ruin for citizens across the country. Connecticut was not spared the pain that was ushered in with the stock market crash of October 24, 1929. The Great Depression hit Naugatuck's companies hard.

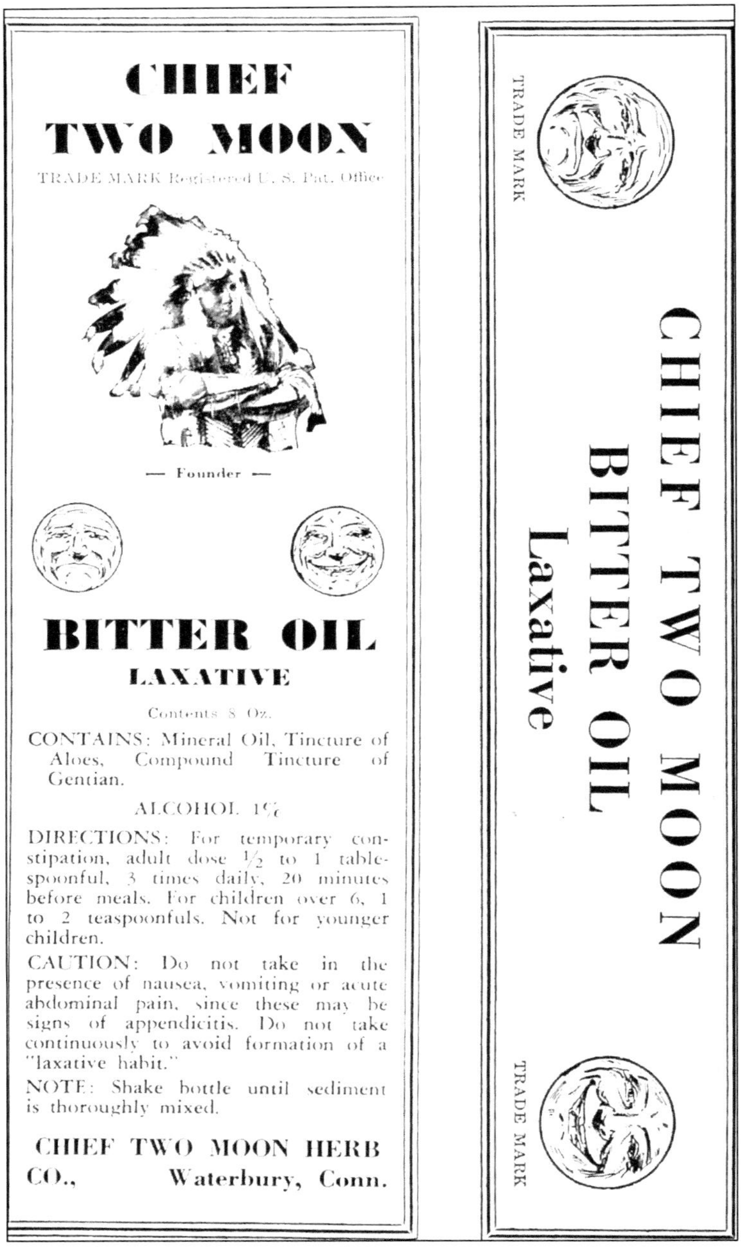

A Little Big Horn Connection. Naugatuck has a connection to Gen. George Custer and the Battle of Little Big Horn through Chief Two Moon, a storied local American Indian herbalist. Some of the American Indians who fought against the men of the 7th U.S. Cavalry in that battle on June 25, 1876, stayed at Chief Two Moon's Naugatuck estate. Chief Two Moon, whose given name was Chico Colon Meridas, was born on August 29, 1888, and died on November 2, 1933, at age 45. He was made an honorary member and chief of the Ogallala Lakota Sioux tribe in 1930. He gained an international reputation for the various elixirs he concocted and produced in Waterbury, Naugatuck's mother city to the north. He also had a home there at 33 Wales Street.

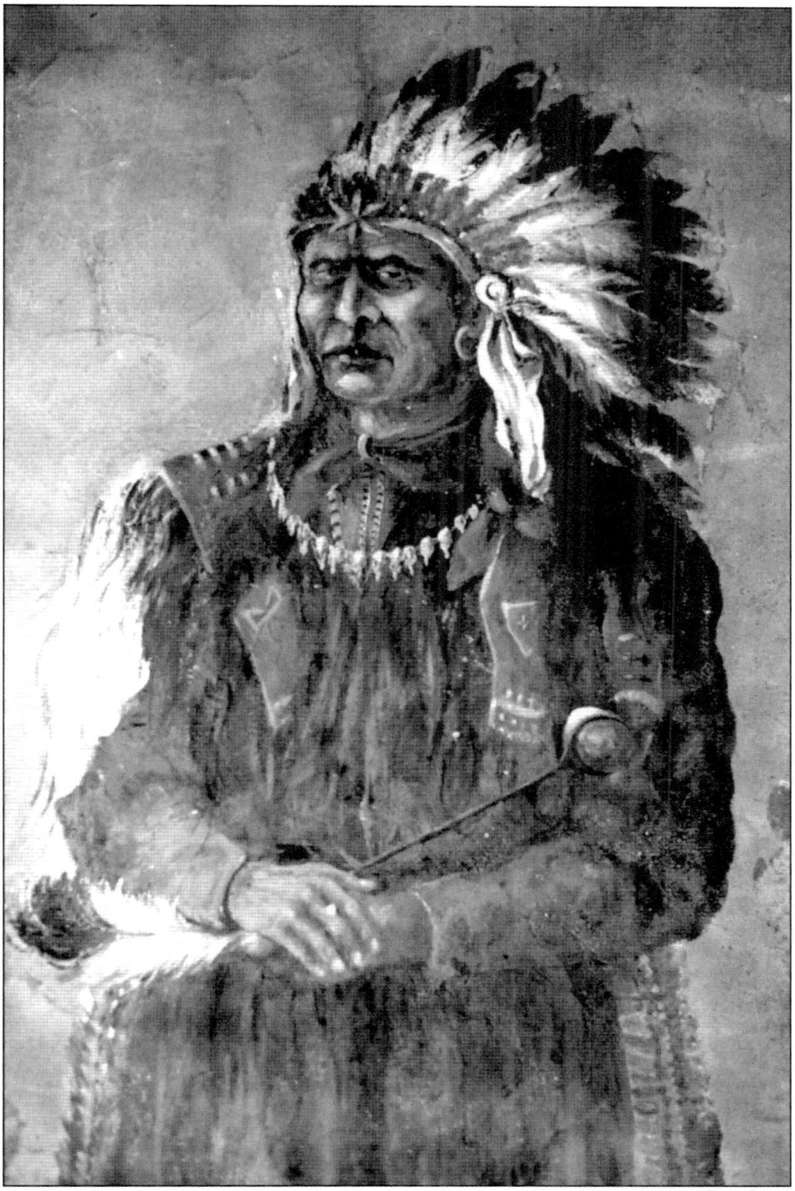

CHIEF TWO MOON. The wealthy chief owned a 300-acre estate in Naugatuck on Beacon Valley Road, on the site of the old fairgrounds. He maintained a lodge-style camp there, where this portrait of him was displayed, along with numerous other murals and artworks. Although he maintained that he was an American Indian, his attempts to prove his bloodlines were frustrated. In October 1932, he invited a group of 30 American Indians from the South Dakota Pine Ridge Reservation to visit for an extended stay. Many had fought in the Battle of Little Big Horn, also known as Custer's Last Stand. Among them were Chief Standing Bear, Chief Kills Crow, No Water, and Chief Little Bear. Two other guests had been scouting for Chief Sitting Bull and arrived at the carnage after the fighting had ended. Their names were Chief Catches Enemy and Chief High Eagle. Many local and state politicians attended the festivities to honor the guests.

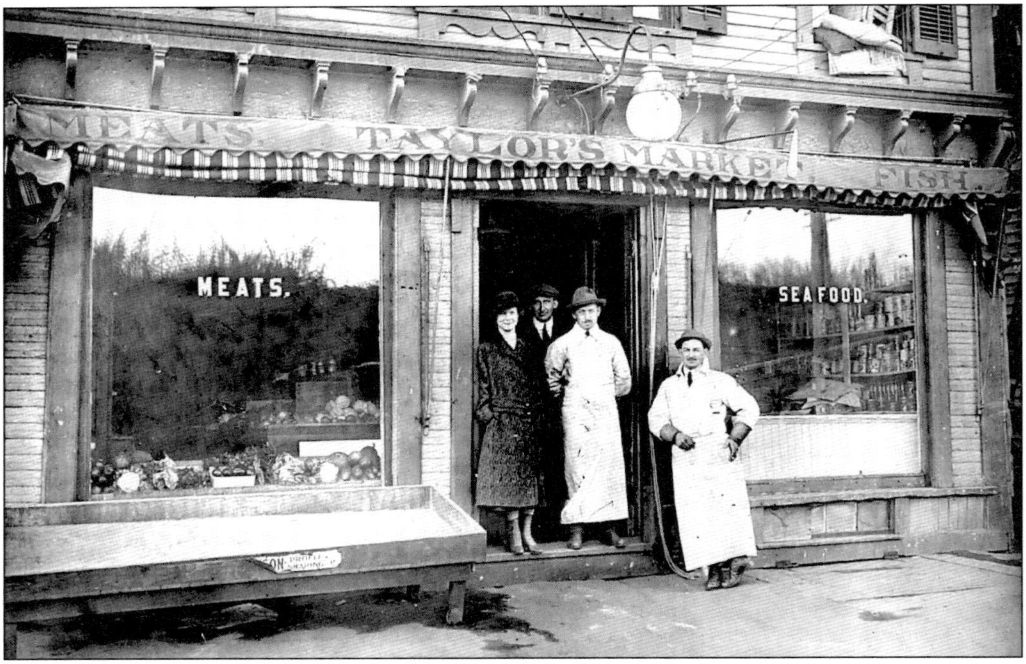

Taylor-Made for Service. Employees of the Taylor store pose for the camera on Water Street. This image is worth exploring closely, perhaps with a magnifying glass. Store windows were like ads inviting customers inside.

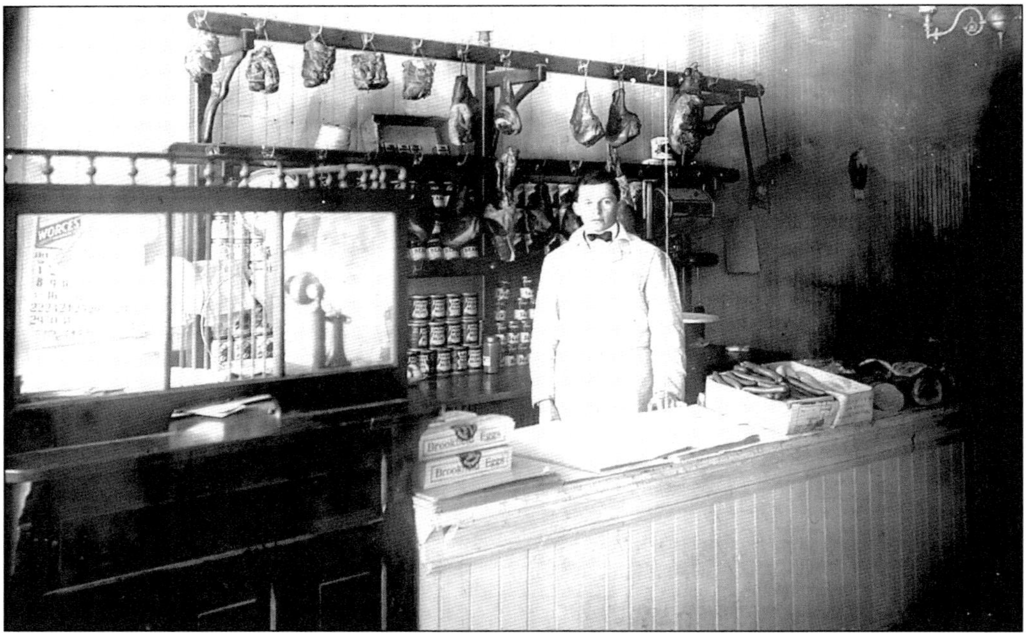

Meat on the Table. This photograph is not labeled, so we do not know the name of the clerk, but he is believed to have been an employee of the Curtiss Market. Hanging meat and canned pork and beans are prominently displayed, ready to be taken home and prepared for the table. A closer examination may reveal details about the companies that provided the packaged goods.

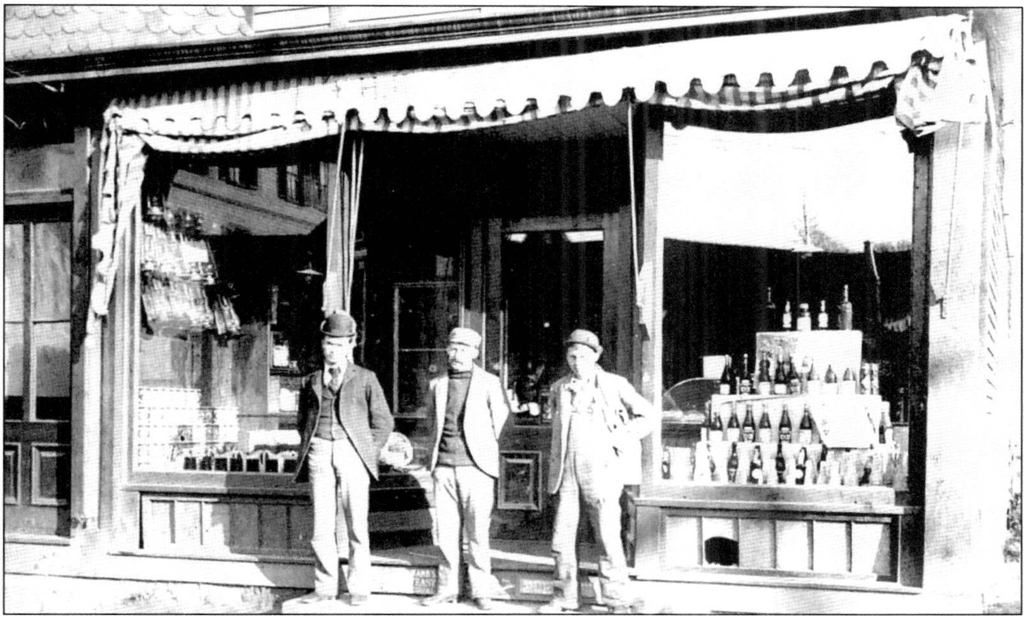

THE SCHOFIELD STORE. The neighborhood convenience store is nothing new. These men posed outside the store for the photographer, taking a short break from their chores around the popular establishment.

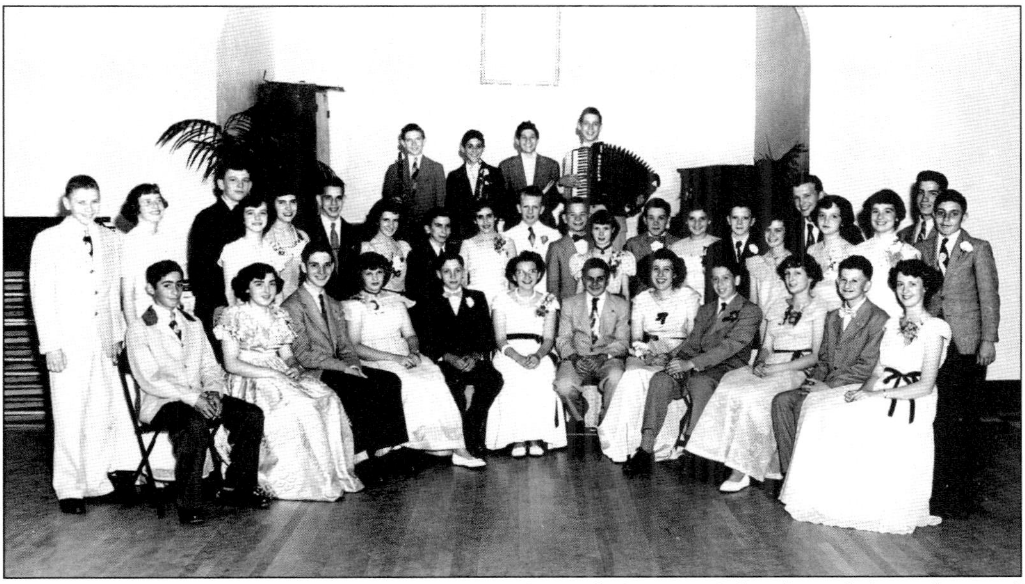

CRISTOFORO COLOMBO DISCOVERS DANCING. Central Avenue School's eighth-graders and their guests attend a dance at the Cristoforo Colombo Hall on South Main Street in 1951. A photographer from the Thibodeau Studio captured the young teenagers in their finery. The band consisted of, from left to right, James Noble, Ronald Squillo, unidentified, and Joseph Speck. Speck is playing the mandatory accordion, one instrument that brought joy to the hearts of most Italians.

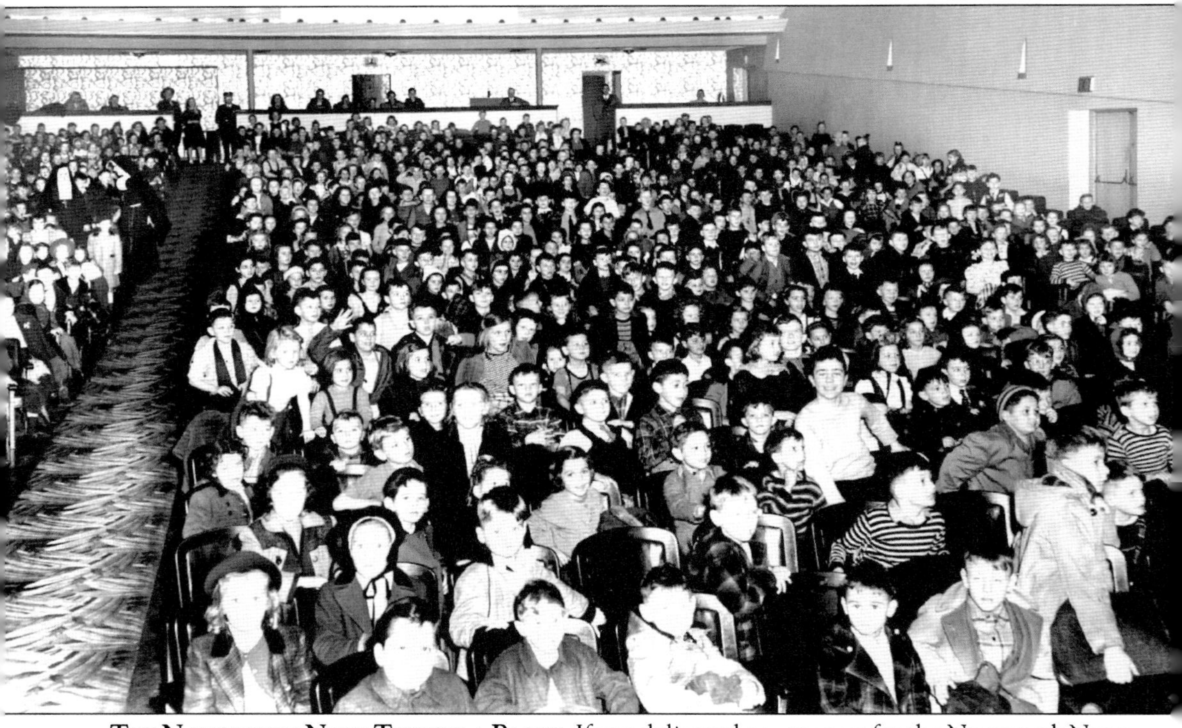

THE NAUGATUCK NEWS THROWS A PARTY. If you delivered newspapers for the Naugatuck News and attended a thank-you party at the Salem Playhouse on Monday, December 23, 1946, get out your magnifying glass; you might be in this photograph. It looks like everyone had a good time. December 23 probably fell during the winter vacation period.

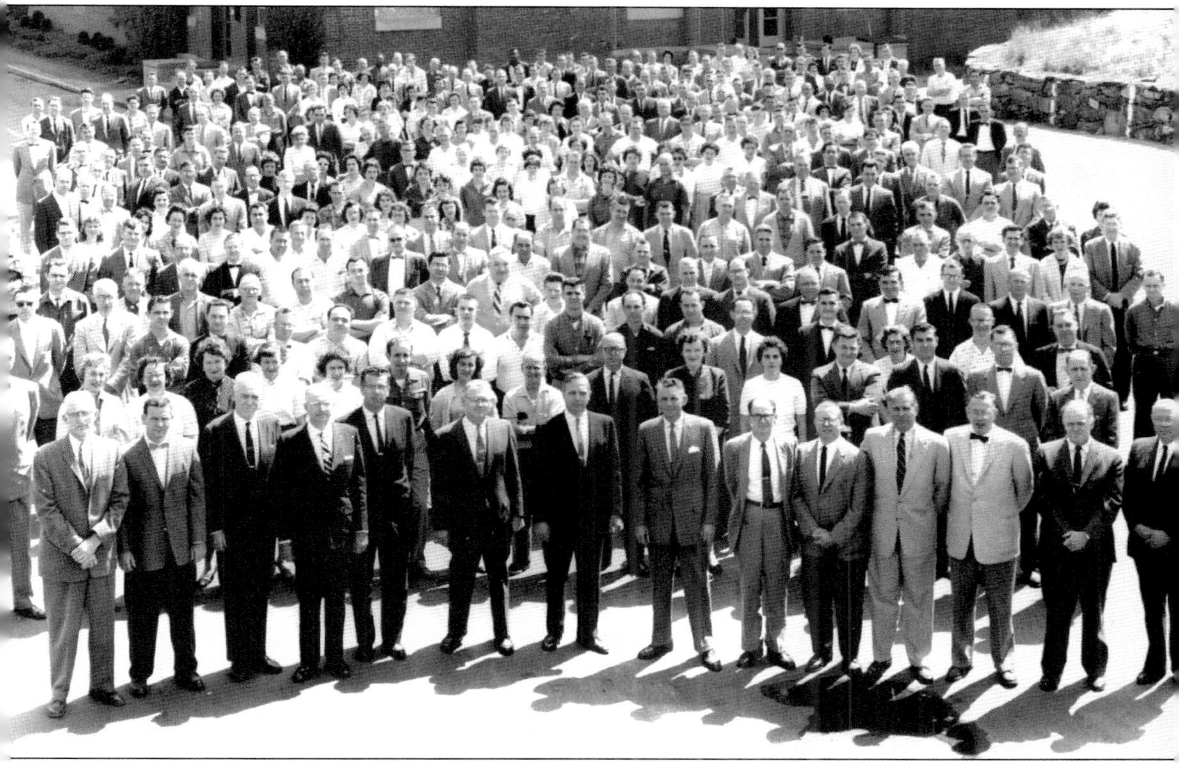

EMPLOYEES OUTSIDE BUILDING NO. 81. This is one of those group photographs that one hardly sees anymore but that were standard fare in the 1940s and 1950s. This photograph was taken *c.* 1954 at building No. 81 by Naugatuck photographer James A. Reynolds. The more than 200 people pictured are all employees of U.S. Rubber's chemical and synthetic divisions. According to the normal protocol of such photographs, the executives are probably prominently arrayed in the front row. This group may hold the borough of Naugatuck's all-time record for the most men wearing bow ties in one spot. Bow ties were much more commonly worn during this time period than they are now.

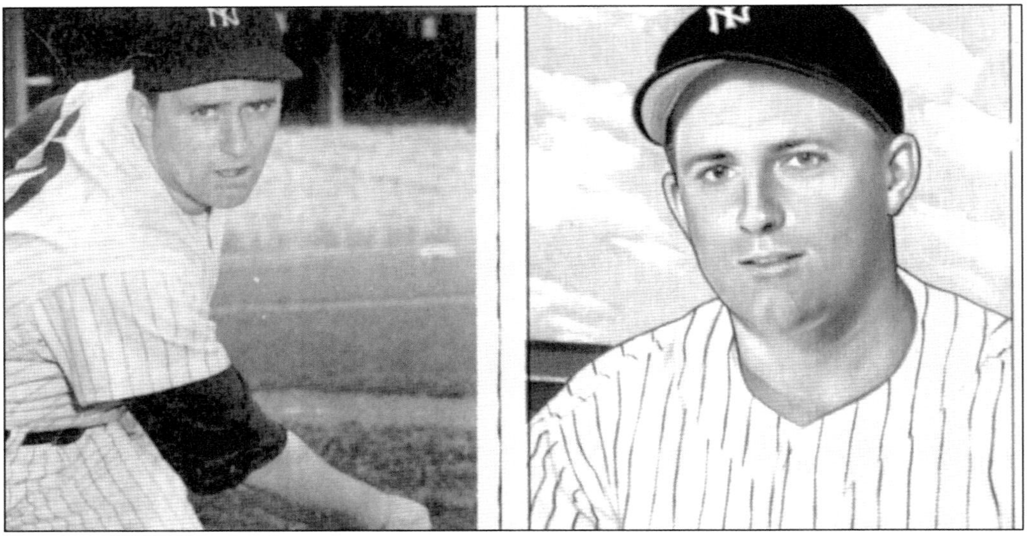

Immortalized on Baseball Cards. Frank "Spec" Shea was a sports legend in his hometown of Naugatuck as well as in his home state of Connecticut. He was born here on October 2, 1922. The New York Yankees showed an interest in him before he graduated from Naugatuck High School in 1939. He pitched brilliantly for the Yanks in 1947. That year, the Naugatuck Nugget, as Shea had been nicknamed by famed sportscaster Mel Allen, led the league as a rookie with the highest winning percentage (0.737 with 14 wins and 5 losses). That same year, Shea also won the All-Star game and the first and fifth games against the Brooklyn Dodgers in the 1947 World Series. Shea was named series MVP and was voted rookie of the year. These cards are Bowman baseball cards from 1950 and 1951 and are reproduced with permission from the Topps Company Inc.

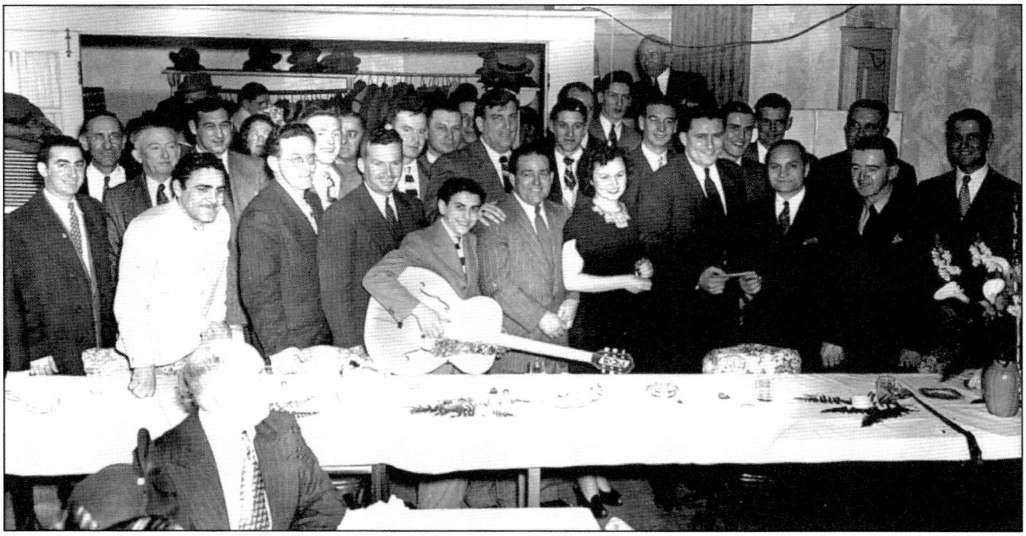

Spec Shea Honored at a Local Banquet. Frank "Spec" Shea was often honored by local groups. In addition to deserving the praise, he was a favorite among the local ticket-buying populace, and his name alone would guarantee excellent attendance. Shea is shown here with his wife, Genevieve, and a large crowd of unidentified men at an event that probably took place in the 1950s or the 1960s.

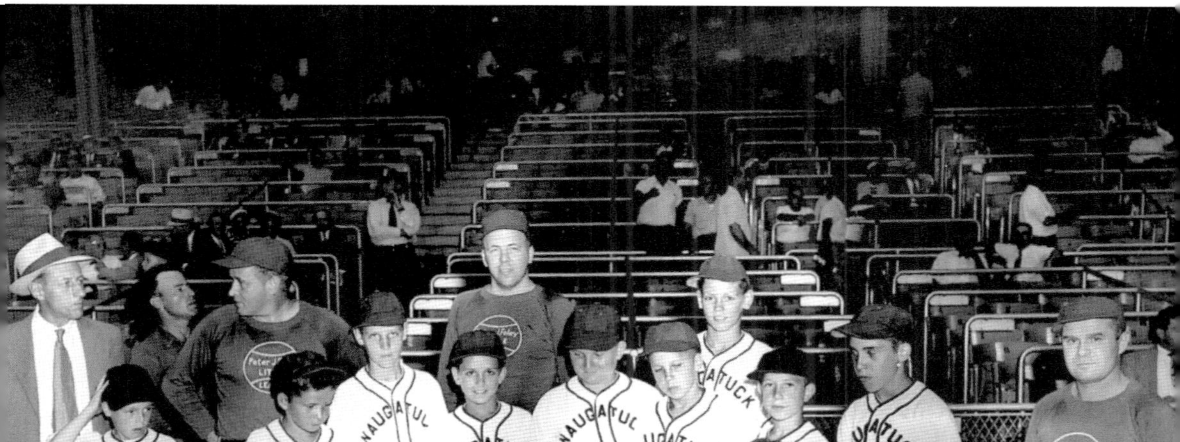

AN MVP AMONG CHAMPIONS. Frank "Spec" Shea was arguably Naugatuck's most famous resident. (Although a case could be made for Charles Goodyear, he never won a World Series game.) Shea was always approachable during his years with the Pinstripers and the Washington Senators. He is pictured here at Yankee Stadium with his favorite fans, kids (especially Naugatuck kids). The Naugatuck Nugget posed for a meet-and-greet with players, parents, and coaches from the 1951 Little League All-Star team, which had traveled to Yankee Stadium to play a three-inning game against a team from Port Chester, New York. Naugatuck beat them 3-0. Pictured are, from left to right, the following: (first row) Tom Kopp, Joey Marinello, Spec Shea, Richie Hoben, Ray Rossi, and Frank Neary; (second row) Billy Stopper, Buddy Kackowski, Bob Carey, Joey Cellelo, Jim Fenton, Ray Kloc, John Crotty, Donny Jones, and Sam Behuniak; (back row) Ralph Stopper, unidentified, coach Danny Walsh, coach Russ Weaving, and coach "Hootsie" Marinello.

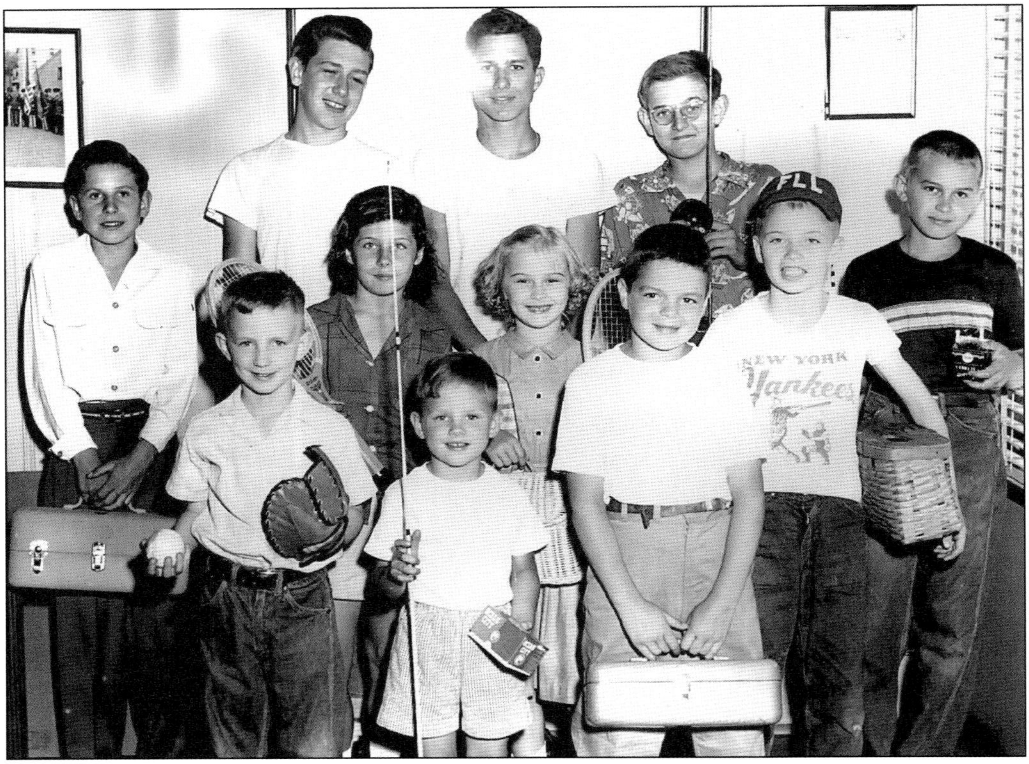

TOP FISHERS. Smiles and prizes were the order of the day for this group of fishing contest winners in 1953. Pictured are, from left to right, the following: (front row) Terry Nolan, Zane Czaplick, and Jim Jones; (second row) Bill Palamar, Judy Sartino, Joan Ploski, Joseph Holland, and Henry Ploski; (back row) Don Oldakowski, David Bravi, and Bob Sharon.

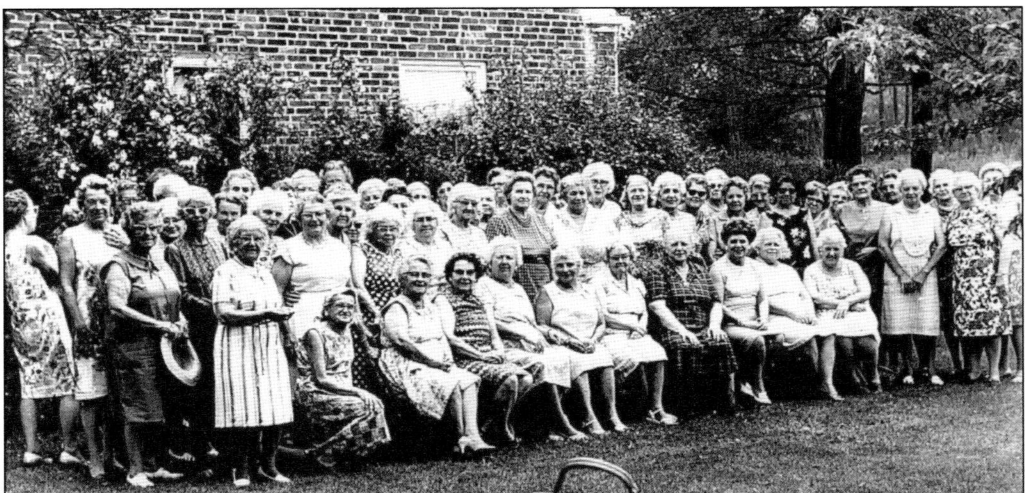

LADIES ON THE LAWN. Julia Mallane's house was the setting for an outing of the Friendship Club. The meeting took place *c.* 1967. Mallane, the dark-haired woman in the middle of the front row, was the president. Jennie Lyons, facing toward the right on the left side of the photograph, was the secretary.

Three

Places, Neighborhoods, and Streets

Naugatuck is known as Rubbertown, the home of Charles Goodyear, U.S. Rubber, and Uniroyal. But there are other historical, architectural, and cultural attractions that were (and in some cases still are) located here that even locals might not know about. The next few pages will provide a tour of the town center and town green area. They will also highlight some of the outlying areas and sections, such as Union City, and popular destinations, such as the Salem Playhouse, the Waldorf, and High Rock Grove. You may even find a treasured childhood memory. Some of the views have changed over the years. Many have remained the same. A few no longer exist. Time, the hand of man, and the forces of nature, sometimes independently and sometimes together, are responsible for most of the changes. And in some cases, only man is responsible for those historic sites that have managed to survive unscathed.

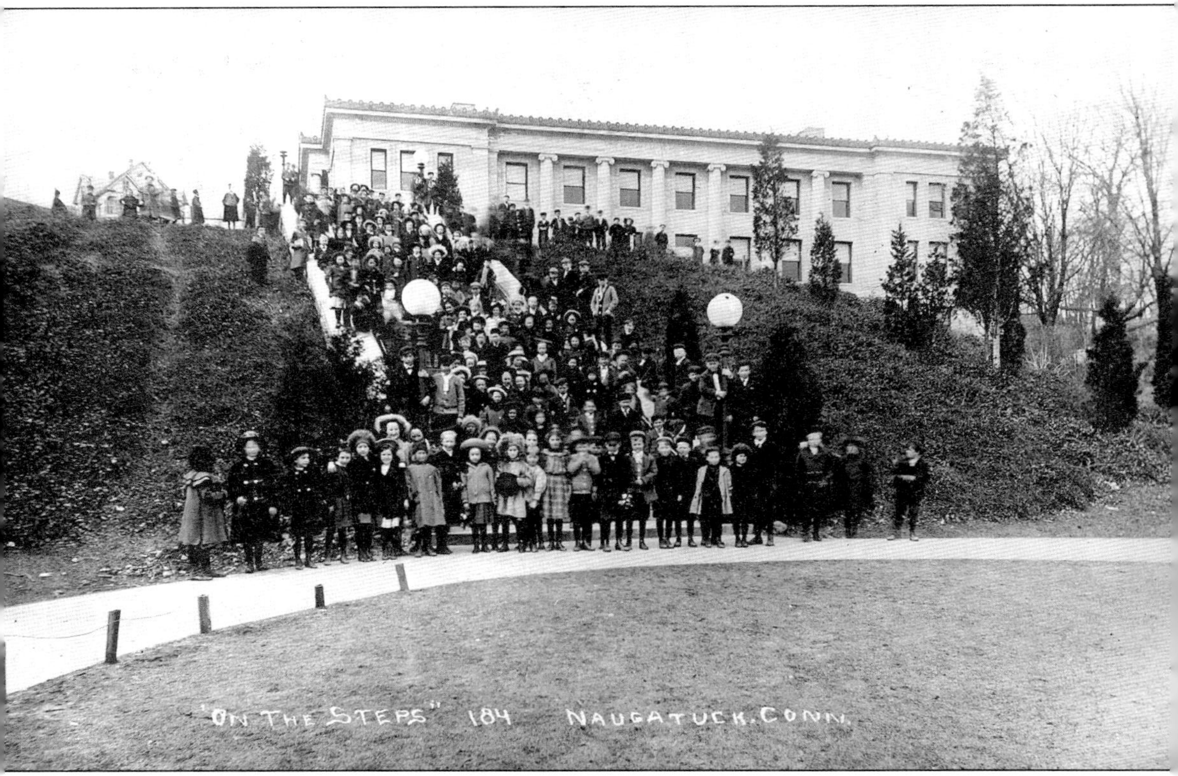

SCHOOL KIDS ON THE STEPS. It was a cool day *c.* 1905 when this group of intrepid elementary school kids, probably from nearby Salem School, posed for a group portrait on the steps leading to Naugatuck High School. The hat styles and the knickers on many of the boys are interesting clues to the time period. These steps were a popular place to pose for group photographs through the years.

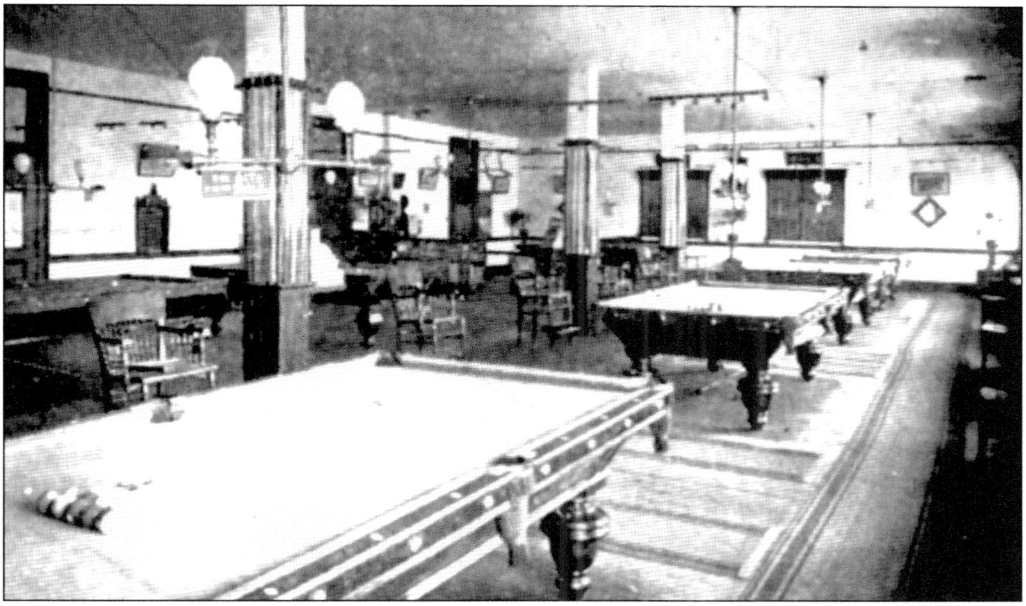

THE LOCAL POOL HALL. "Pool hall" is a term that conjures different images for people of different eras. In the past, pool halls were often thought of as hangouts that truants and gamblers frequented. Today, pool is often played at reputable family- and couples-oriented establishments. The Waldorf, located upstairs in the Neary Building and operated by Breen and Stapleton, appears to have been a high-class place to play pool around 100 years ago.

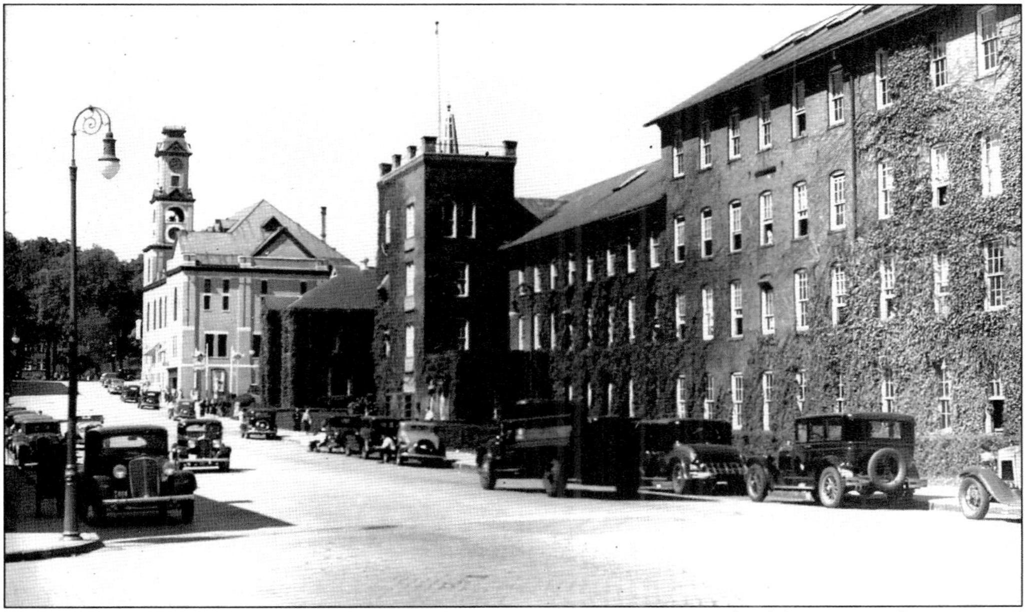

MAPLE STREET, LOOKING WEST TOWARD CHURCH STREET. If you had been traveling toward the green on Maple Street in the 1930s, this is the view you would have seen. The Tennis Mill building, called the Phoenix, is on the right. The building at the corner of Church and Maple Streets is the old town hall, dedicated on July 24, 1882. It was demolished in 1964 by the Stamford Wrecking Company to make way for the new municipal building.

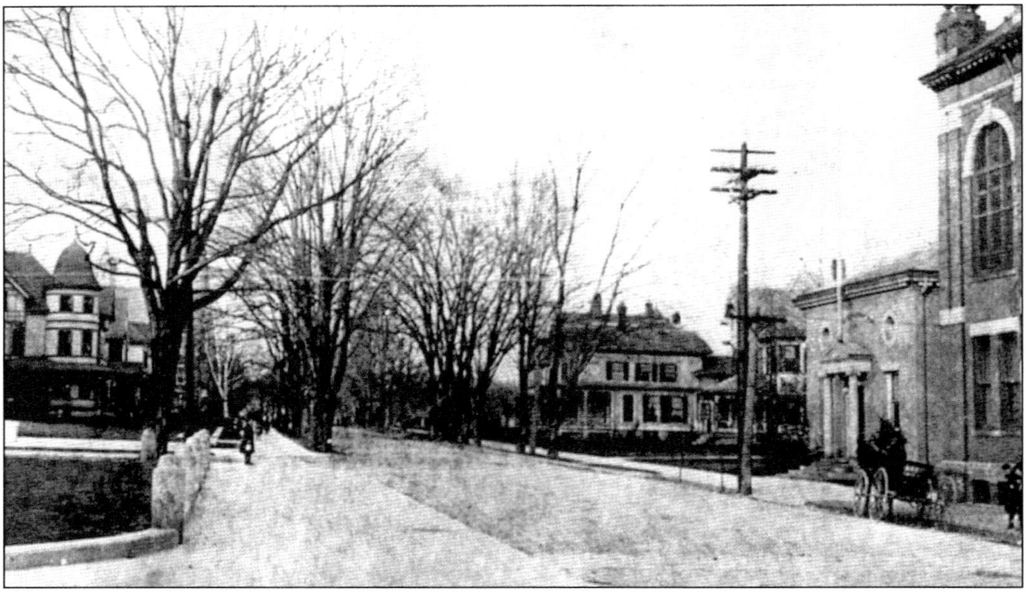

Looking North on Church Street. A close examination of this W. G. Hard image reveals a wagon parked in front of the old town hall. There are a few folks standing about. Next door is the Naugatuck National Bank, built in 1893. The Whittemore Memorial Public Library, built in 1894 just north of the bank, does not seem to be present; the nearby residence seems too close.

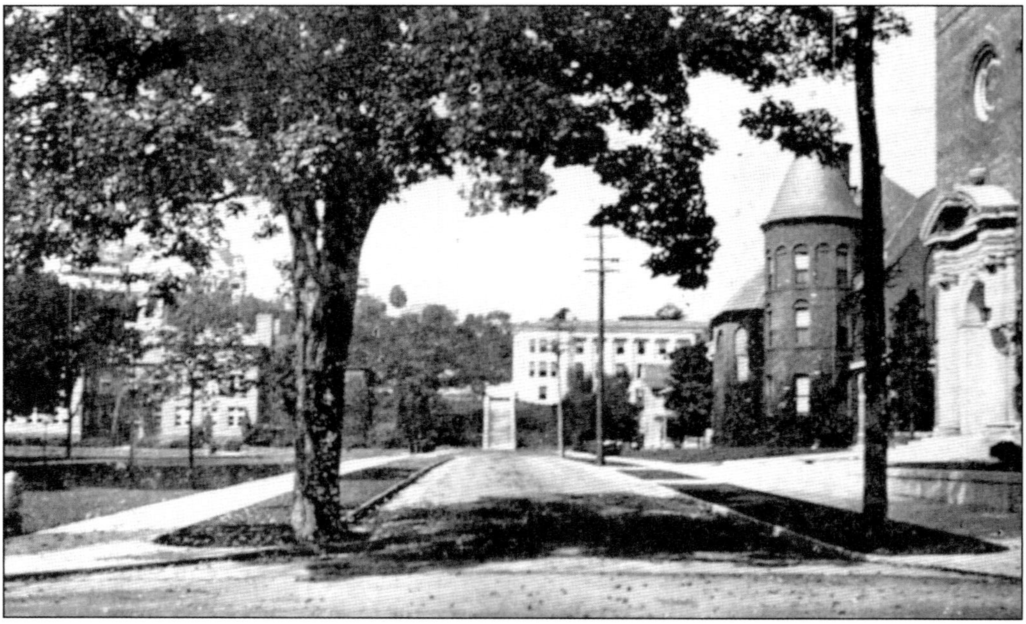

Looking West from Town Hall. Another postcard in W. G. Hard's series is this scene at the north end of the green, looking west through Division Street from Church Street. The building on the far left is Salem School. At the end of the street are the steps to what was then Naugatuck High School. The castlelike building on the right is the parish house of the Congregational church, the building partially visible on the right.

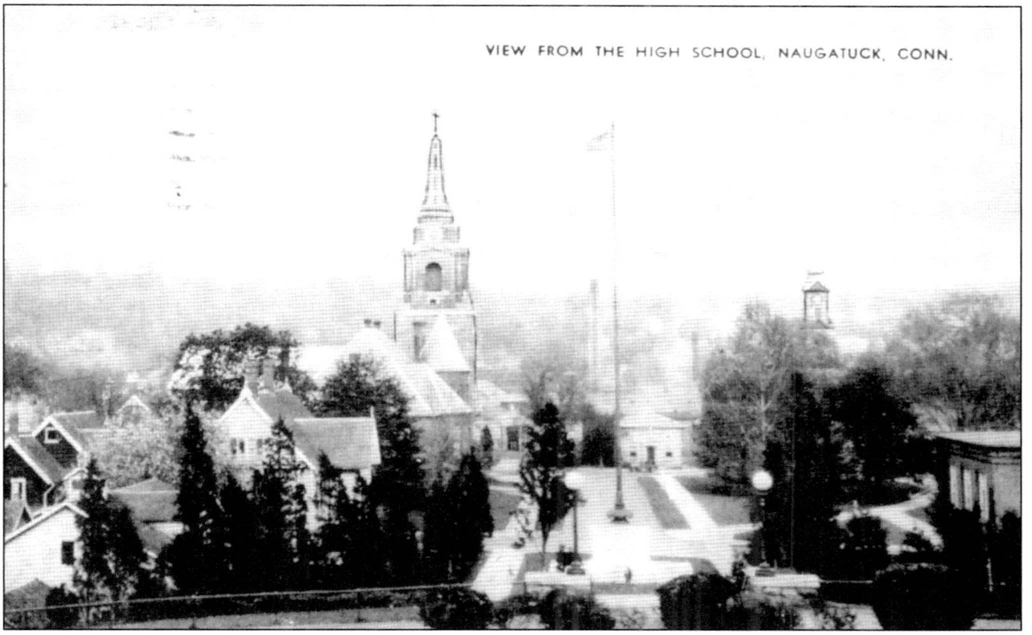

LOOKING EAST TOWARD TOWN HALL. This postcard was mailed on September 30, 1941, from Naugatuck. If you had been standing at the high school, looking toward the Naugatuck River, you would have seen the Congregational church on the left, the front door of the Whittemore Memorial Library, the Children's Library, the spire of the town hall, and the north side of Salem School on the right. The green is in the center.

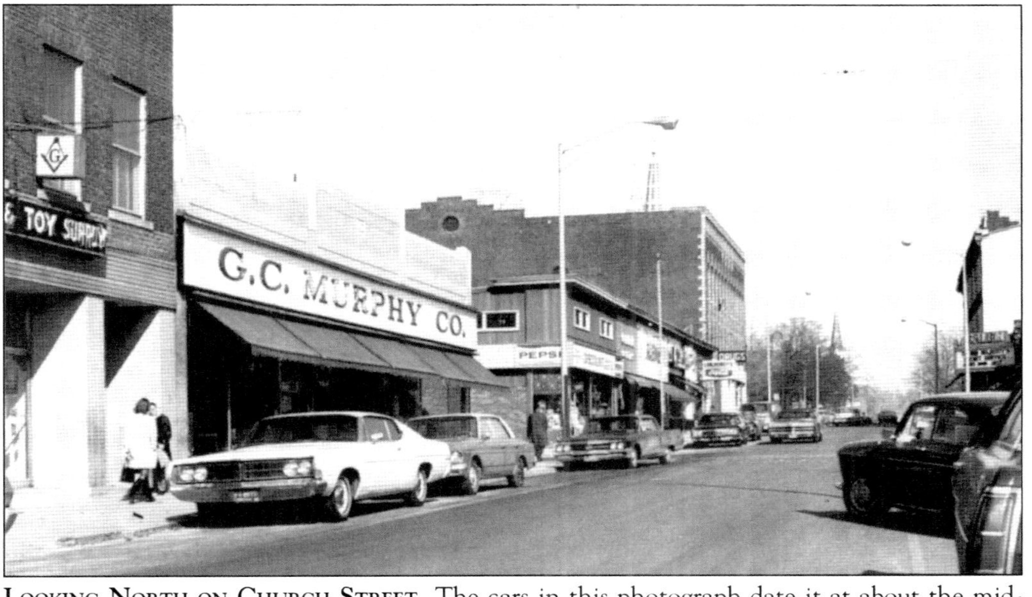

LOOKING NORTH ON CHURCH STREET. The cars in this photograph date it at about the mid-1960s. Naugatuck Historical Society member Sandra Clark remembers the G. C. Murphy Company as a department store that was fun to shop in "because if you couldn't find something anywhere else, they would have it there." The building to the left of it housed a toy store. At the far end of the street on the right is the Salem Playhouse.

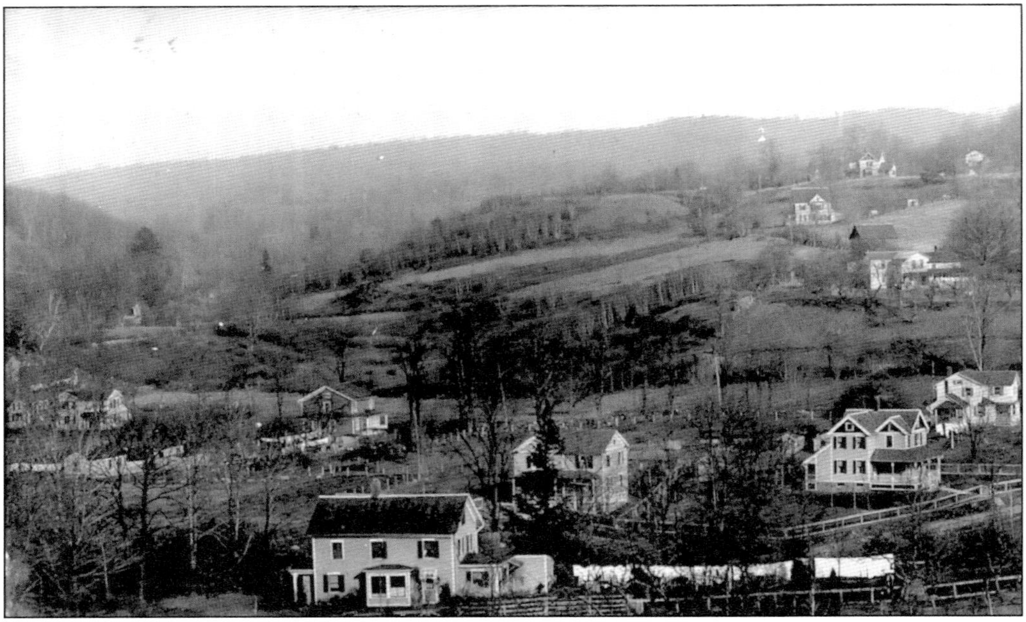

WASHDAY IN THE HILLS OF NAUGATUCK. This is a fine example of a real-photo postcard, a card not produced on a printing press but printed directly from a negative. It is dated December 12, 1912. Many of the neighbors had chosen this day to hang their laundry to dry on their clotheslines. The message on the back of the card explains that it was taken by someone standing near Jim Coen's (possibly on City Hill) and that the first house is the Keelings'.

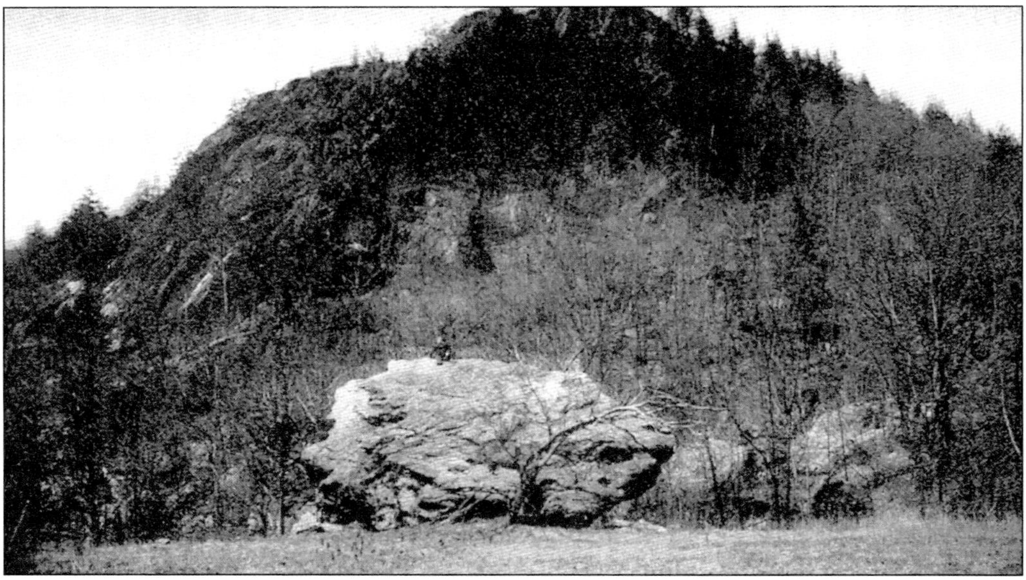

HIGH IN THE HILLS. B. Benander and Company of Naugatuck published this color postcard of Skating Rink Rock at High Rock Grove, located on the border between Naugatuck and Beacon Falls. It was built and owned by the Naugatuck Railroad and described in their advertising as noted for its "romantic and weird-like scenery and the first class accommodations." They claimed it attracted 50,000 visitors in 1880.

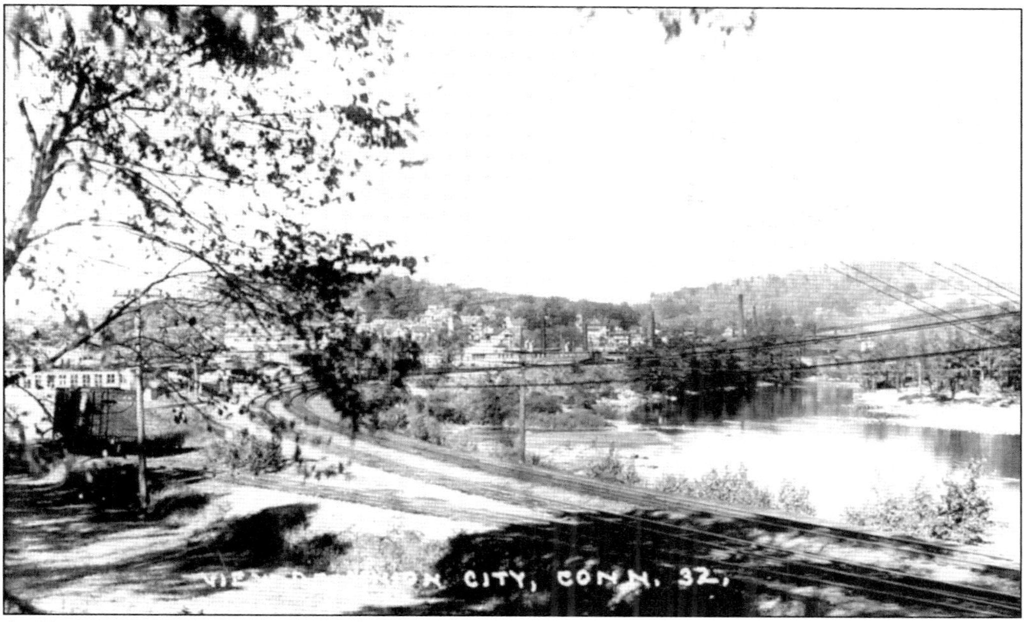

A View of Union City. Another real-photo postcard features this scene of Union City, a section of Naugatuck that was home to many Polish and Swedish residents. It was taken facing north from central Naugatuck.

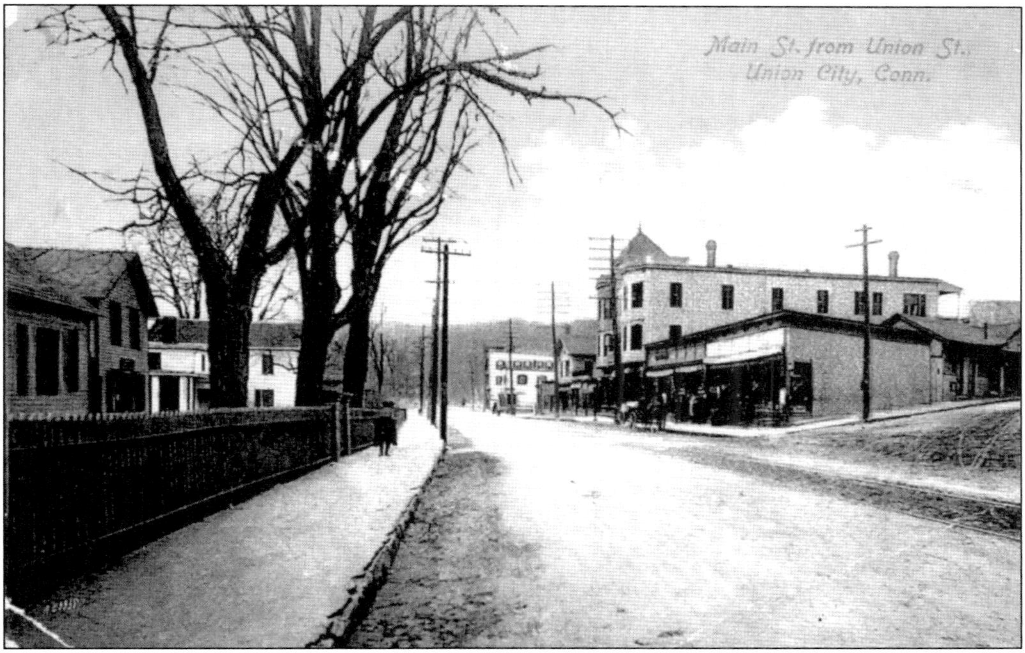

Downtown Union City. This postcard reveals a quiet scene on Main Street in Union City, looking north. A small child is walking on the sidewalk toward the photographer; shops are visible in the background. This view of a quiet New England town would have been in stark contrast to the industrial sections of Naugatuck in operation at the same time. The home of Charles Goodyear, now gone, appears on the left of the postcard.

Admit One

THE SALEM PLAYHOUSE

Naugatuck, Connecticut

.... MGR.

ADMIT ONE

THE SALEM PLAYHOUSE

NAUGATUCK, CONN.

GOOD THRU ....

....MGR.

DESIRABLE DUCATS. These were two of the most desirable pieces of paper in all of Naugatuck: free passes to the Salem Playhouse, the place to be on the weekend. They were granted to deserving individuals with the authorization of the manager.

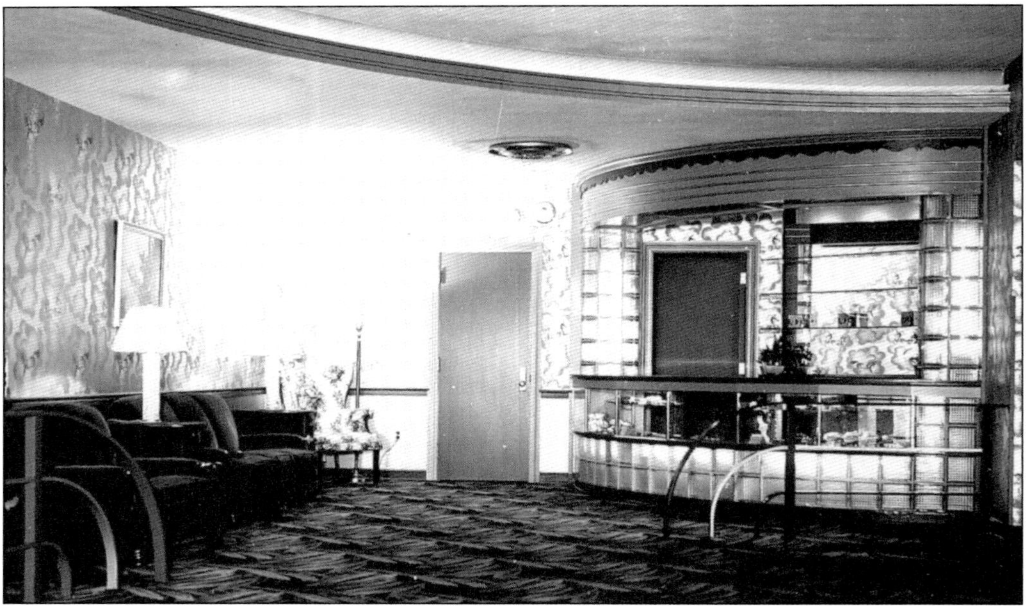

THE PROMISED LAND. The lobby area of the Salem Playhouse, located on Church Street, should be readily recognizable to most longtime residents of Naugatuck. For many years, especially in the days before television, this was the home of entertainment and weekend dating rituals as well as Saturday afternoon "kiddy matinees." Decorating with thick glass bricks, popular in the heyday of the Salem, is now in vogue again.

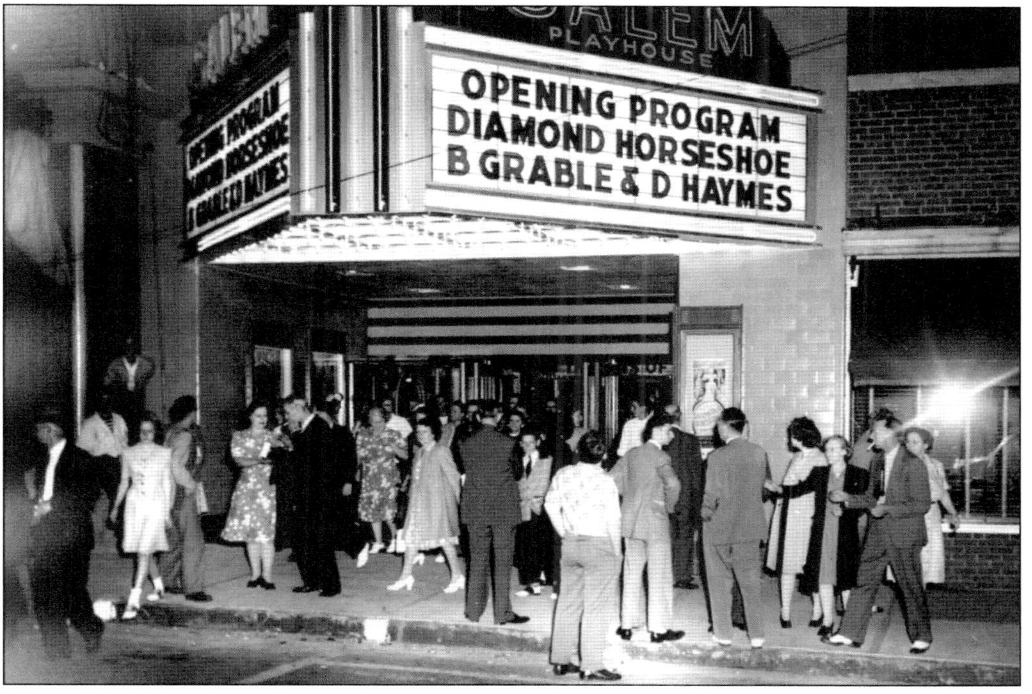

Opening Night? *Diamond Horseshoe* starred Betty Grable and Dick Haymes and was released in 1945. This photograph, taken by Thibideau, shows some of the crowd exiting the theater in their moviegoer finest. It would be hard to find people dressed like this—men in white shirts and ties, and ladies in high heels—at movie theaters today.

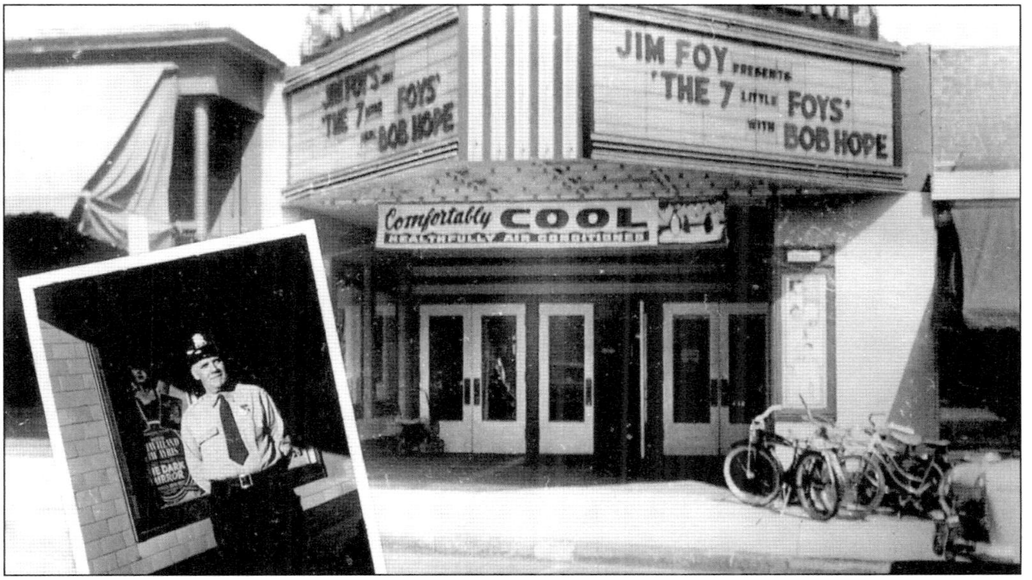

Foy Foibles. *The 7 Little Foys* was released in 1955 and starred Bob Hope and James Cagney. The reason the marquee reads, "Jim Foy Presents" is that Jim Foy was the ticket taker at the theater. He had also been on the Naugatuck police force. The management was promoting the last-name coincidence.

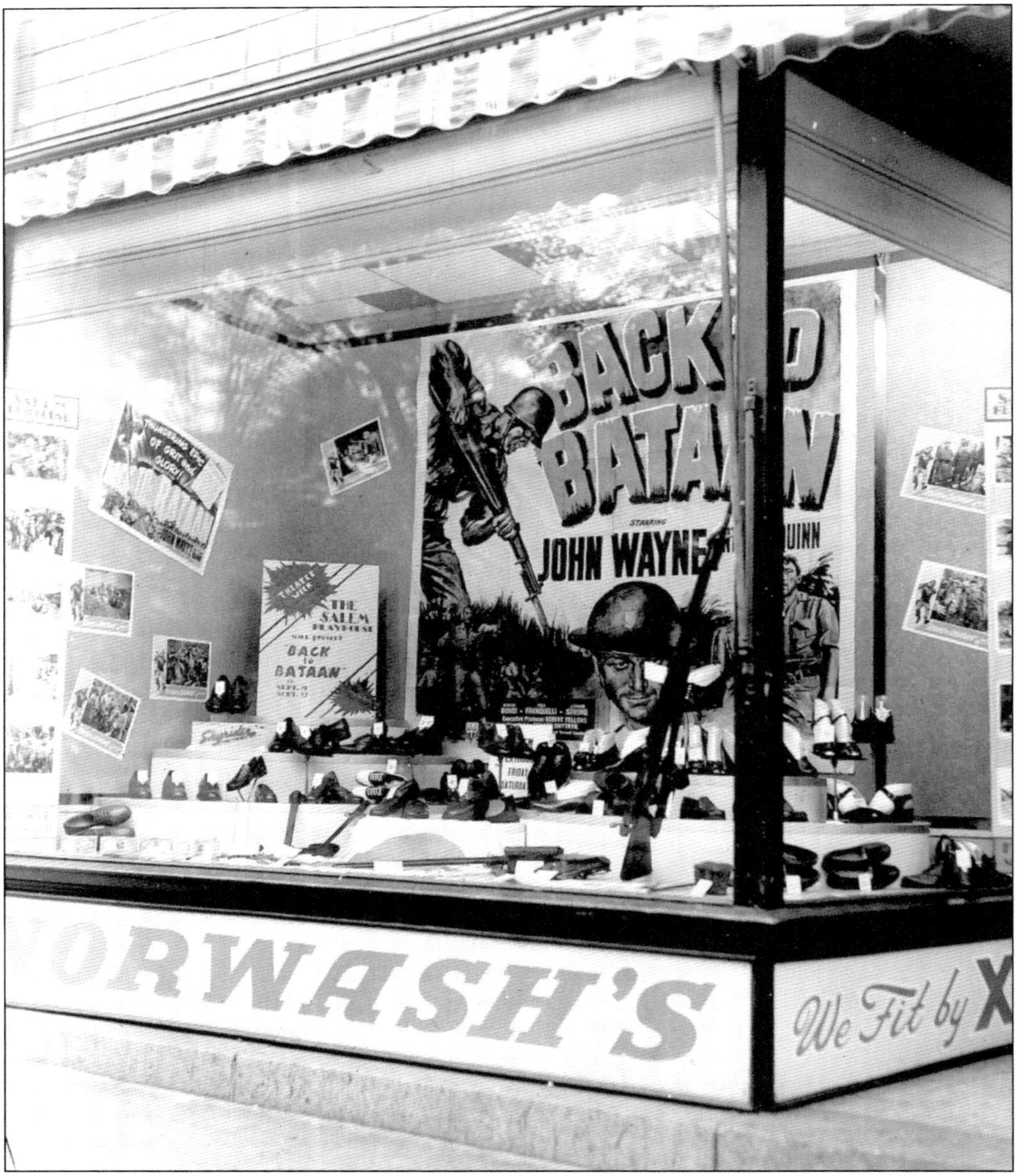

CROSS-PROMOTION: WAR, WEAPONS, AND SHOES? This Thibodeau image is almost surreal, at least when viewed through the lens of today. The display window at Norwash's store features a large poster of the latest John Wayne and Anthony Quinn action movie, *Back to Bataan*, released in 1945. Smaller posters and stills from the movie are distributed around the window. The September 26 and 27 viewing dates and the statement "NHS Presents" appear on a poster. This may have been a fundraising event. One would expect to find shoes in a shoe store display window, but this extravaganza has rifles! Also, notice the sign in the bottom right-hand corner. The full message is "We Fit By X-Ray." Customers, especially fascinated children, used to place their feet in a pair of shoes and then into an x-ray or fluoroscope unit to "see through" the shoes to check the fit. Considering that this method caused customers to be exposed to radiation every time they bought shoes, it is little wonder that it is no longer used.

Four

BUSINESSES, PRODUCTS, AND SERVICES

Manufacturing and Naugatuck have been almost synonymous since 1707, when the proprietors of Waterbury first permitted Samuel Hickox Jr. to establish a mill that would pass and dry cloth on Fulling Mill Brook. The mill started producing in 1711 or 1712, beginning a tradition of manufacturing that continues to this day in Naugatuck. Buttons, knives, clocks, candy, sneakers, chemicals, and safety pins are just a few of a long line of items that originated in Naugatuck and that brought that name around the world. Company names like Salem Bridge, U.S. Rubber, Uniroyal, Risdon, and Peter Paul and product names like Keds, Naugahyde, Almond Joy, and Mounds were well known internationally and helped to put Naugatuck on the world map.

One little-known story of a strange way our borough became a player on the international scene involved the open seas far away from Naugatuck's inviting hillsides. After Pearl Harbor was attacked, the Peter Paul Company could no longer obtain coconut from the Philippines to feed their candy-making machines at the factory on New Haven Road. A new source was found in the Caribbean and Central America. The company's fleet of schooners, too small to be a target for German submarines, provided the U.S. Navy with valuable information about the location of the enemy's subs. Who could have imagined such a scenario—a candy company "spying" for the military in time of war?

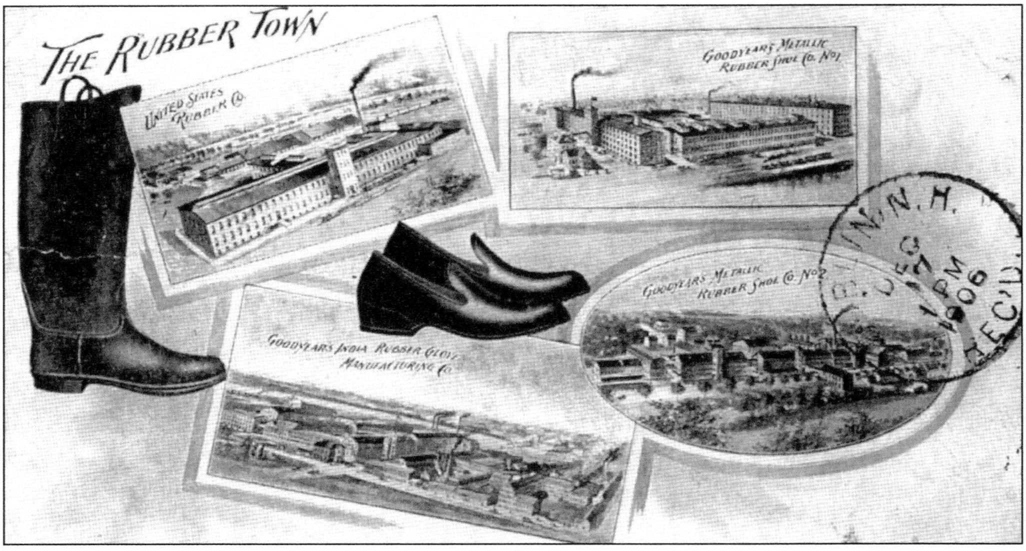

Advertising Rubbertown on a Postcard. This Perry Press postcard was sent on its way on December 15, 1906, from Union City. It is basically an advertisement for "the Rubber Town of Naugatuck." It portrays the local factory complexes engaged in the production of various rubber items and features articles of rubber footwear.

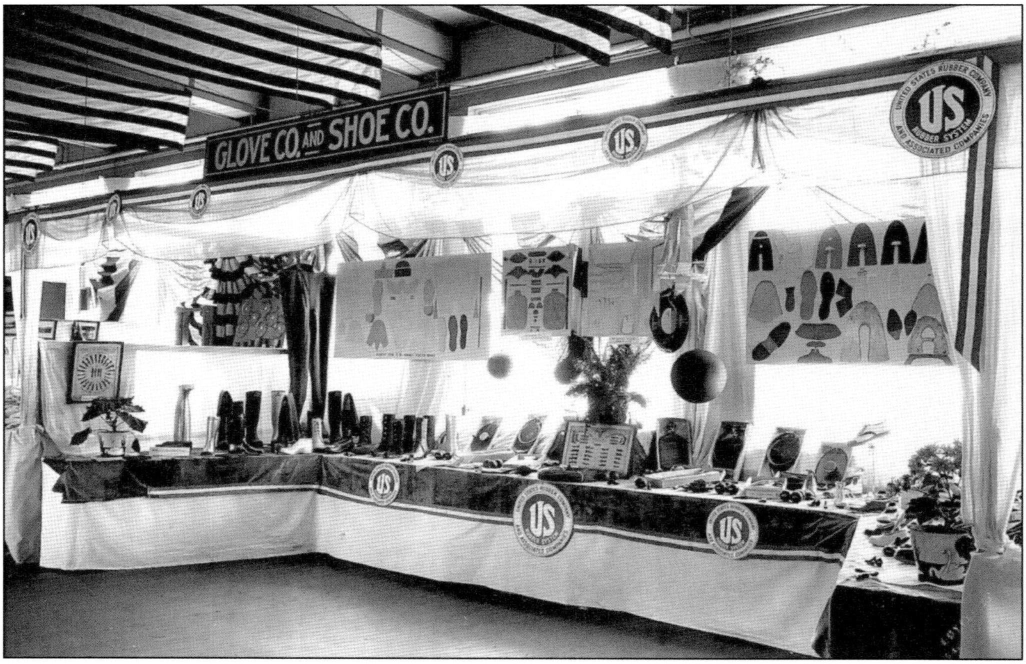

A Company on Solid Footing. The Naugatuck Chamber of Commerce sponsored a trade show in the early 1920s at its building on Bridge Street. Most local industries were represented. This appealing booth belonged to the Glove and Shoe Division of the U.S. Rubber Company and displayed the company's latest footwear and "handiwork." This photograph was taken by the Lovine Studio.

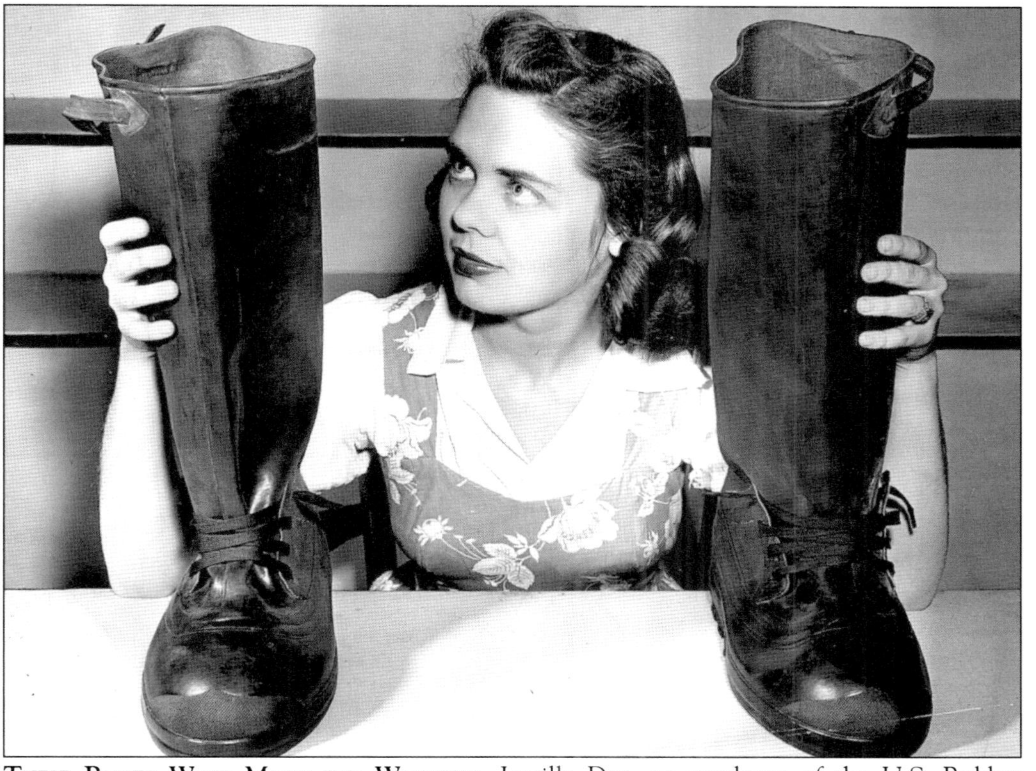

These Boots Were Made for Working. Lucille Dee, an employee of the U.S. Rubber Company in the Industrial Relations Department, was asked to pose for a series of photographs with these rather large rubber boots. Her attractive looks landed one of the photographs in an issue of *Popular Mechanics*. The photo session took place at the plant *c.* 1945. The U.S. Rubber Company later became the Uniroyal Company.

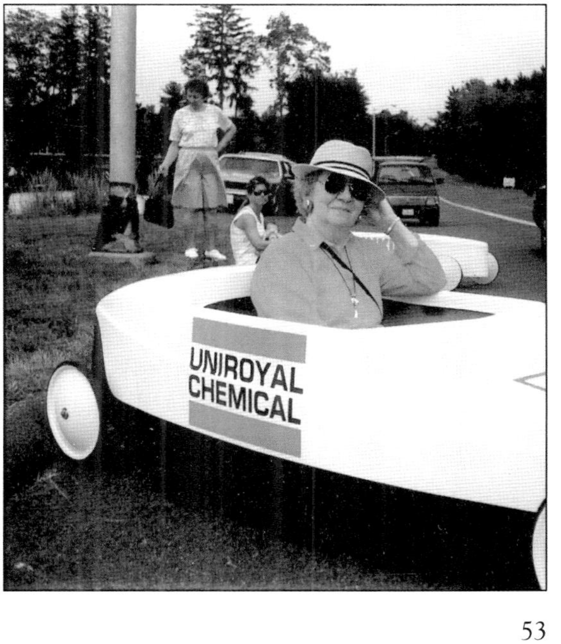

Invest in Plastics? Kraylastic is a hard latex that the Uniroyal Chemical Division developed for use as a lightweight material for automobile bodies. Uniroyal employee Frances Jackson is shown in a prototype at the industrial park off Union City Road in 1995. While Kraylastic may never have been used in automobile bodies, it was used to make small plastic items such as letter openers.

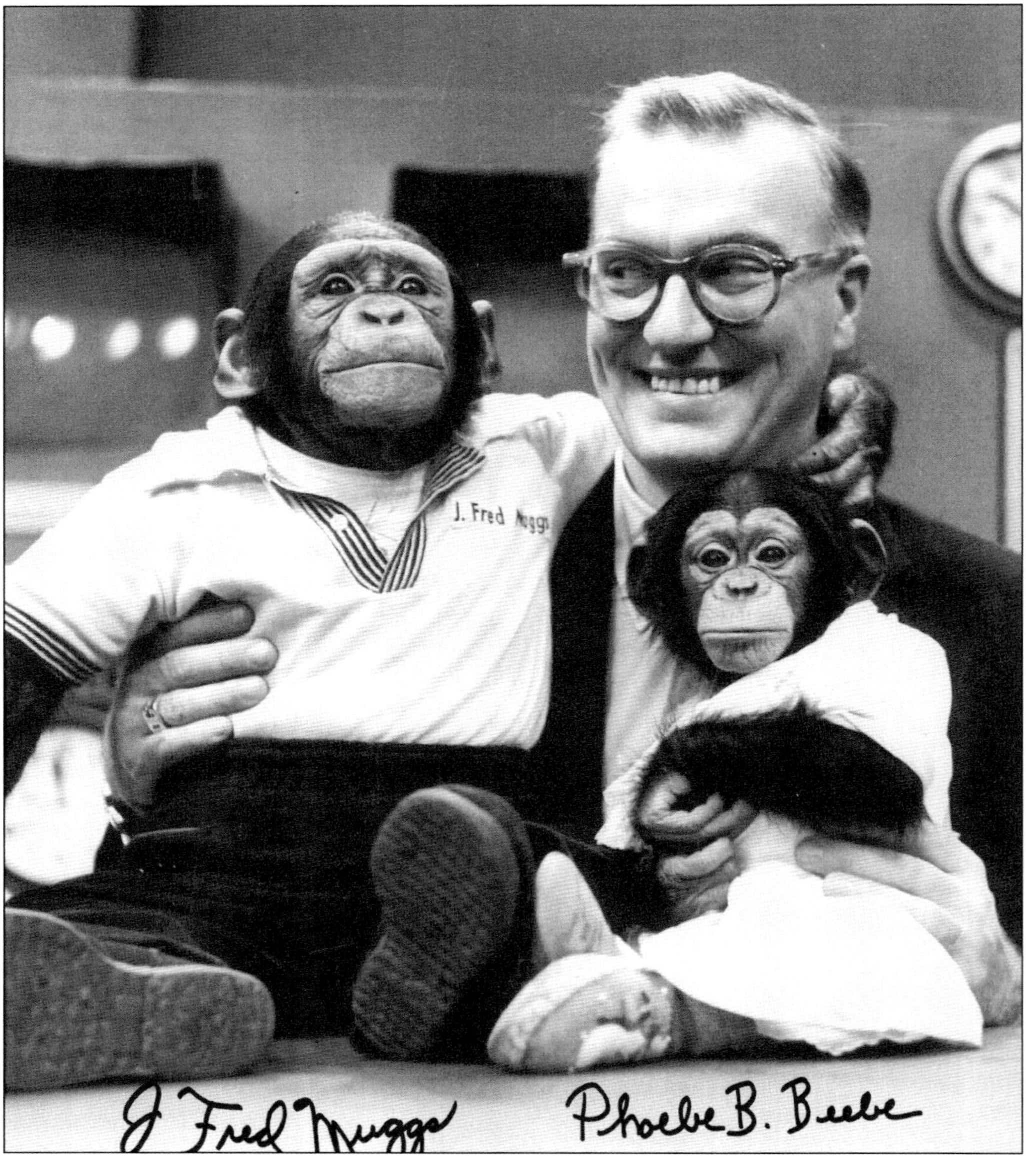

A PRIMETIME PRIMATE. The Naugatuck Historical Society Museum, located in the former railroad station on Water Street, is the home for this jungle-related photograph. Dave Garroway was the first host of NBC's still popular *Today Show*, which began in January 1952. The chimp shown above, J. Fred Muggs, was added a year later in February 1953 and continued as co-host through March 1957. Of course no self-respecting television co-host could run around barefoot, so it was decided he needed sneakers. Twice a year, J. Fred and his trainer made the trek to Naugatuck to the U.S. Rubber Company, where Fred was fitted for his size 8 1/2 extra wide sneakers. In 1999, the pair on display in the photograph was offered at auction on eBay. Naugatuck Historical Society member Greg Nole led the effort to find the funds to buy them. With the help of society member Bob Stauffer and his fellow members of "Club 47" of Naugatuck High School's graduating class of 1947, the money was raised, and the sneakers came back to their original hometown.

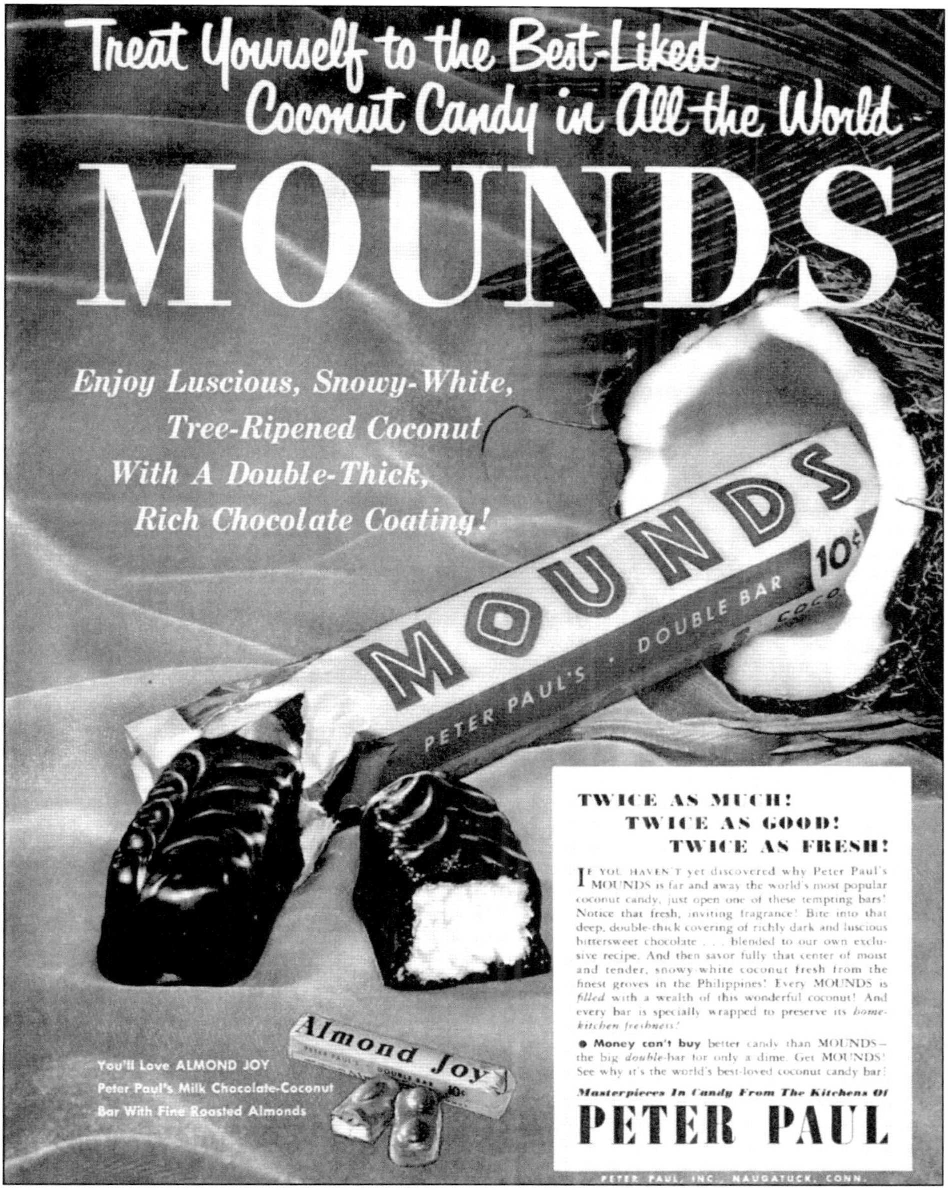

THE INFLUENCE OF TROPICAL PLANTS ON NAUGATUCK. This advertisement from the October 24, 1950, issue of *Look* magazine promotes the most famous edible products from Naugatuck: Mounds and Almond Joy candy bars, made by the Peter Paul Candy Company. Two of the major ingredients in these confections are chocolate, made from the cocoa bean, and coconut, made from the meat of the nuts taken from certain types of palm trees. Both are grown in tropical climes. If you consider that the recipe also calls for sugar, harvested from sugar cane raised on plantations in many tropical countries, the three plants cement Naugatuck's connection to and dependence upon tropical countries. And if you were to add the rubber tree, the plant that was mostly responsible for Naugatuck's growth, into the equation, it would become even more clear that this municipality would never have attained its international stature if not for nature and the entrepreneurial use of her tropical bounty.

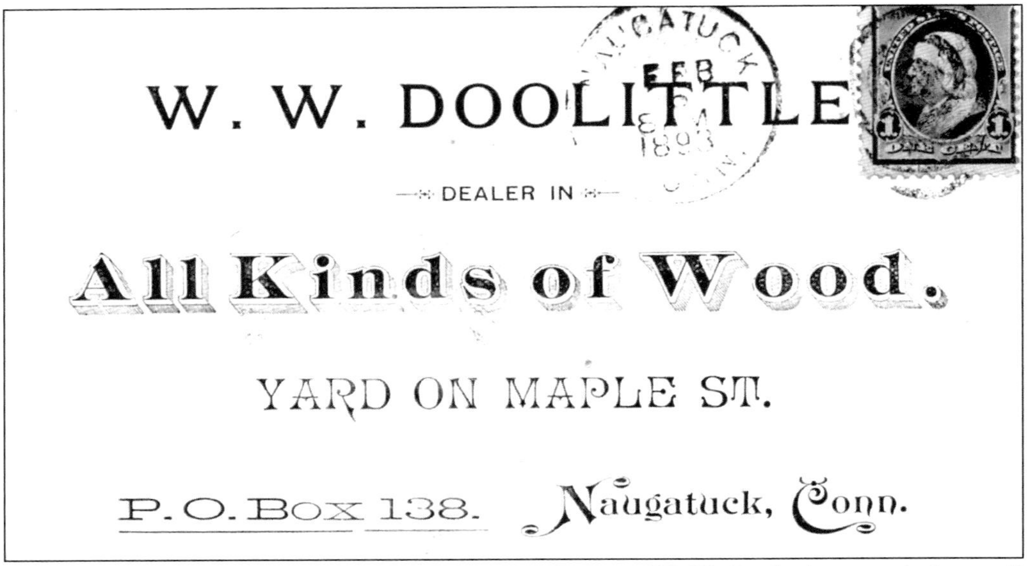

W. W. DOOLITTLE

DEALER IN

All Kinds of Wood.

YARD ON MAPLE ST.

P. O. BOX 138. Naugatuck, Conn.

NAUGATUCK FEB 6 1893 CONN.

GOOD WOOD, APPROPRIATELY LOCATED ON MAPLE STREET. W. W. Doolittle was a dealer in all kinds of wood and had a wood yard on Maple Street. This order form and advertisement has a postal cancellation dated February 6, 1893, and was sent from John A. Anderson of Aetna Street.

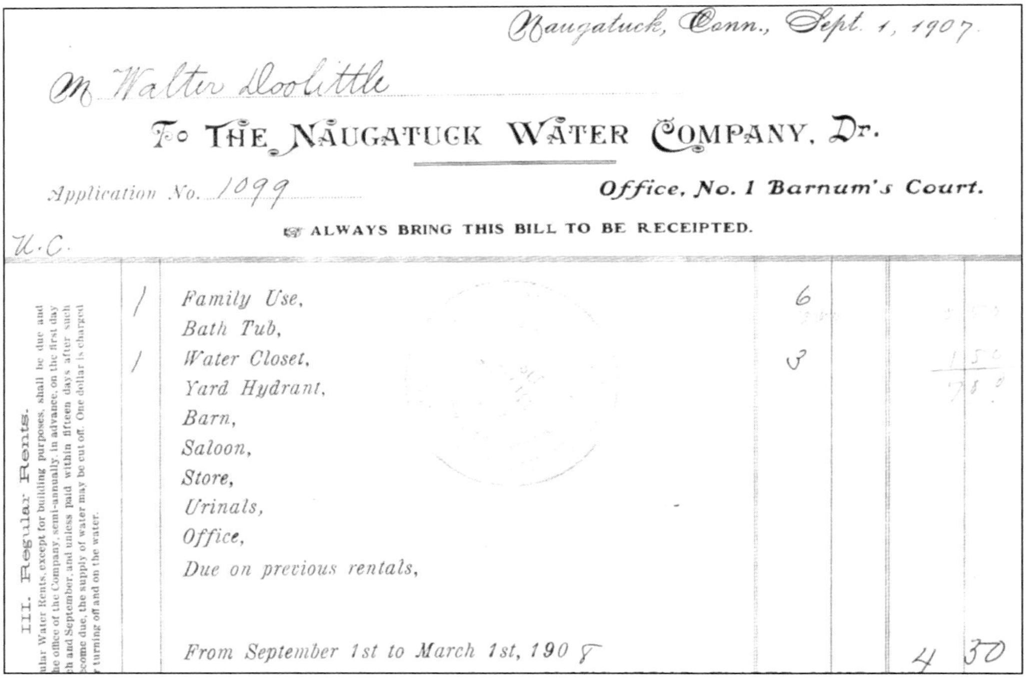

Naugatuck, Conn., Sept. 1, 1907.

M Walter Doolittle

To THE NAUGATUCK WATER COMPANY, Dr.

Application No. 1099

Office, No. 1 Barnum's Court.

ALWAYS BRING THIS BILL TO BE RECEIPTED.

U. C.

III. Regular Rents.

...ular Water Rents, except for building purposes, shall be due and ...he office of the Company, semi-annually, in advance, on the first day ...h and September, and unless paid within fifteen days after such ...ecome due, the supply of water may be cut off. One dollar is charged ...r turning off and on the water.

1	Family Use,	6		
	Bath Tub,			
1	Water Closet,	3		
	Yard Hydrant,			
	Barn,			
	Saloon,			
	Store,			
	Urinals,			
	Office,			
	Due on previous rentals,			
	From September 1st to March 1st, 1908		4	30

NO SHORTAGE OF WATER IN NAUGATUCK. Unlike many municipalities, Naugatuck turned down the opportunity to establish a water company. Instead, the state of Connecticut recognized a group of businessmen who administered this precious resource. This may have been wood dealer Walter Doolittle's bill. It was paid on September 6, 1907. Water bills of the era were itemized and stamped with the date and time in an interesting fashion.

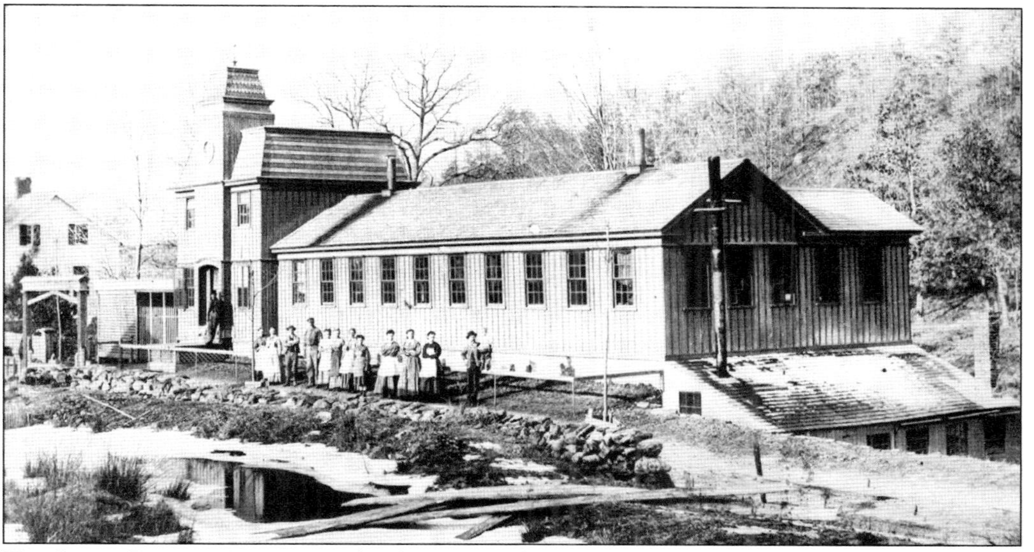

The Smith Button Factory. This factory was located on Prospect Street in Union City. The Smith company manufactured "vegetable ivory" buttons, made from part of a tropical plant. One of the assembled employees has a child on his shoulder who was undoubtedly "as cute as a button."

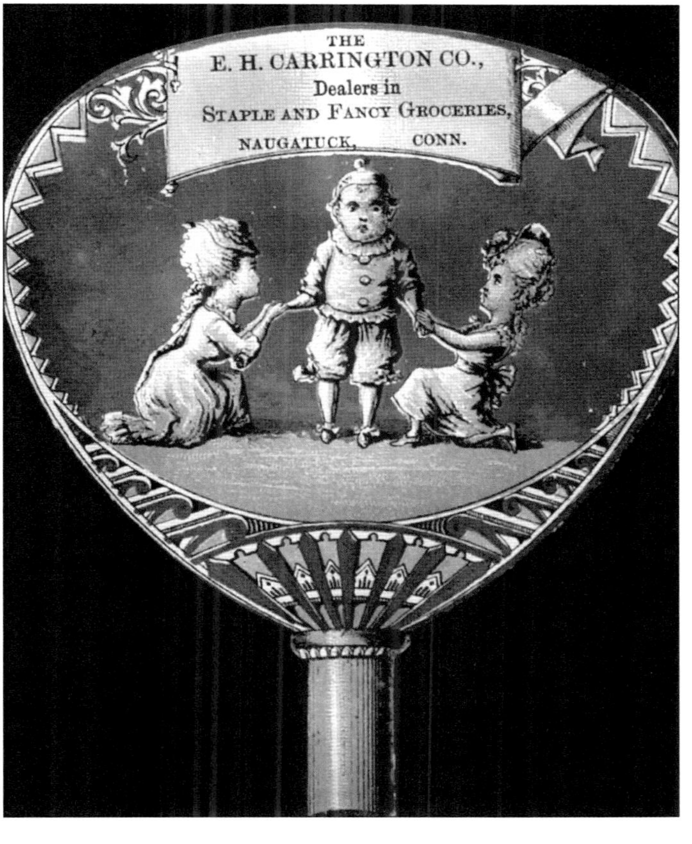

A Fan for Their Fans. Edward H. Carrington decided to promote his store with this impressive-looking miniature fan. In 1891, the store was located on Maple Street opposite the railroad depot (where the fire station is now). Carrington sold "staple as well as fancy groceries." The golden background and rich look of this piece accomplish Carrington's intent: it looks high-class and expensive and presents the image of a ritzy store.

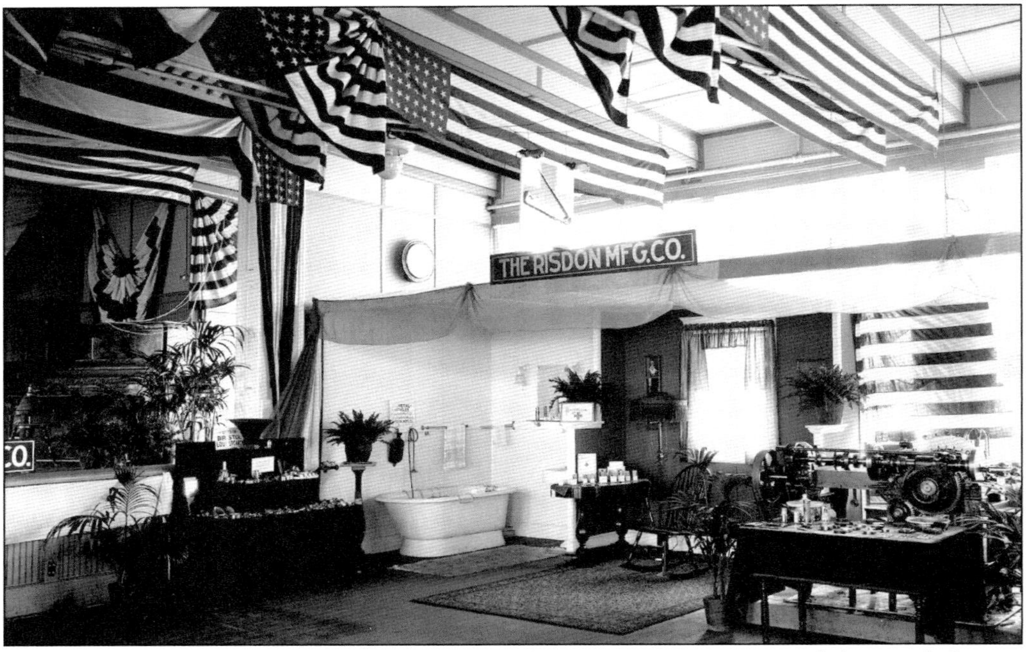

RISDON RISES. In 1910, the Risdon Tool Manufacturing Company was a failing tool shop in Waterbury. An infusion of new investor money led to a move to Andrew Avenue in Naugatuck *c.* 1913, when Lewis Dibble began 50 years of service as general manager. This photograph, taken at an early-1920s trade show sponsored by the Naugatuck Chamber of Commerce, shows that Risdon became a thriving manufacturer of metal goods, including safety pins, pins, movie cameras, cosmetic containers, Colt 45 cartridge clips, and whistling toy canaries.

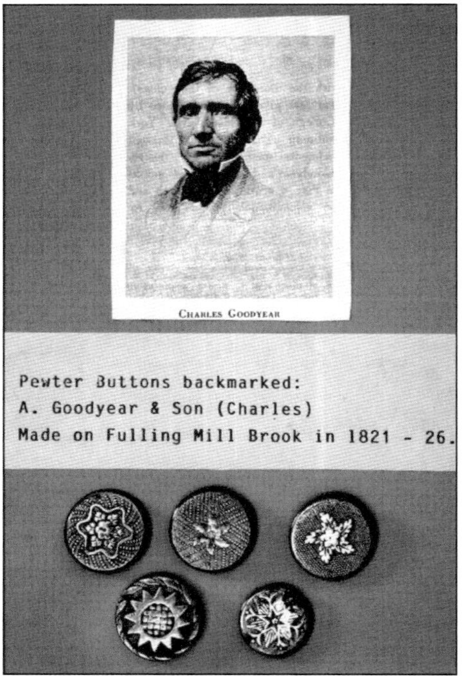

BUTTON, BUTTON, WHO'S GOT THE BUTTON. Amasa Goodyear, father of Charles, produced a high-quality line of buttons *c.* 1820. He was the first to create pearl buttons in the United States. He and his son also opened the first hardware store in America, in Philadelphia in 1826. The rare and valuable buttons in this photograph were collected, researched, and donated to the Naugatuck Historical Society Museum by society member and button dealer Marilyn Nichols.

THE WHITE HOUSE

WASHINGTON

August 27, 1974

Dear Chris,

Thank you for your recent letter concerning your son, Mac's, candidacy for Congress from the First Congressional District of Connecticut. He has my sincere congratulations on winning the Republican nomination at the state Republican Convention. I know that you are justifiably proud of him.

In reference to your interest in financial assistance from the national level, the National Republican Congressional Committee will be reviewing their allocation of funds following the respective state primaries.

It is good to know that young leaders of high caliber are running for public office at every level. Our nation is depending on their leadership today and in the future. My sincere best wishes to you for your efforts on your son's behalf, and to Mac for a highly successful campaign and victory in November.

Warm regards.

Sincerely,

Gerald R. Ford

Mr. Christopher H. Buckley
Chairman of the Board
Risdon Manufacturing Company
Naugatuck, Connecticut

A Letter from a President to a President. This letter was one of three discovered by the author under a pile of magazines in Joe's Antiques Store on Church Street. It had been sent to Christopher Buckley, president of Risdon, by Pres. Gerald Ford. Interestingly, the signatures on each letter were different, possibly because they were signed by a secretary or by auto-pen. The signature on this letter is closest to POTUS Ford. "POTUS" was a Secret Service code meaning "president of the United States."

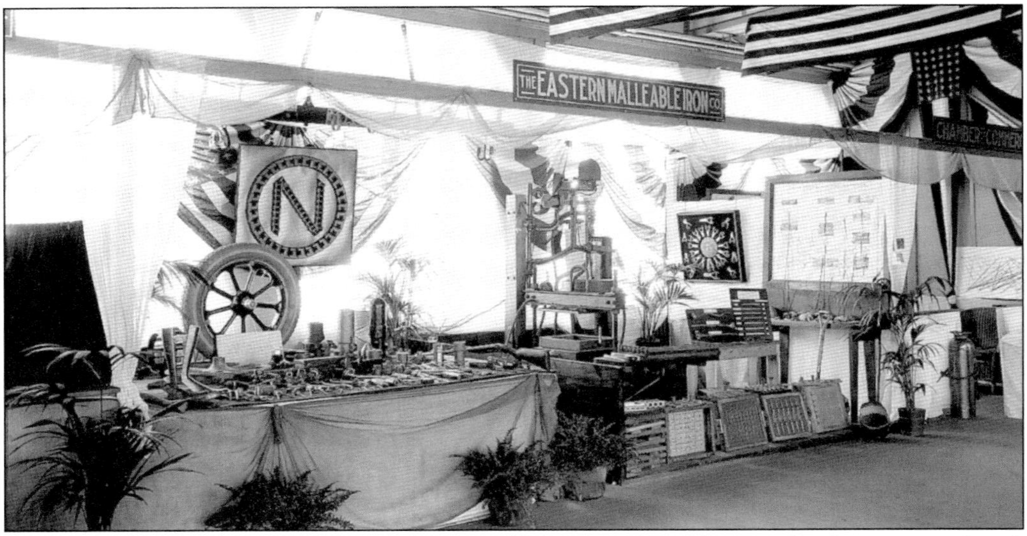

Iron at Its Core. John H. Whittemore arrived here in 1858, and soon after, he partnered with Bronson B. Tuttle to found the Naugatuck Malleable Iron Company, which eventually became one of the foremost producers of malleable iron in the country. Malleable iron was used when a product was required to be flexible and strong. The factory provided wheel hubs for carriages and Union army caissons as well as plates to hold railroad ties together.

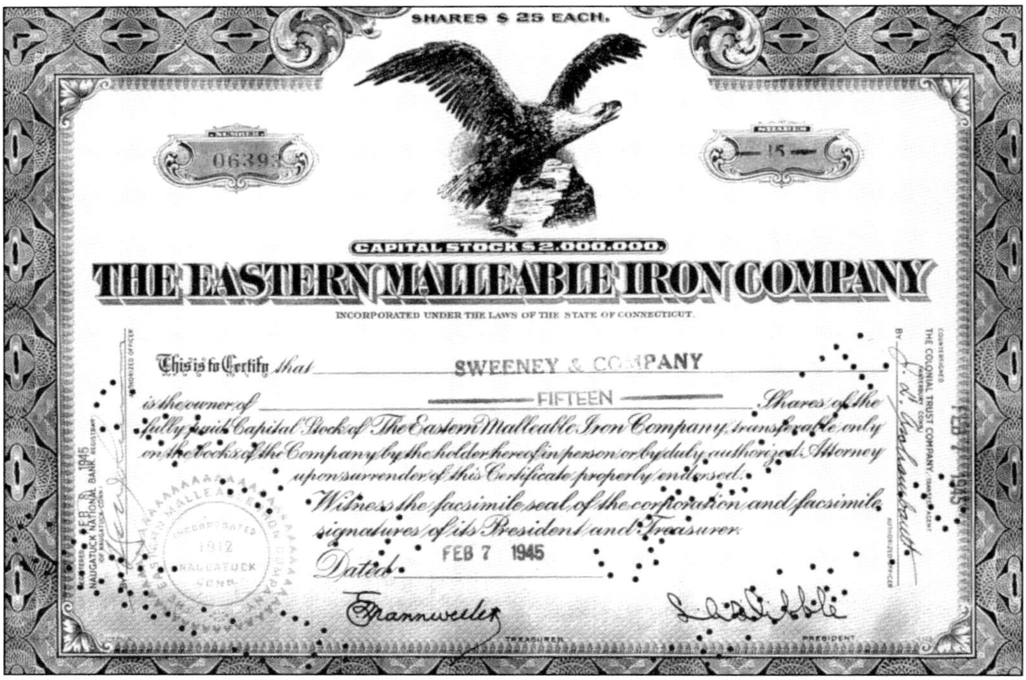

Taking Stock in the Eastern Malleable Iron Company. In 1945, Sweeney and Company purchased 15 shares in the Eastern Malleable Iron Company. This document reflects the ornate nature of stock certificates then and now. At one time, the Eastern Malleable complex covered numerous acres in Naugatuck, and the company had plants in other cities in the country. The company eventually became known as the Eastern Company.

Five

The Military, Monuments, and Moving Moments

Naugatuck has had a lengthy history of supporting our country's military in times of peace and in times of war. Numerous companies that were located here provided materiel to the military juggernaut. Naugatuck's citizens have served proudly during the wars and conflicts in which the United States has fought. As in many other communities, there have been numerous monuments, plaques, and honor rolls prominently positioned throughout the town over the years. The green features two monuments, the Great War Memorial and the Soldiers' Monument. This chapter will acquaint the reader with some of the ways the citizens of Naugatuck have chosen to honor those who fought and died for democracy.

Also to be found in this chapter are accounts of some of the individuals who shipped out to the war front, putting their lives and families on hold to become a part of a fighting unit or support group. Some fought in conflicts within our boundaries; others served in far-flung locations and countries they had never studied in local schools' geography lessons.

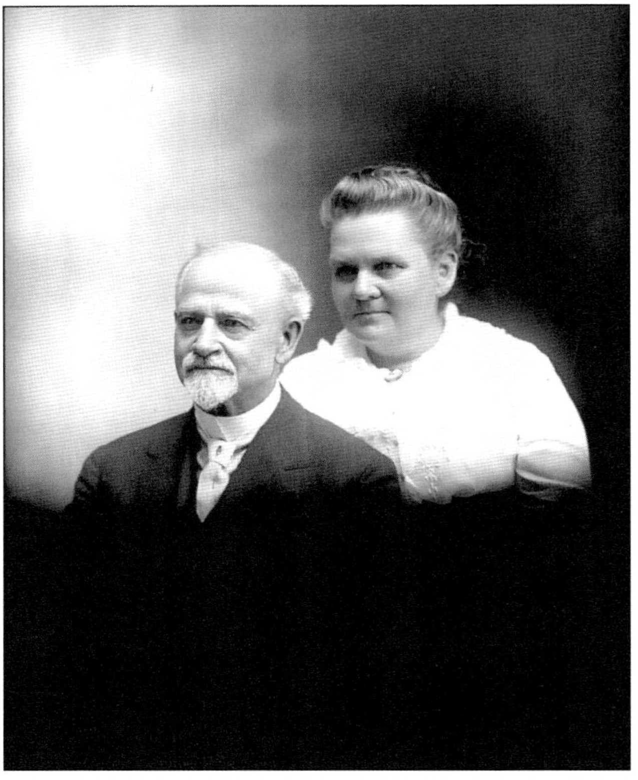

Sheldon and Nellie Hoadley Payne. Sheldon Franklin Payne, Naugatuck's longest-surviving veteran of the Civil War, was born in Naugatuck on October 2, 1842. He served in Company H of the Connecticut 23rd Regiment. Payne was one of the oldest members of the Masons in the state and was also a member of the American Society of Engineers. He installed a majority of the heavy machinery in Naugatuck's rubber factories. Payne died on December 7, 1939, at his home in Naugatuck.

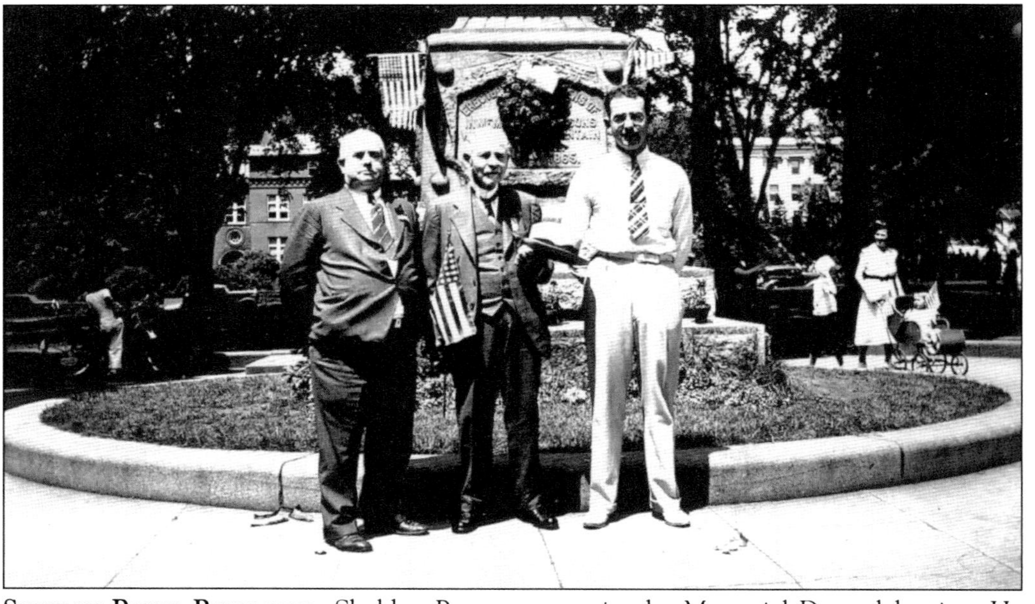

Sheldon Payne Remembers. Sheldon Payne never missed a Memorial Day celebration. He attended his last one on the green at age 96 and answered proudly during the roll call. This photograph was taken on May 30, 1937, and includes Walter Payne Sr., Sheldon Payne, and Walter Payne Jr. They are posed in front of the Soldiers' Monument on the green.

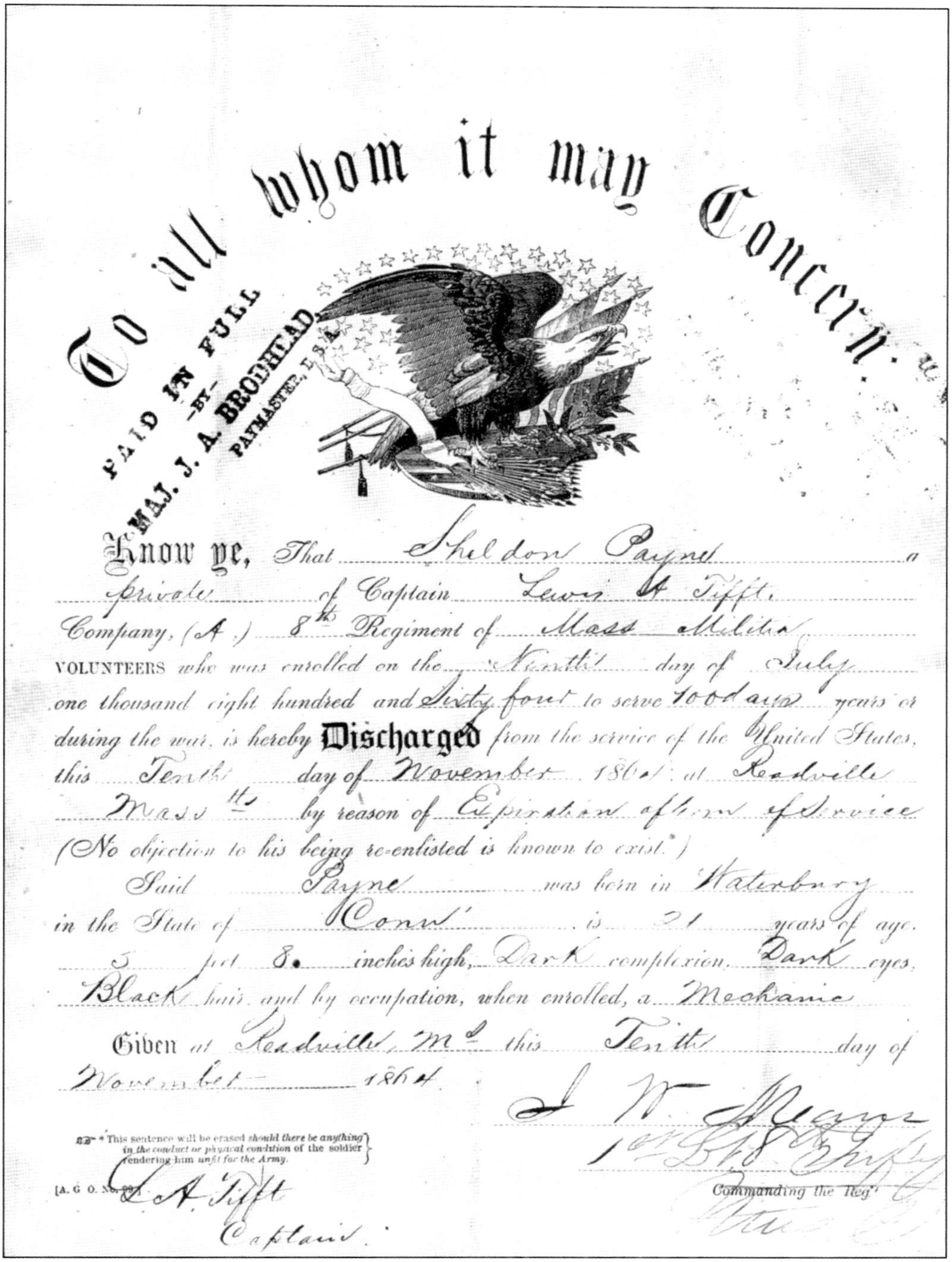

To all whom it may Concern.

PAID IN FULL
-BY-
MAJ. J. A. BRODHEAD,
PAYMASTER, U.S.A.

Know ye, That Sheldon Payne a private of Captain Lewis H Tifft Company, (A) 8th Regiment of Mass Militia VOLUNTEERS who was enrolled on the Ninth day of July one thousand eight hundred and Sixty four to serve 100 days years or during the war, is hereby Discharged from the service of the United States, this Tenth day of November 1864 at Readville Mass tts by reason of Expiration of term of Service (No objection to his being re-enlisted is known to exist.*)

Said Payne was born in Waterbury in the State of Conn is 21 years of age, 5 feet 8 inches high, Dark complexion, Dark eyes, Black hair, and by occupation, when enrolled, a Mechanic

Given at Readville Ms this Tenth day of November 1864.

*This sentence will be erased should there be anything in the conduct or physical condition of the soldier rendering him unfit for the Army.

[A. G. O. No. 99.]

L. A. Tifft
Captain

J. W. Meyer
1st Lt 8th Infy
Commanding the Reg.

TO ALL WHOM IT MAY CONCERN. This is the official discharge form of Sheldon Franklin Payne, dated November 10, 1864. It states he was born in Waterbury because Naugatuck was still part of that city in 1842, when Sheldon was born. Most soldiers are pleased when they finally get this document in their hands. It signifies a return to the lives and families they left behind.

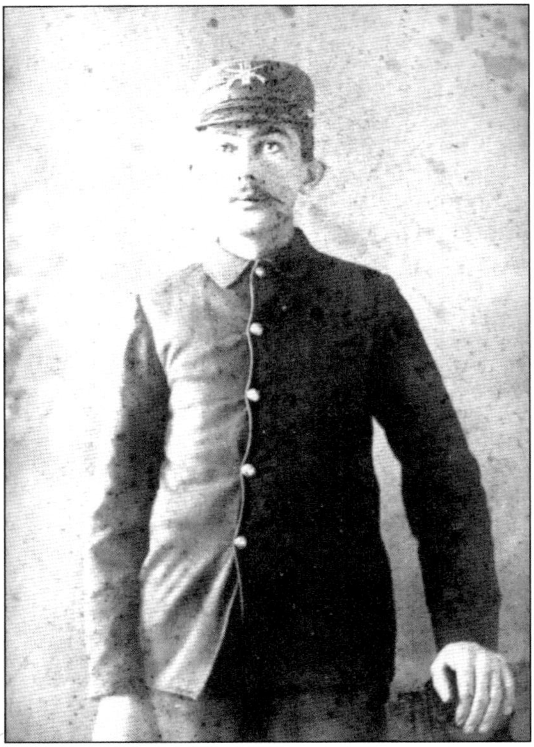

A Proud Soldier. Clifford Culver poses proudly in this uniform. It looks like it is from the Civil War era, but there are no insignias, and the symbol on the hat could not be identified. The back of the photograph reveals that he had two sisters, Fannie and Sarah, and a son, Russell, who had no children.

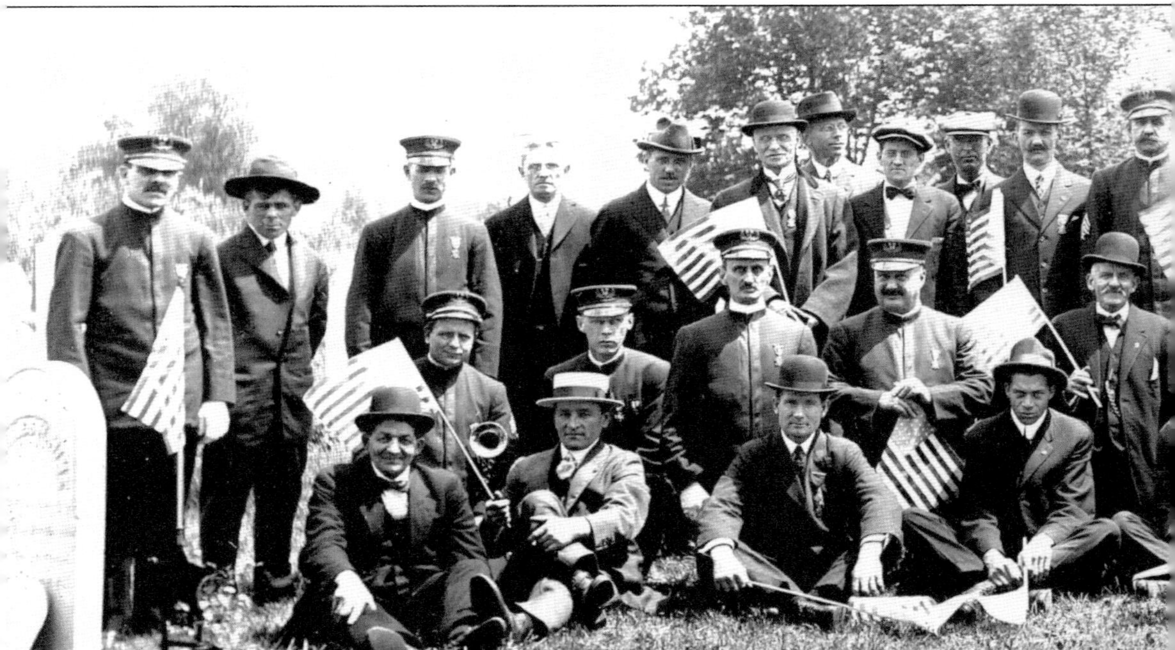

Men of History Celebrating History. Naugatuck's remaining Civil War veterans gather for a group photograph among the graves of their departed comrades. No date or location was listed

A World War I Casualty. J. Edward Dooley fought in World War I. On the back of this photograph it states, "He died for his country on the battlefields of France." He was killed on October 12, 1918.

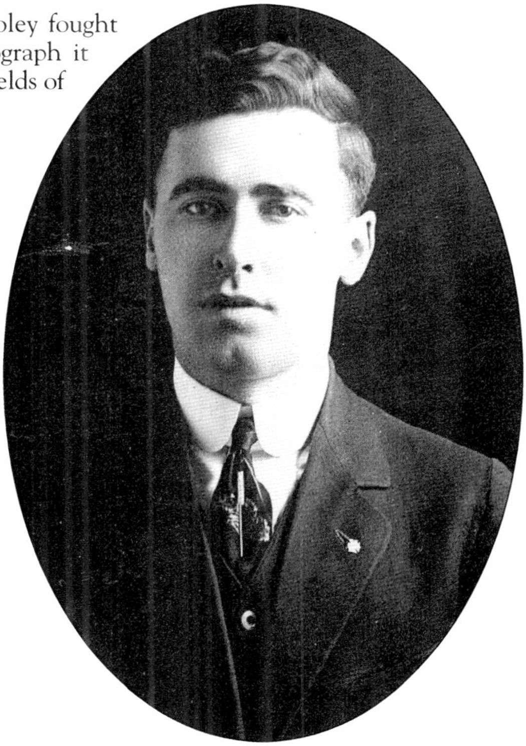

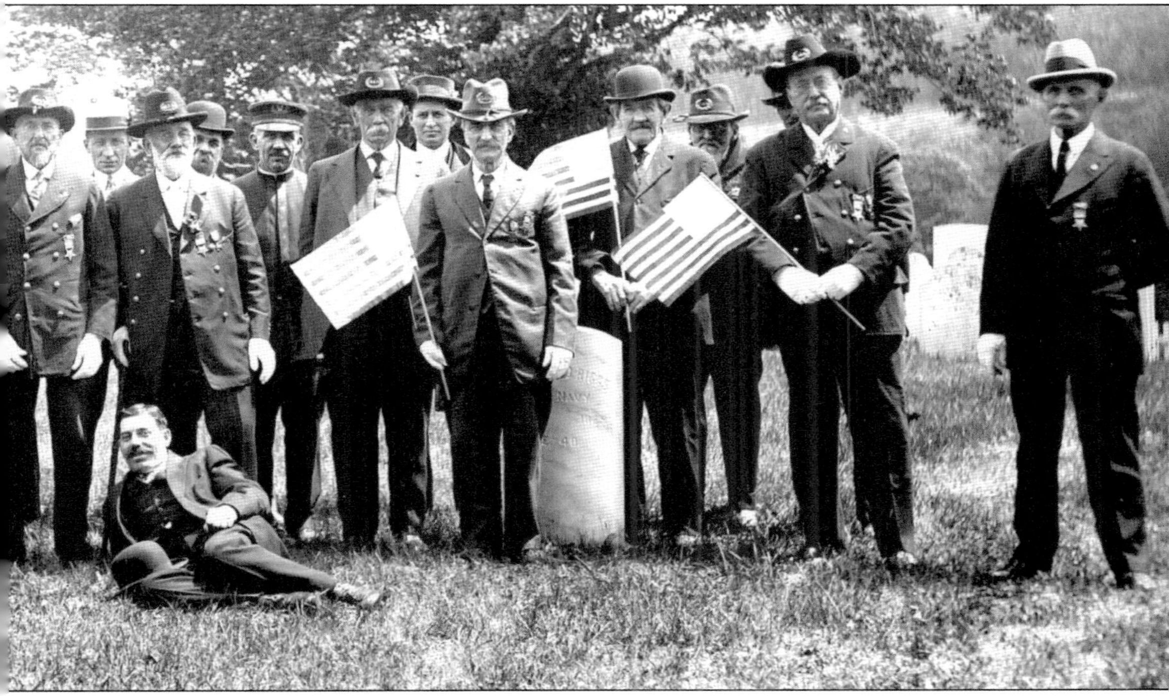

for this image. The man on the extreme right appears to be Sheldon Payne; he outlived all of the men in this photograph.

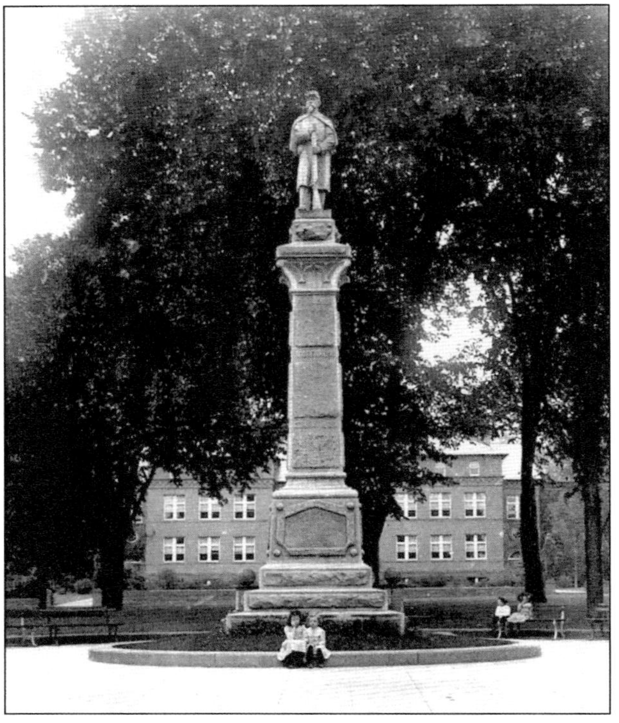

The Soldiers' Monument on the Green. This imposing statue was dedicated on May 30, 1885, on what was then called Decoration Day. The memorial celebrated the 236 of Naugatuck's men who fought in the Civil War, 29 of whom did not return. The monument is made of granite and cost over $3,000.

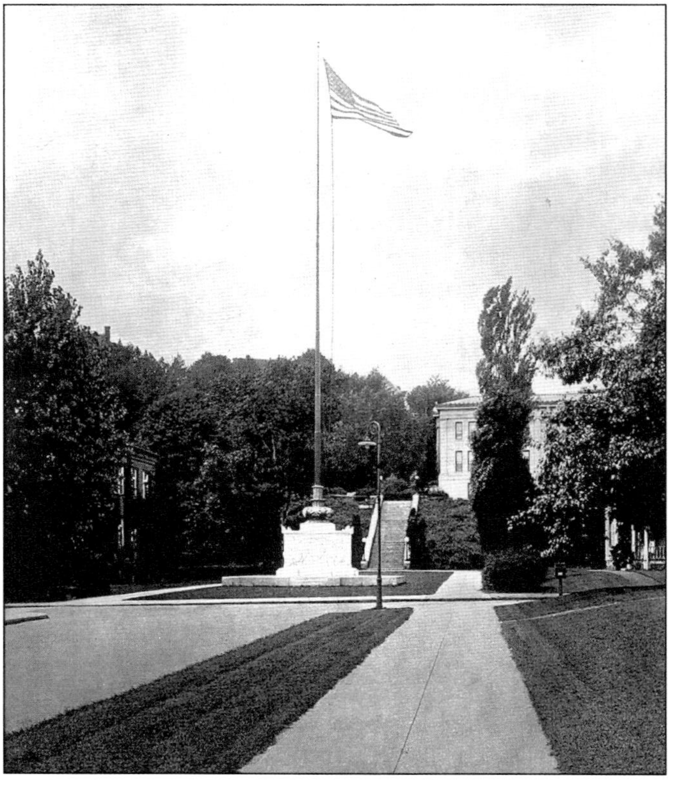

The Great War Memorial on the Green. This memorial, by Evelyn Beatrice Longman, was dedicated in 1921. Its base is made of Italian marble and resembles an altar, a symbol of the sacrifice our soldiers made. Figures representing war and victory are carved in bas-relief on its east face. The names of 30 soldiers who gave their lives are carved on the west face.

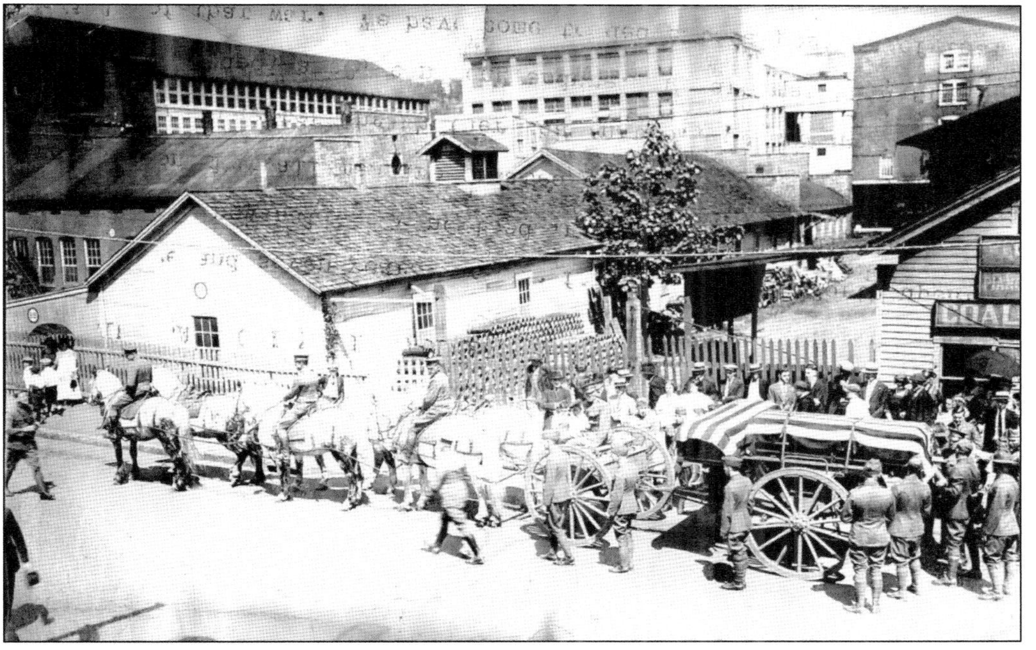

The Caisson Goes Rolling Along. Soldiers prepare to march in a Naugatuck parade, probably the Memorial Day parade. A group of onlookers watches them prepare the caisson and get into formation.

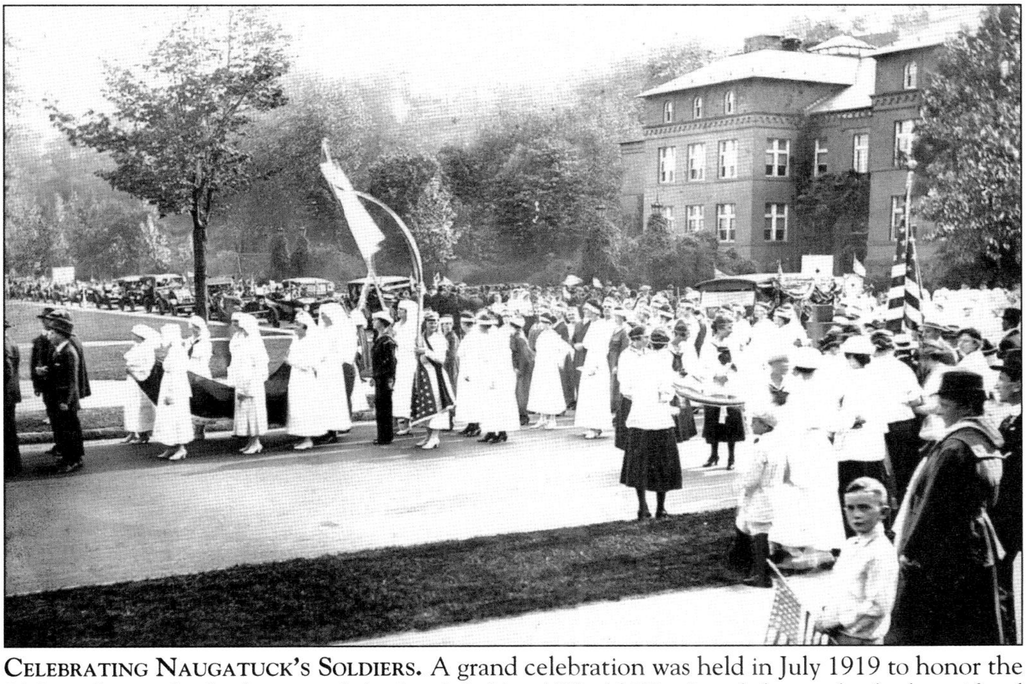

Celebrating Naugatuck's Soldiers. A grand celebration was held in July 1919 to honor the 836 residents who had survived the battlefields of World War I and those who had sacrificed their lives defending their country. This image shows a parade proceeding in front of Salem School and eastward down Division Street. It is likely a Fourth of July celebration.

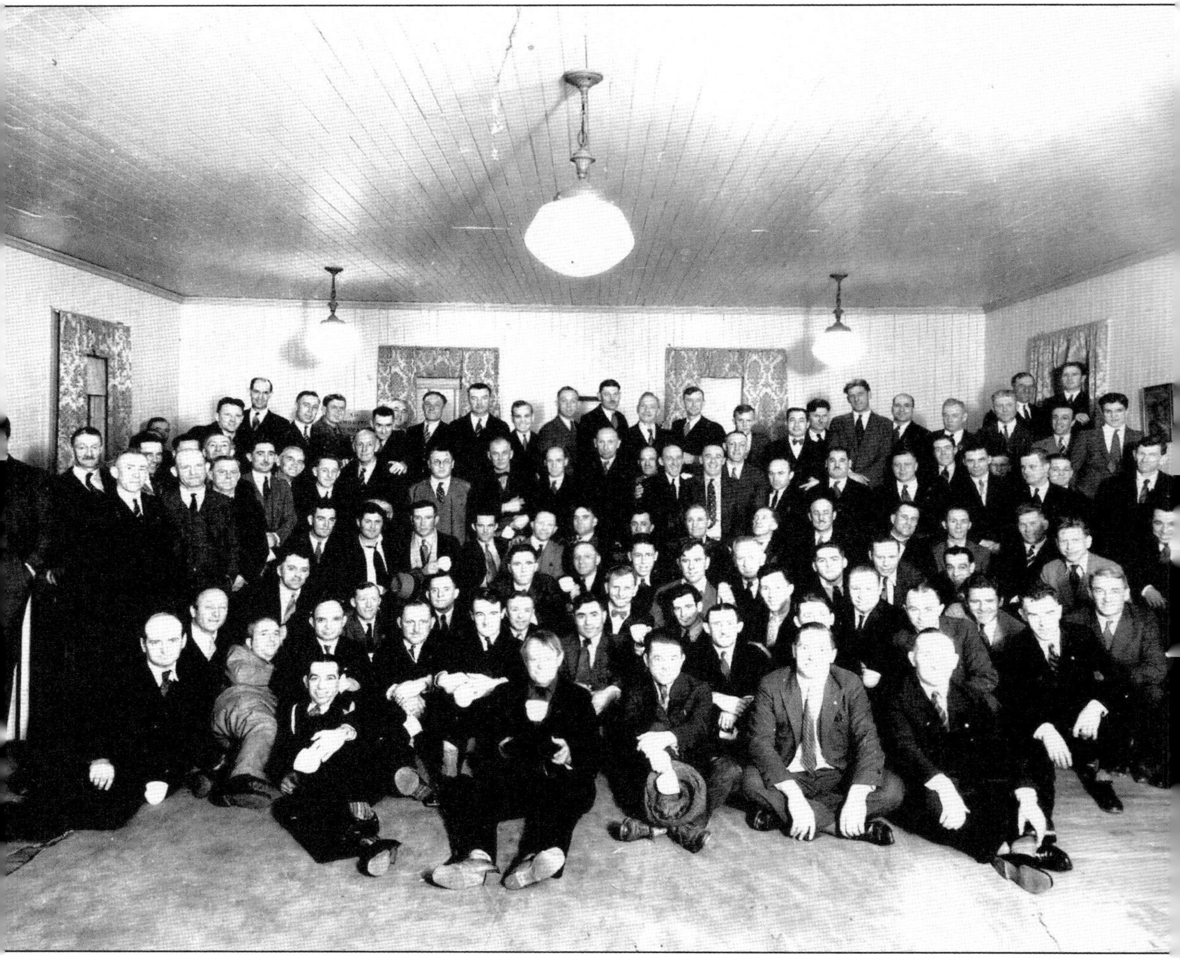

MEN AT THE VETERANS OF FOREIGN WARS HALL. The Veterans of Foreign Wars (VFW) hall was the setting for many happy and poignant moments, tales of battlefield heroics, and toasts to those who never returned. This assemblage of Naugatuck veterans posed there in the late 1920s or early 1930s. Three men have been identified. The gent in the center of the front row with the cup on his bowler is Wilbert Jordan. John Jordan, his son, is in the second row, to Wilbert's right. Another son, Wilfred Jordan, is in the back row in front of a window, although we do not know which window.

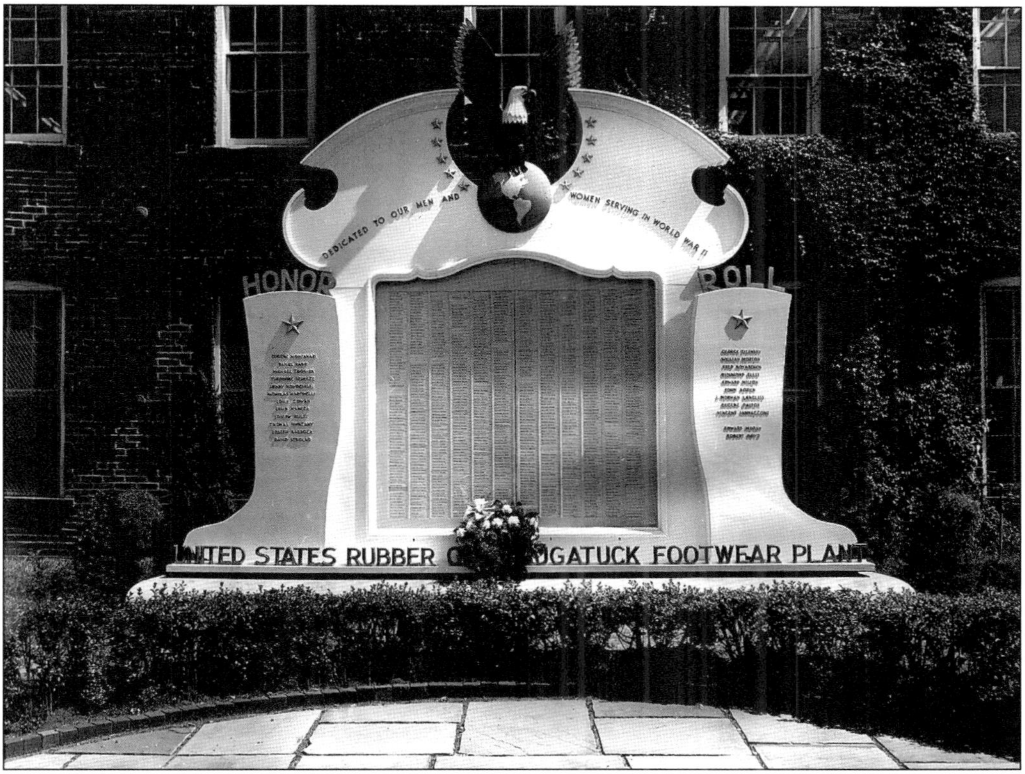

The U.S. Rubber Honor Roll. An impressive monument was erected by the U.S. Rubber Company to honor its employees who had served in World War II.

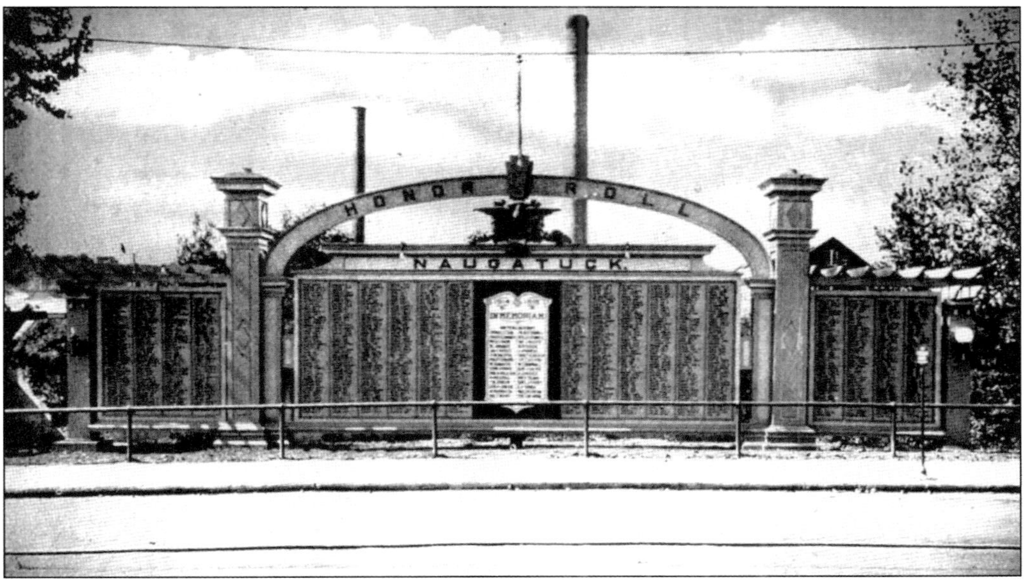

Naugatuck's Honor Roll. Naugatuck chose to honor it residents who had served the country in time of war with this massive honor roll. It no longer greets pedestrians; it is said to have been washed away in the flood of August 19, 1955.

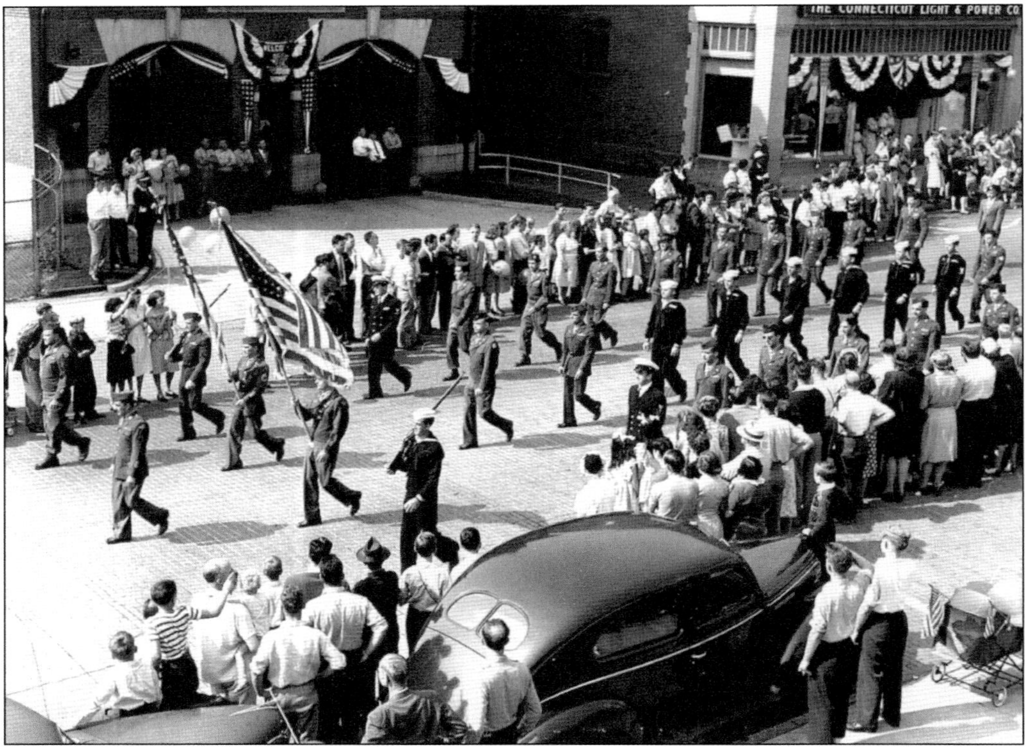

THE WELCOME HOME PARADE. Maple Street was the scene of this 1946 parade welcoming home Naugatuck's veterans from the battlefields of World War II. The firehouse is visible on the left side of the photograph. All branches of the service were represented among the marchers.

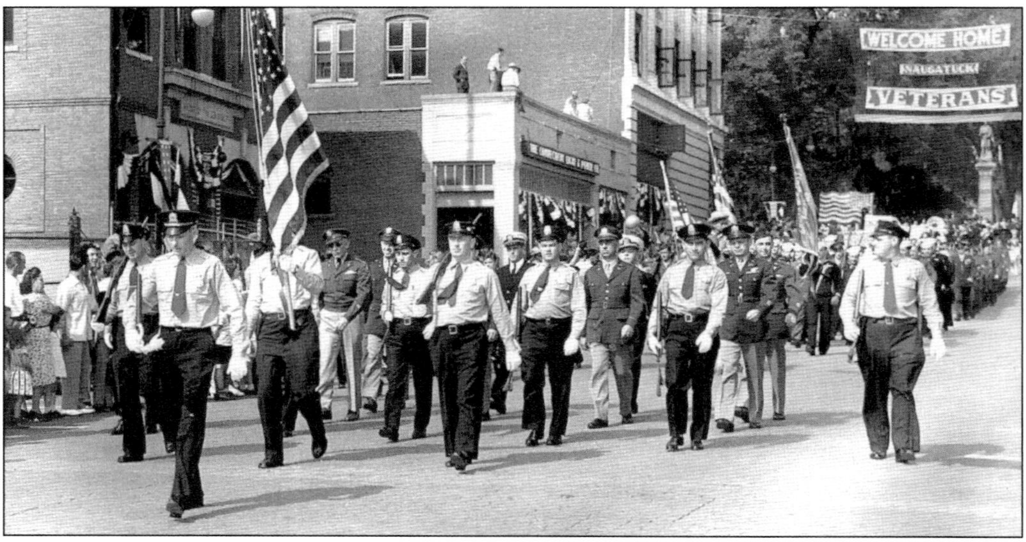

IN AMONG THE MARCHERS. The banner stretched across Maple Street proclaims the purpose of the parade for all to see. A few lucky folks have positioned themselves on a nearby roof for an unobstructed view. The photographer has captured a ground-level angle of the police department honor guard marching in front of one of the military units.

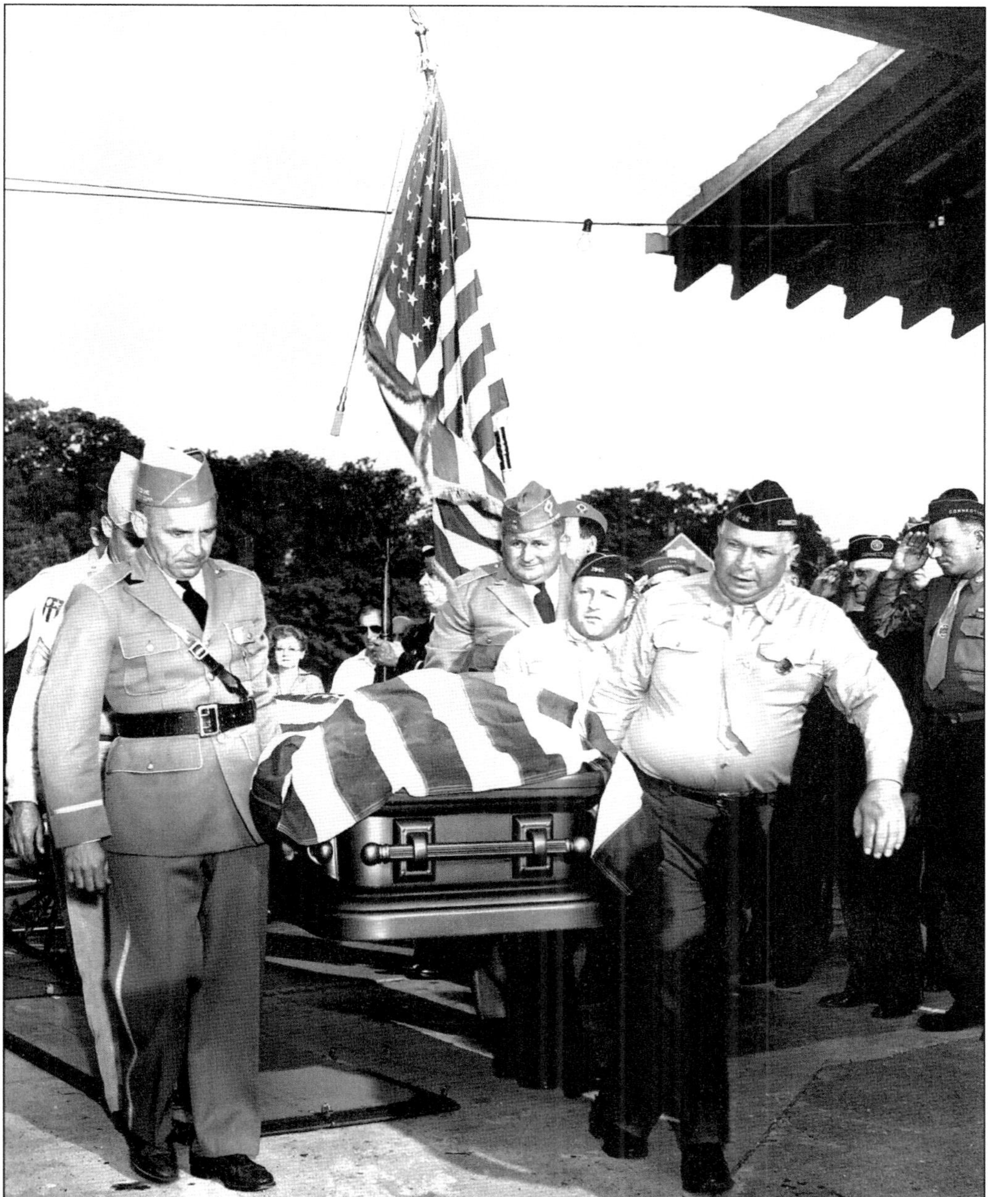

PALL BEARERS. A flag-draped coffin contains the remains of a Naugatuck resident who lost his life in defense of his country. Although the photograph contains no identifying information, it is likely that the person died in World War II or in the Korean War. The distinctive roof identifies the site of this touching scene as the rear of the railroad station. Two of the participants have been identified. At the front of the coffin, holding it with his left hand, is a gentleman whose last name is Fratesi. Directly under the flag is Henry Racki.

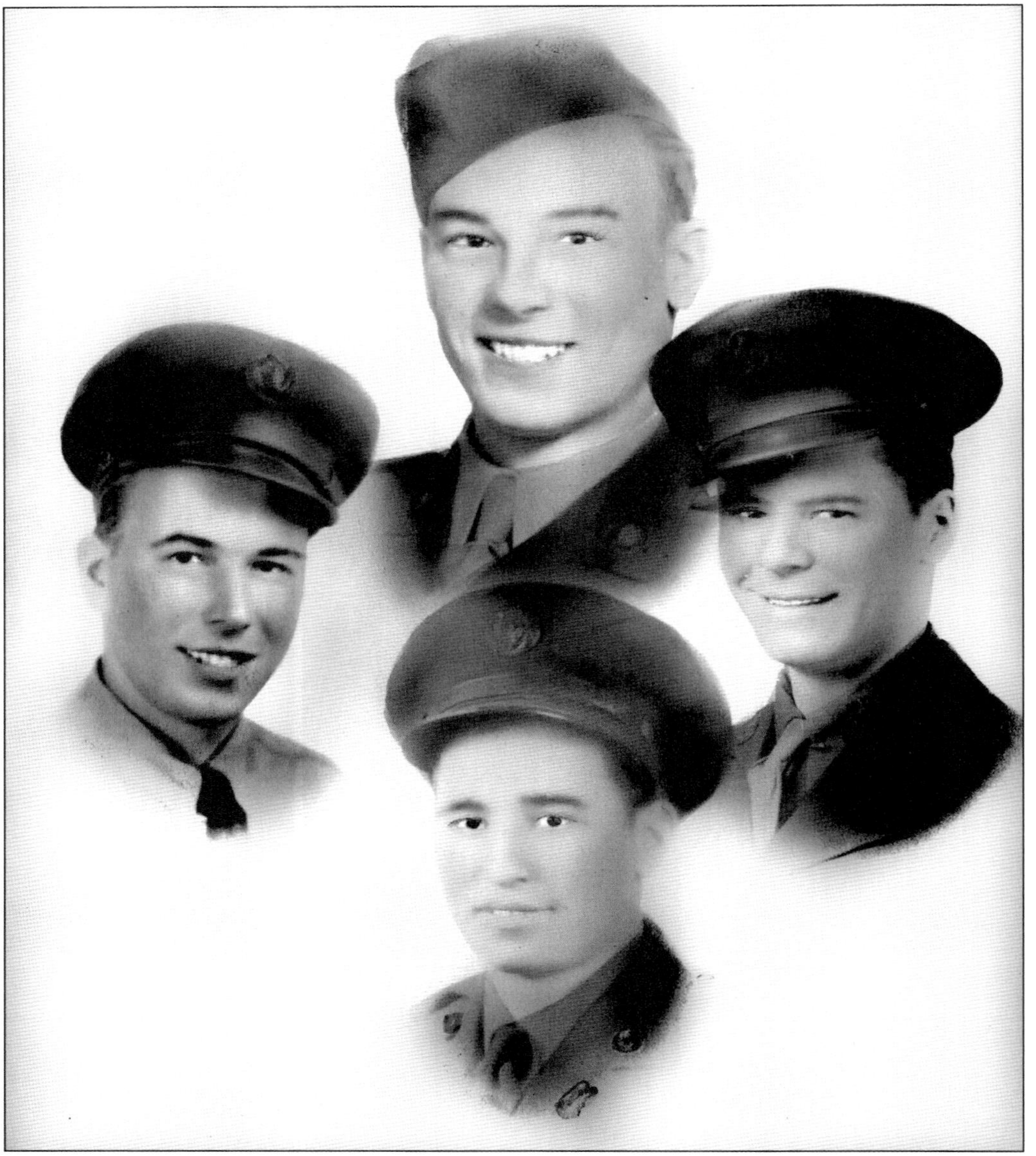

The Doback Brothers. One Naugatuck family could boast of five members who served their country. Charles, Michael, Andrew, and John Doback and their step-brother, Michael Borsos, all participated in World War II. Another brother, George, attempted to join but was not accepted. In this montage, Sgt. John Doback is on the bottom. He served in the 8th Air Force from 1942 to 1945 as a tail gunner on a B-17. His plane was shot down over Germany on May 24, 1944. John "hit the silk," parachuting into German hands. He was a prisoner of war for 11 months. Pfc. Charles Doback, on the left, also served in the 8th Air Force from 1942 to 1945. He was a gunner for a time, stationed in England, and then served in the infantry in Czechoslovakia. Sgt. Michael Doback, seen at the top, served from 1941 to 1945 in the U.S. Army Air Force and was stationed at Harding Field in Louisiana. Pfc. Andrew Doback, on the right, served from 1943 to 1945 in the Aviation Engineers and was stationed in Iceland. Not pictured is Pvt. Michael Borsos, who served in Germany.

Six

Government and Municipal Departments

For those of you who aren't quite as thorough
As Walter Cronkite or Edward R. Murrow,
You can bypass your sources.
There's no need to take courses.
Our state has just nine spots labeled borough.

—Ron Gagliardi, "Naugatuck Is Almost Unique"

Yes, Naugatuck is one of only nine boroughs in the state of Connecticut. It became a borough in 1844. One of the differences between a borough and a city or town is the title of the elected officials. Naugatuck does not have councilors or aldermen; the town leaders are called burgesses. There is an elected mayor, and some fairly well known individuals have occupied that position over the years, including Charles Clark, William Rado, and Joan Taf (the first woman mayor of Naugatuck).

Borough government also has the normal complement of departments, including a parks and recreation department, a public works department, a board of education, fire and police departments, a building inspection department, and a health department. Speaking of health, one of the town's ordinances shows how much its citizens care for its streets. An ordinance prohibiting "spitting upon the floor, or steps of any public building, hall, church, opera house, theater . . . also on any public walks" appeared on the books on January 5, 1904, and still appears in Article I, Section 13-2.

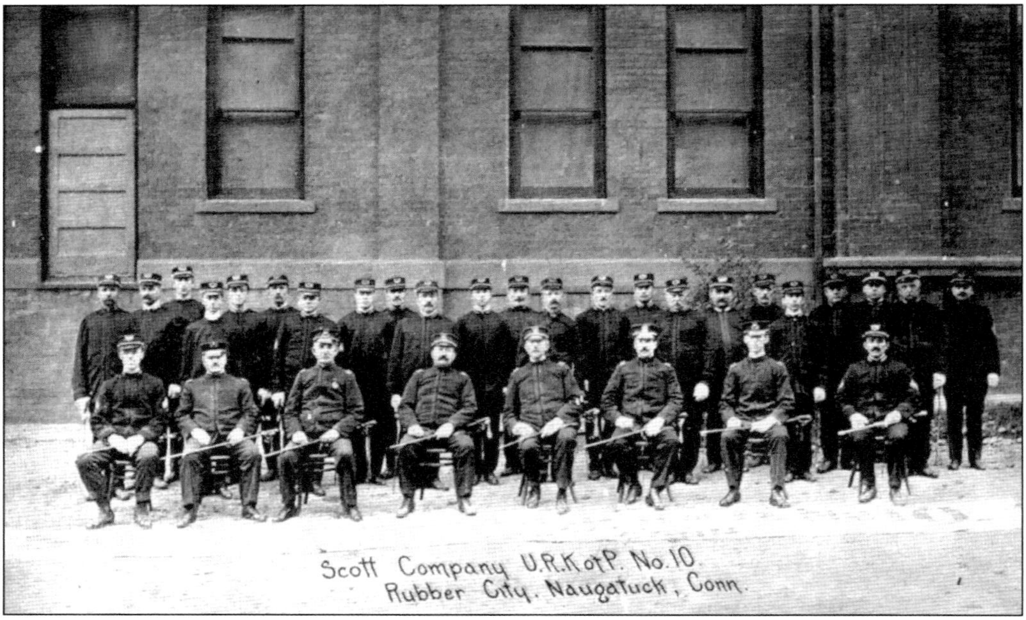

THE PRIVATE FIRE DEPARTMENT. Prior to 1883, firefighting was performed by volunteers. Bucket brigades responded to fires within their membership area. In 1883, the Goodyear India Rubber Glove Manufacturing Company purchased its own equipment for use in its factory complex and for a few subscribers. The town paid $100 per year for fire protection for the town hall and for the new steel bridge. In 1888, the town set up its own group of volunteers.

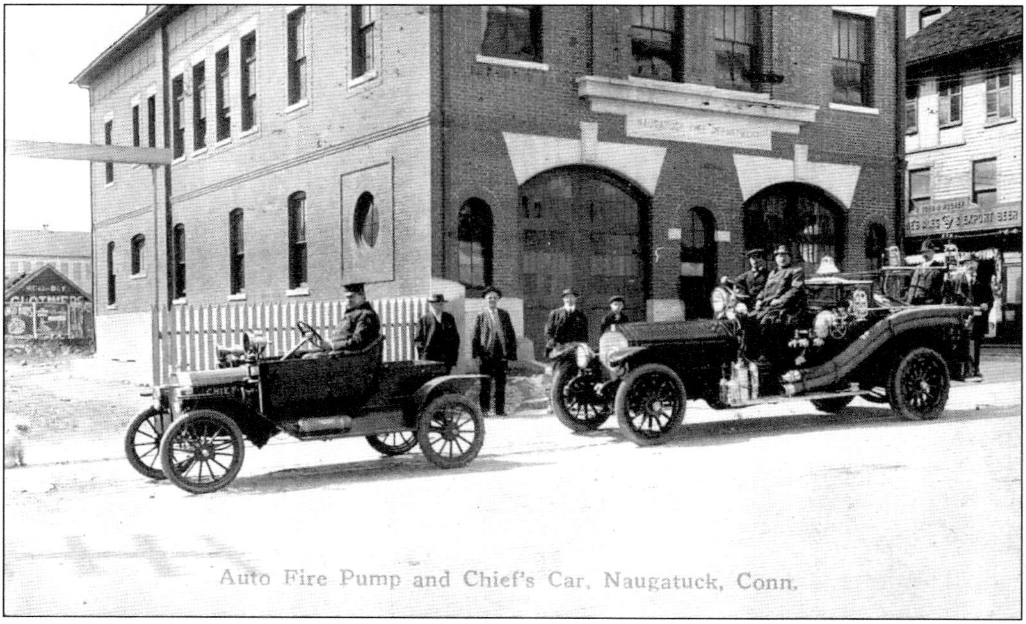

WATERPOWER ON DISPLAY. This photograph was taken in front of the new firehouse on Maple Street. It had to have been taken after 1909, the date construction on the building began. Note the name "Auto Fire Pump" on the postcard, a name that was eventually replaced by the term "fire engine." The chief's car has been identified as a pre-1915 Model T Ford.

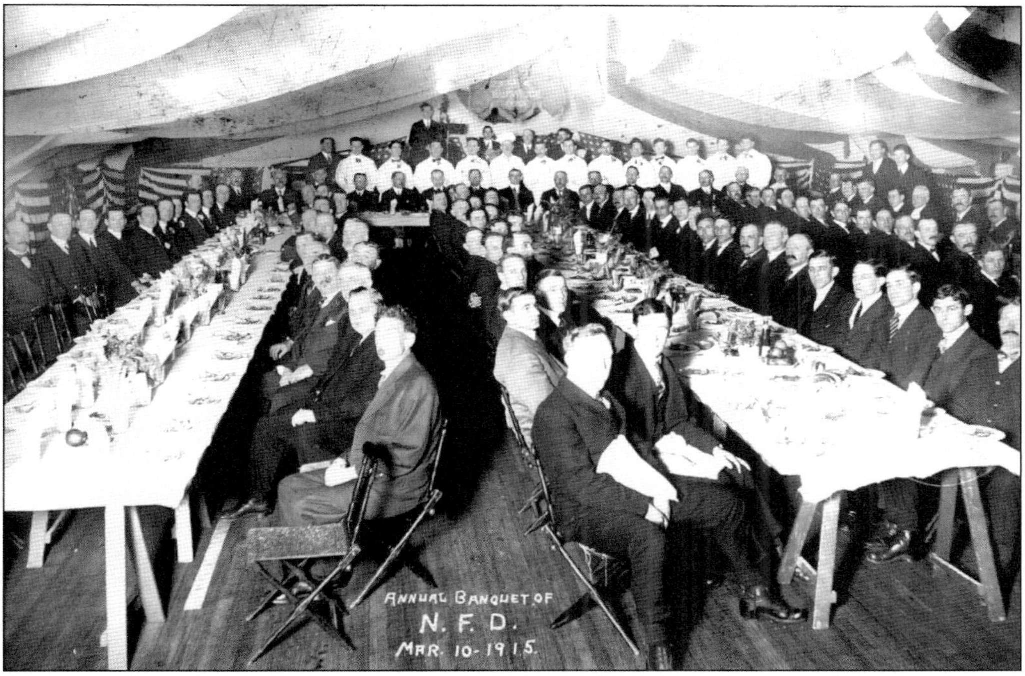

A Fire Department Feast. March 10, 1915, was the date of the annual banquet for the Naugatuck Fire Department. No attendees were identified on the photograph, but the studio hired to take the shot was Bernander of Naugatuck.

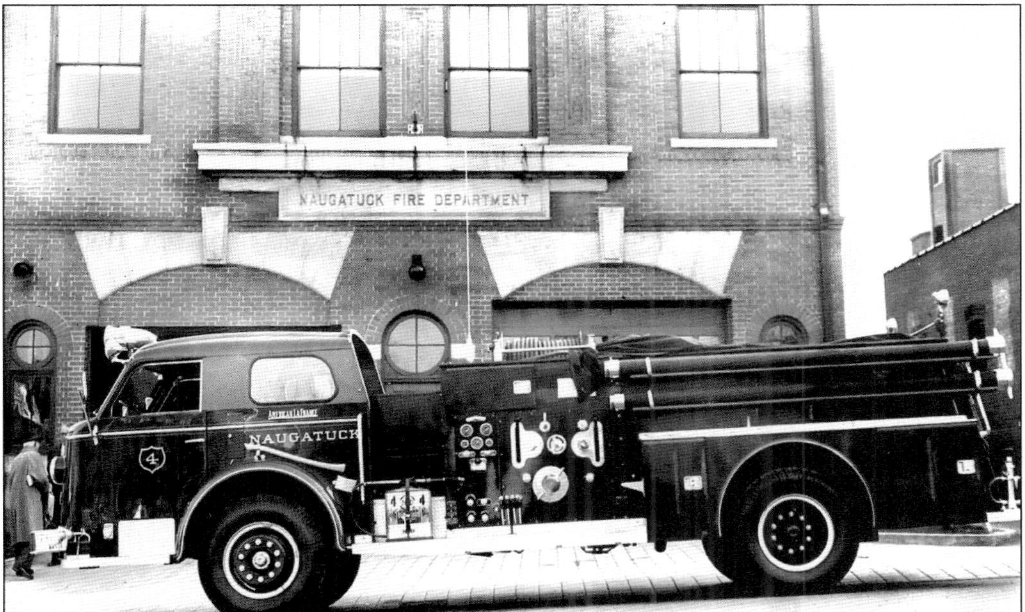

Vive LaFrance. The Naugatuck Fire Department was justly proud of this state-of-the-art American LaFrance fire engine, seen here gleaming in front of the fire department headquarters on Maple Street after 1956.

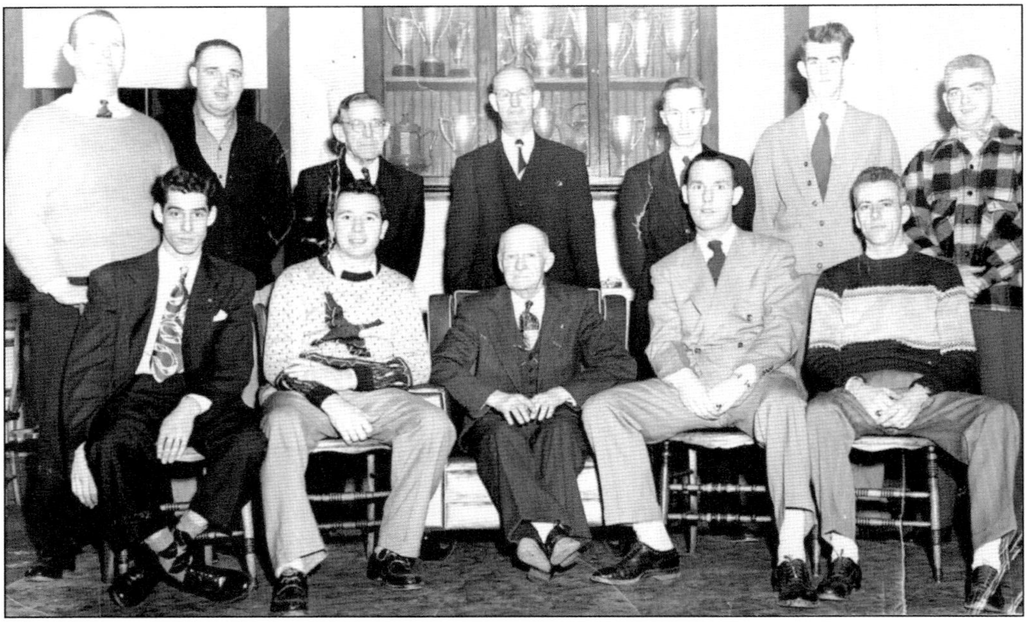

The Fired-Up Officers of Company No. 1. These men were the officers of Hose, Hook and Ladder Company No. 1 of the volunteer fire department for the years 1950–1951. The photograph was taken in March 1950. Pictured are, from left to right, the following: (seated) T. K. Weaving, Francis Canfield, Herbert Cockcroft, William Sullivan, and Robert Lawlor; (standing) William Passeck, Thomas Feeley, William Wood, Garrett Joyce, J. J. Foley, and Francis Feeley.

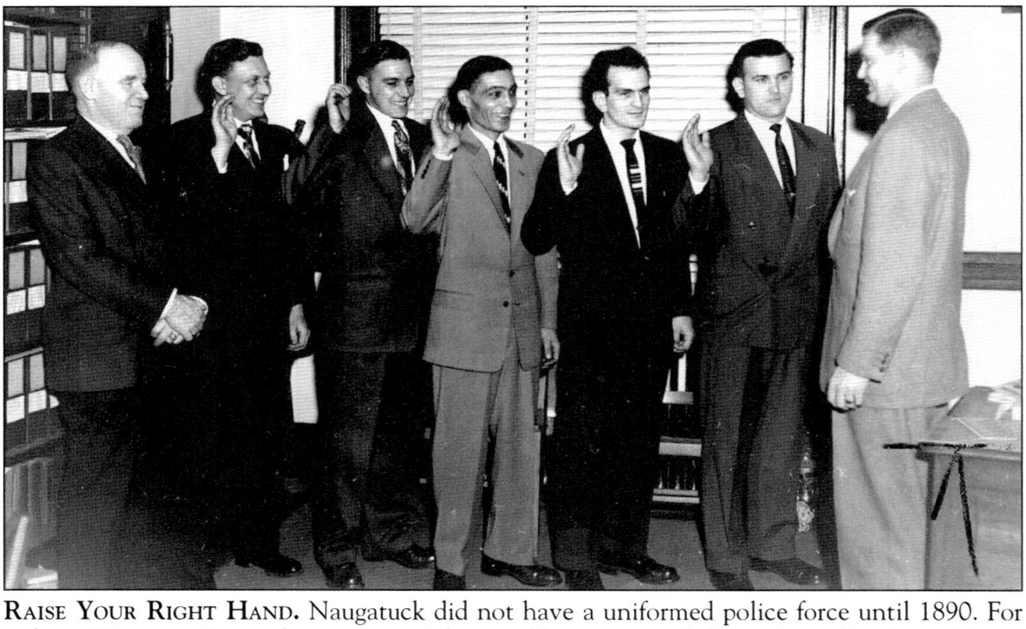

Raise Your Right Hand. Naugatuck did not have a uniformed police force until 1890. For at least 20 years prior to that, one special constable constituted the entire police force. Mayor Charles Clark is pictured on the right swearing in these new policemen, who are ready to continue in that proud tradition as they begin their law enforcement careers in the 1950s.

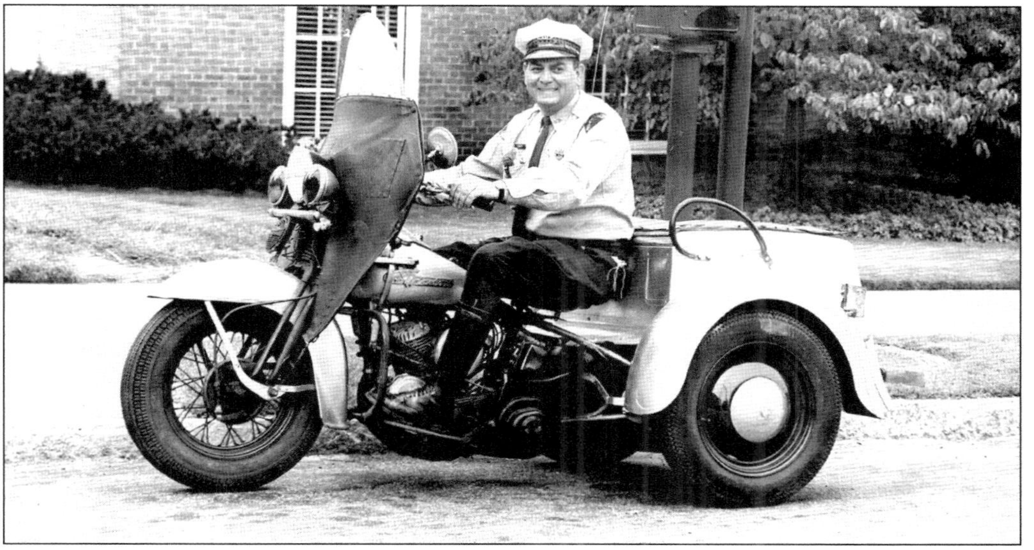

The Least Desirable Ticket in Town. Officer Jerry Sirica had many duties, including that of driver for Mayor Bill Rado. Riding herd on illegally parked cars in Naugatuck on his three-wheeled Harley Davidson motorcycle apparently was one of Sirica's main jobs, based on the memories of some longtime residents and on the parking tickets protruding from his left pocket.

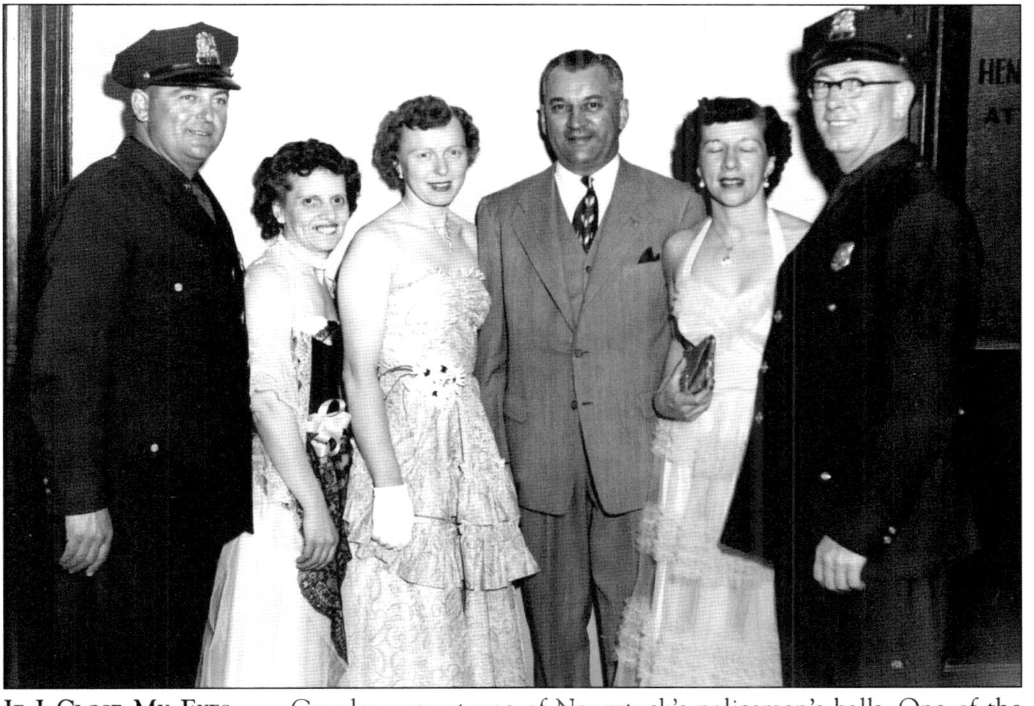

If I Close My Eyes. . . . Couples pose at one of Naugatuck's policemen's balls. One of the women happened to blink at the precise moment the image was recorded, making it appear that she could have been picturing herself elsewhere, perhaps at her senior prom. The dresses look like they date from the 1940s or 1950s. Pictured are, from left to right, Mr. and Mrs. Frank Mariano, Mrs. and Mr. Dimitro Pawchyk, and Mrs. and Mr. James Fenton.

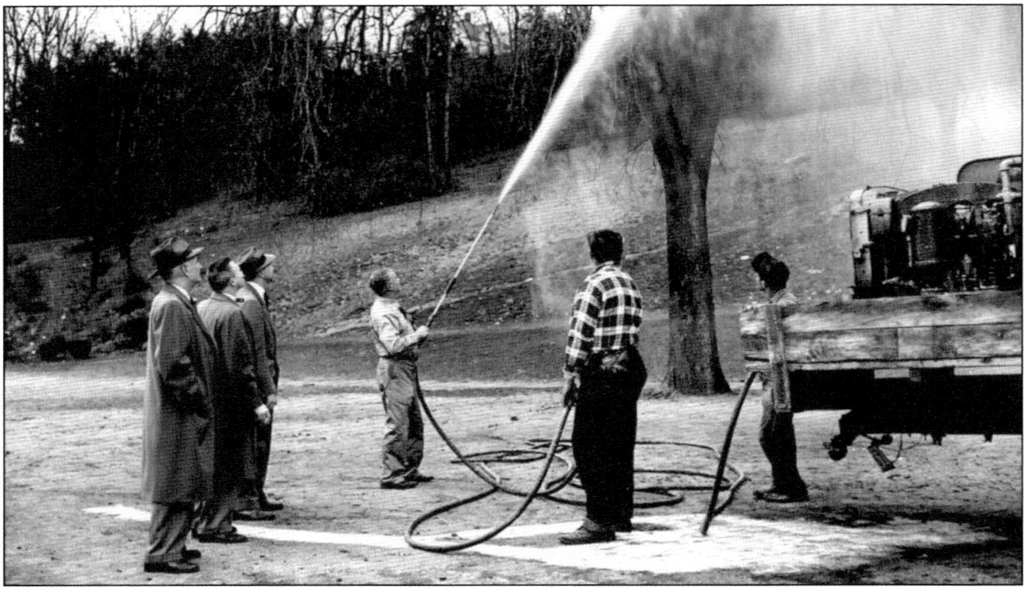

THE SPRAY OF THE DAY. "Spraying Elms, 1953" is the title written on this photograph. The crew was spraying insecticide on the tree, probably to combat Dutch elm disease. The photograph was likely taken in early spring, the customary season for spraying trees. The last names of the well-dressed men, who may be supervisors, are, from left to right, Fellows, Nyde, and Neklutin. Two of them wear fedoras, which were as ubiquitous then as the baseball cap is today. The sprayer is identified as a Mr. Billetti. The others are unidentified.

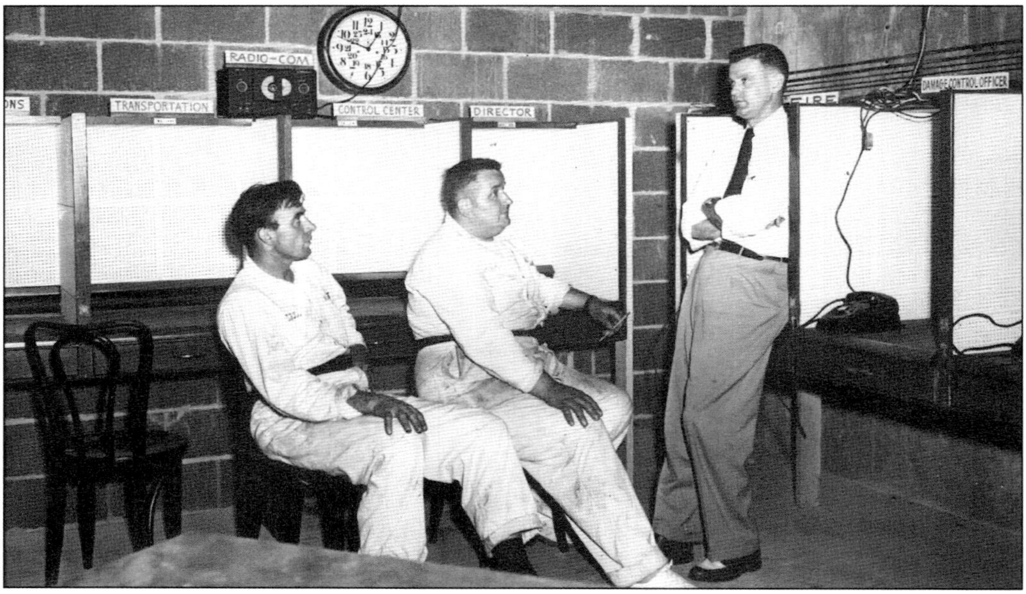

THE CIVIL-DEFENSE HEADQUARTERS. The setup of this basement nerve center indicates that it was probably civil-defense headquarters. The gentleman on the right has been identified as Charles Clark, who served as mayor of Naugatuck from 1953 to 1957. The gentleman in the center is Henry Racki, civil-defense director; the person to his right has not been identified. This photograph was probably taken around the period of the devastating 1955 flood.

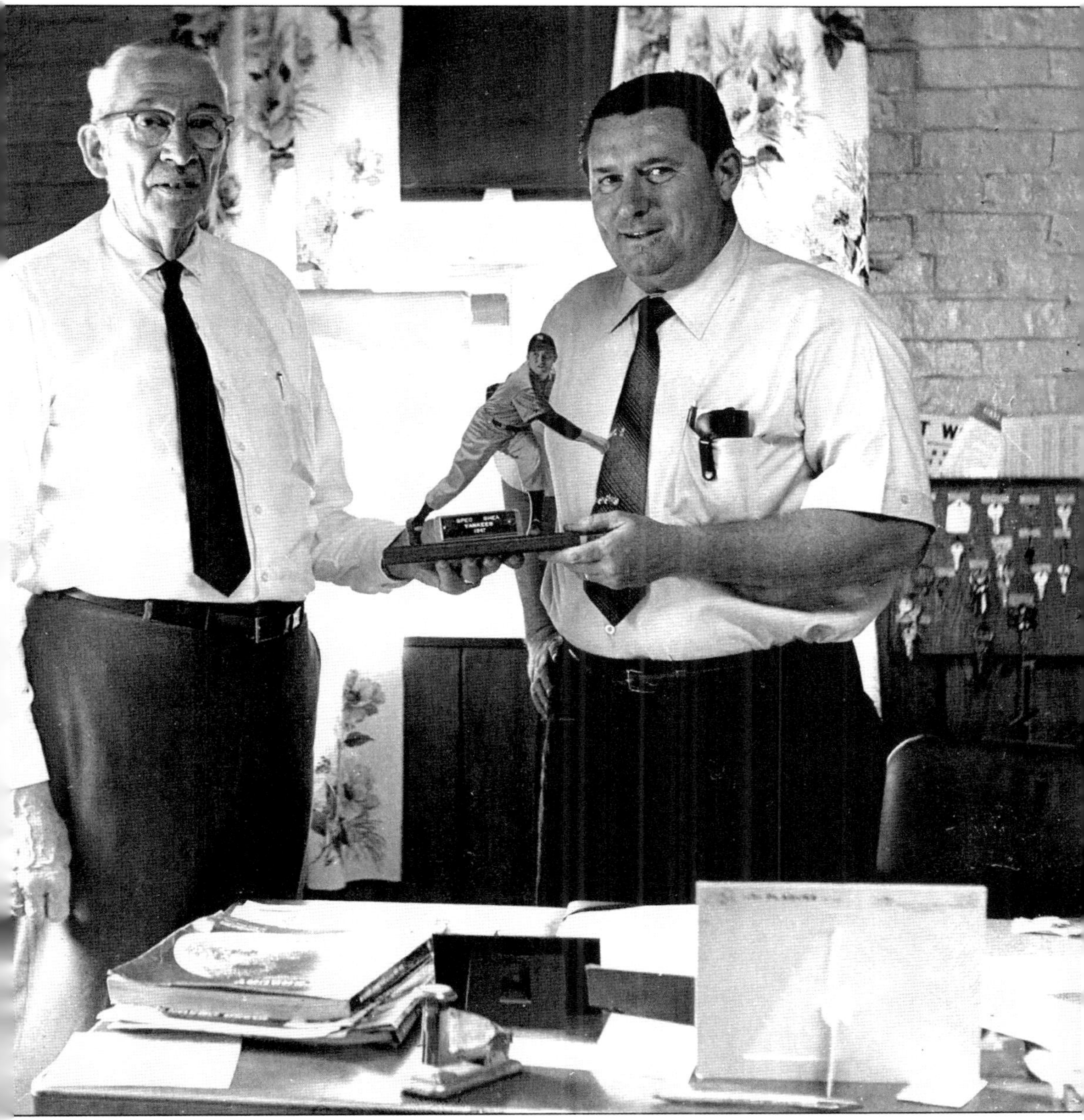

The Good Old Days. Frank "Spec" Shea holds a cutout photograph of himself labeled 1947, the year he was selected the World Series MVP as a pitcher for the New York Yankees. The Naugatuck Nugget was the borough's superintendent of parks and recreation from 1969 until his retirement in 1989. Here he poses in his office with Tom Chiswell, the maintenance supervisor for the Bristol Company and a tireless advocate for the elderly in Naugatuck.

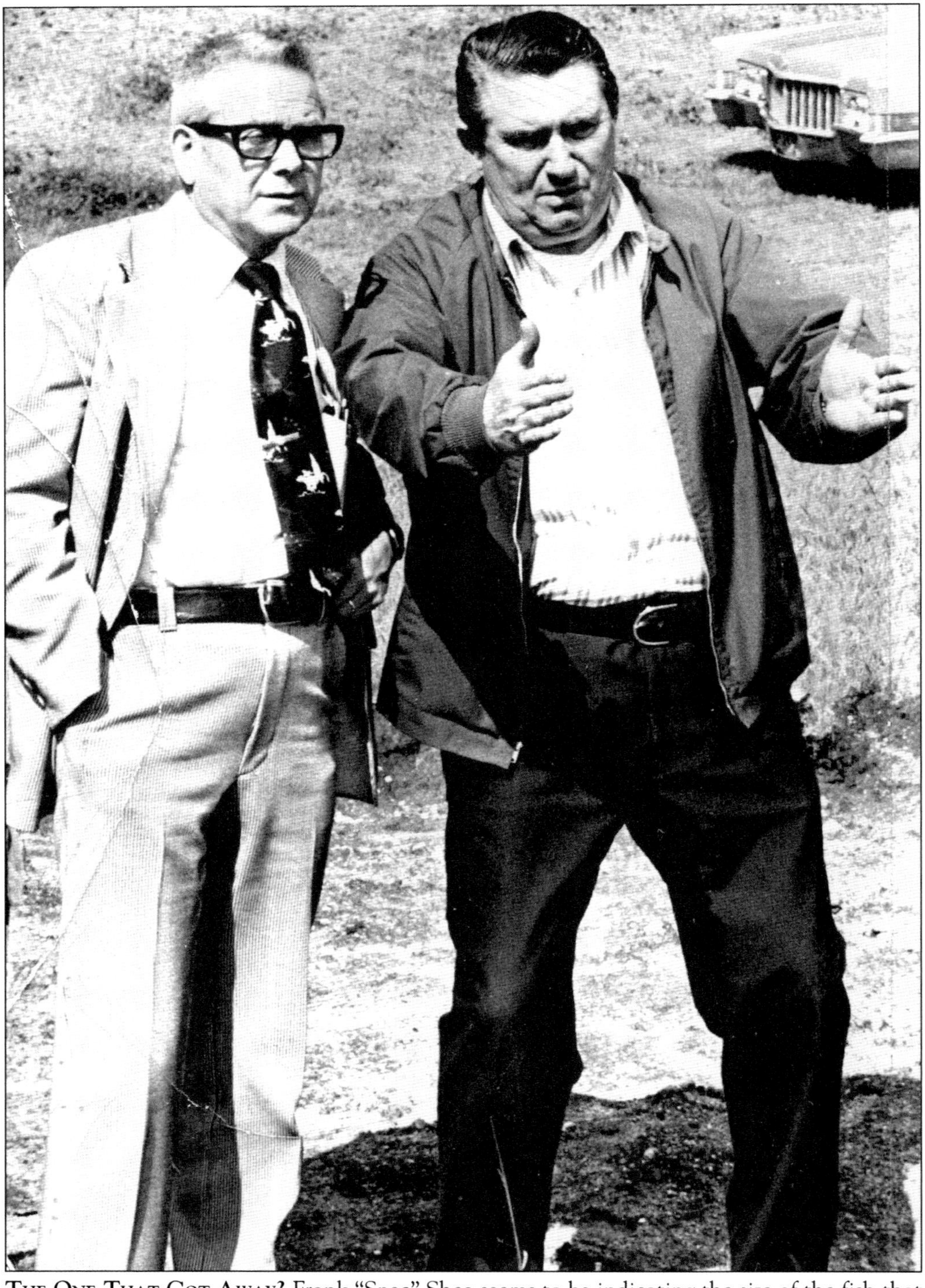

THE ONE THAT GOT AWAY? Frank "Spec" Shea seems to be indicating the size of the fish that got away to Mayor Bill Rado in this photograph by Don Cousey. More likely, he is pointing out some detail at a construction site for a new ball field in town.

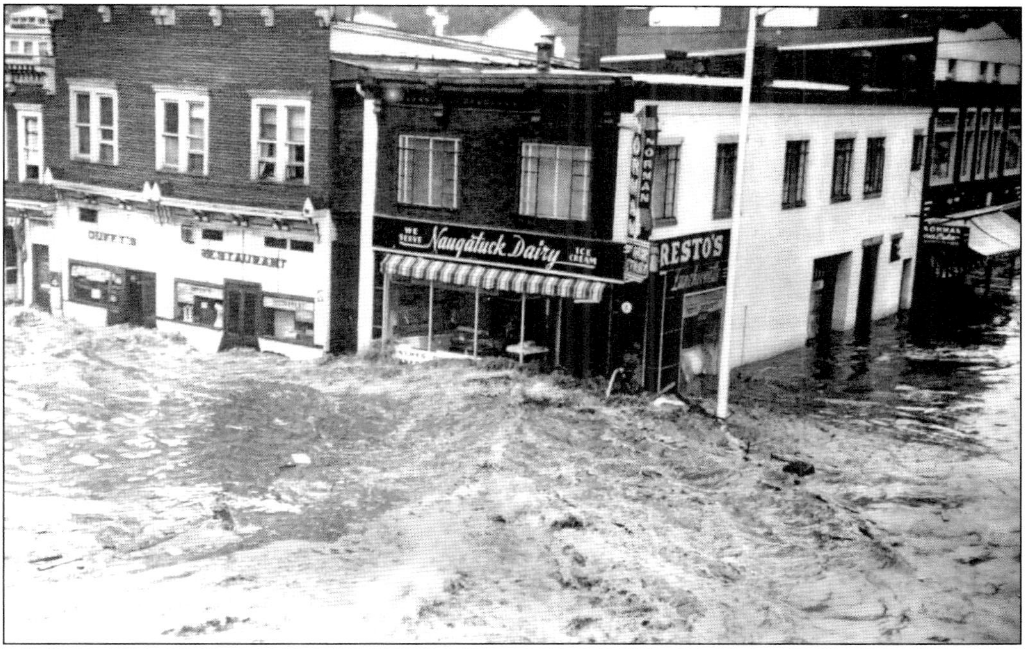

SWEPT AWAY. Floodwaters swept through Naugatuck on August 19, 1955, destroying businesses and homes and putting commerce on hold in Naugatuck. This photograph was taken on Maple Street.

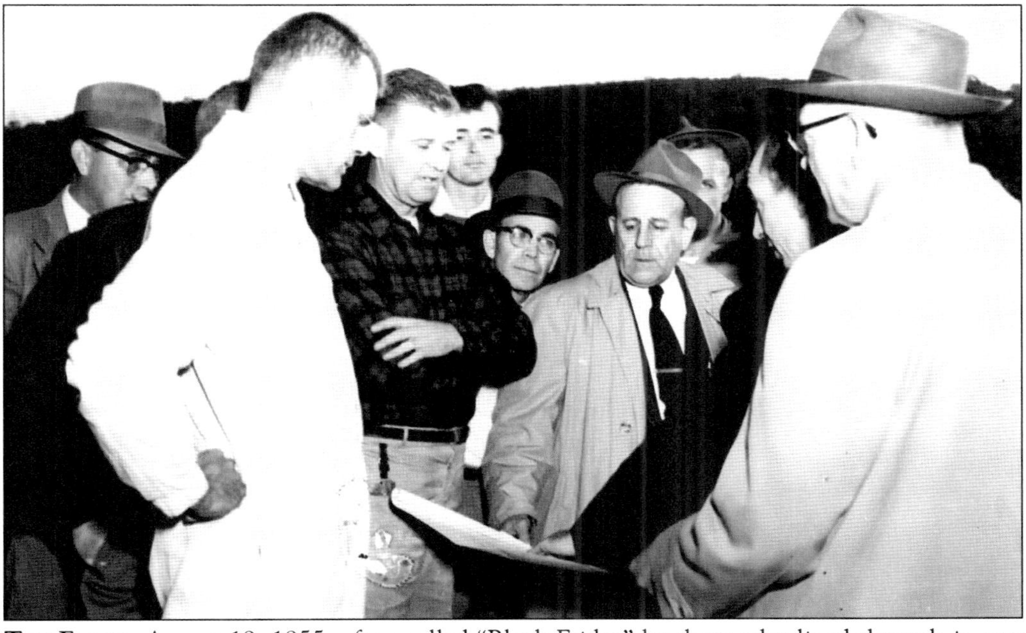

THE FLOOD. August 19, 1955, often called "Black Friday" by those who lived through it, was the day the Naugatuck River overflowed its banks. These men are formulating a plan to deal with the devastation. The gentleman in the white coveralls is probably from the Civil Defense Department. His uniform is the same as those worn by the men in the photograph on page 78. Mayor Clark is the man with his arms folded.

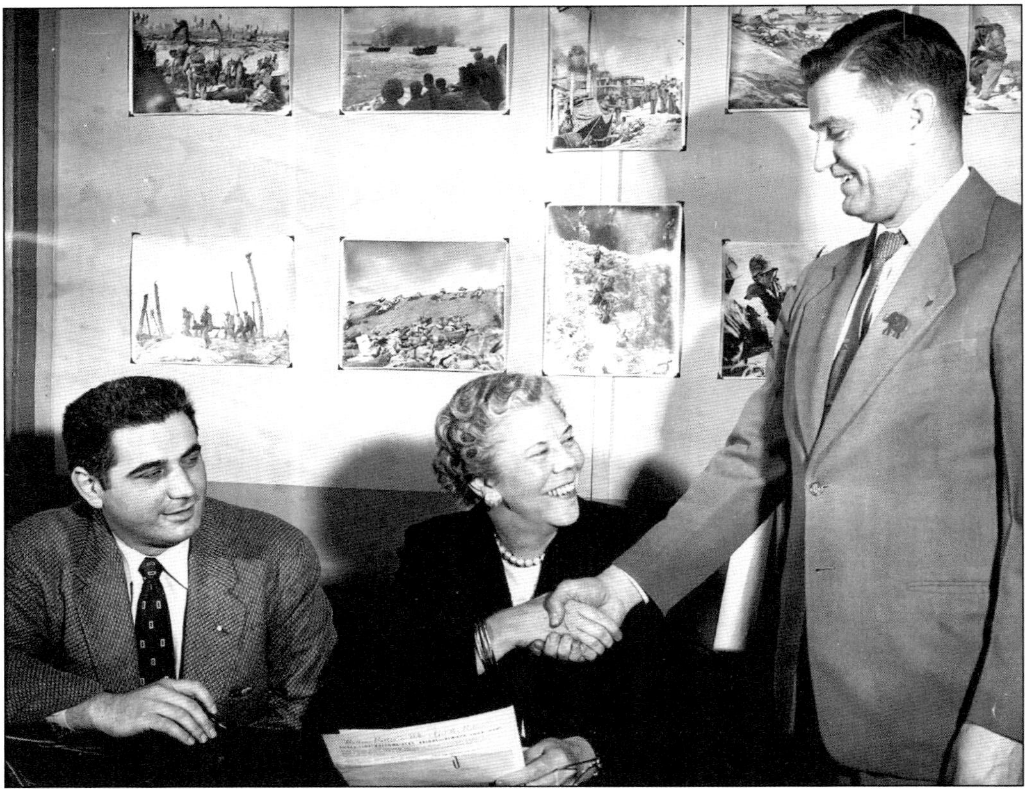

WELFARE FARES WELL. Mayor Charles Clark is pictured welcoming the new superintendent of welfare, Catherine Brennan, into the community. Former superintendent Mike Rizzuti was nearby to show her the ropes. The photographs on the wall deserve closer examination. They appear to be military related and are possibly from the Korean War.

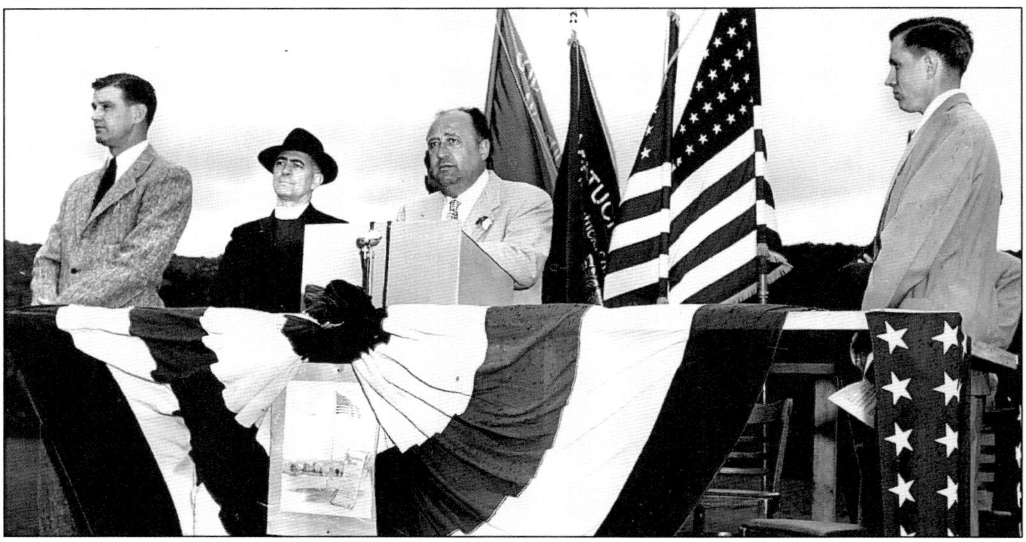

A PARK DEDICATION. Mayor Charles Clark (far left) and Rev. Albert Taylor are shown at a 1950s dedication ceremony. The other men and the location are unidentified.

Seven

ARCHITECTURE

Naugatuck is one of those rare communities whose architectural heritage is so pervasive that walking its streets feels like the equivalent of strolling the halls of a museum or art gallery. Buildings, monuments, and a historic bridge contribute mightily to the image of this architects' haven. Naugatuck has more pillars, polished marble, and granite than a borough its size would normally be expected to possess, especially one with the reputation of a factory town. In fact, it was the wealth derived from manufacturing and the philanthropic nature of industrialists like the Whittemores that permitted Naugatuck's architectural renaissance.

The casual stroller here will see work by the firms of McKim, Mead and White; Jallade, Lindsay and Warren; and such noted architects as Theodate Pope Riddle, James Murphy, and Henry Bacon, the designer of the Lincoln Memorial in Washington, D.C. Take a tour among the next few pages and give some thought to visiting the actual sites of the "architectural museum" that can be found along the streets of Naugatuck.

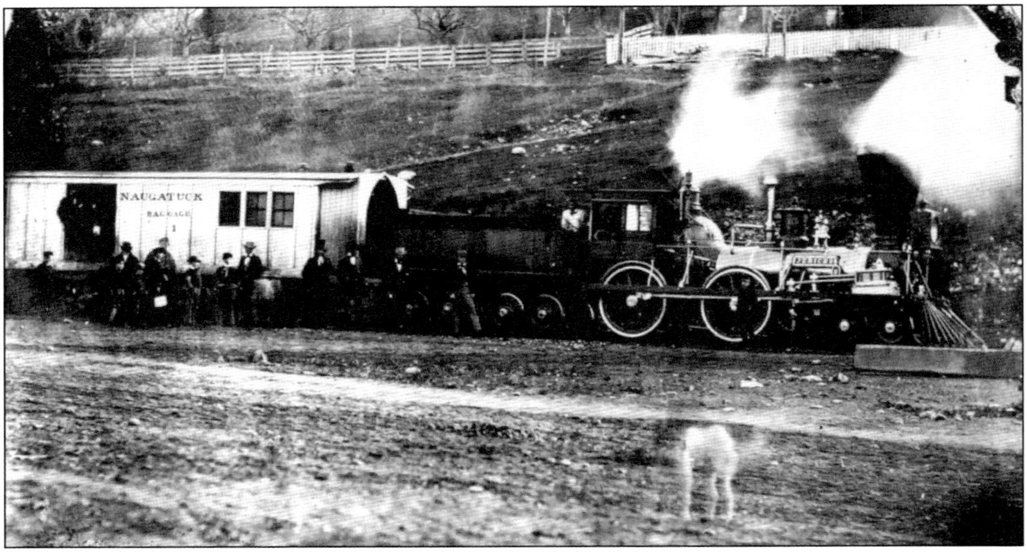

The Land of Jericho. The Naugatuck Railroad was granted a charter by the state of Connecticut in 1845 and began operations in 1849. Alfred Bishop and a group of investors were responsible for getting it up and running and eventually stretching the tracks from Winsted to Bridgeport. The railroad was a major factor in promoting Naugatuck's prosperity, permitting its factories and businesses to receive raw materials and to ship out finished products. It was an invaluable connection to the rest of the country. This print from an original glass-plate negative depicts the 4-4-0 road engine *Jericho* with a Naugatuck baggage car. Ferroequinologists (students of what American Indians called the iron horse) will be interested to note that the picture was probably taken in the 1860s.

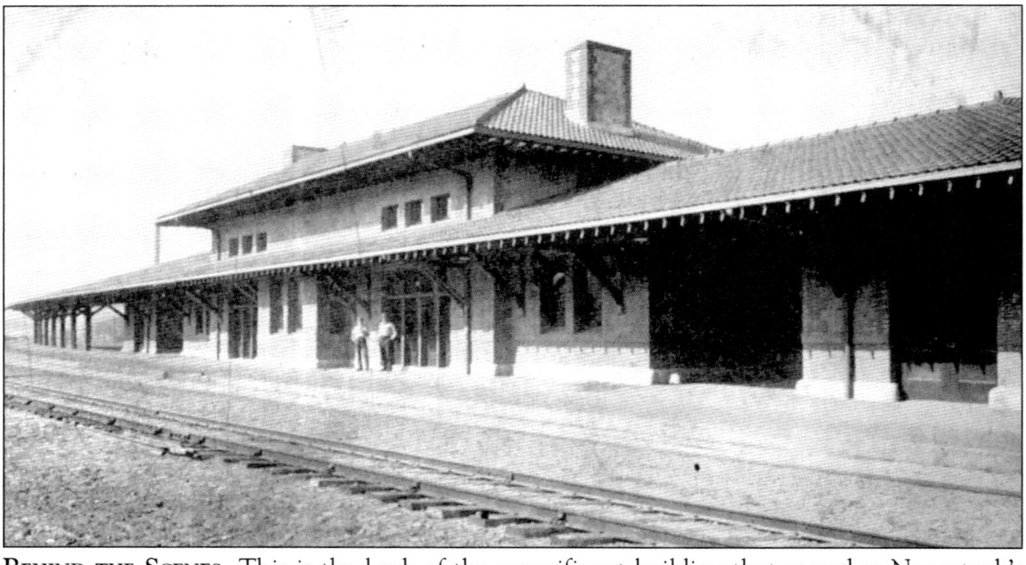

Behind the Scenes. This is the back of the magnificent building that served as Naugatuck's railroad station for decades beginning in 1910. The station was designed by Henry Bacon. The *Naugatuck Daily News* operated here for many years. The borough purchased the building and leased it to the Naugatuck Historical Society. It was transformed by a small army of dedicated volunteers into the museum that now occupies it.

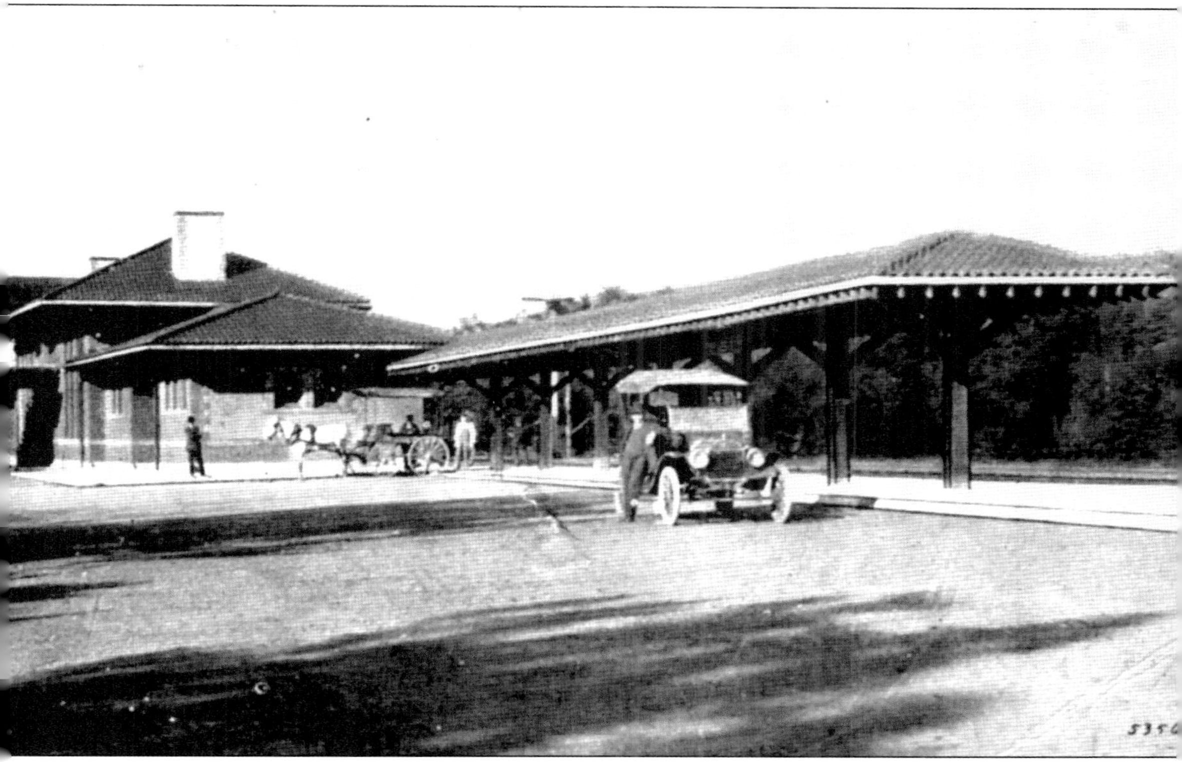

Three Modes of Transportation. The horse, the iron horse, and horsepower, three ways of transporting people and freight, are represented in this postcard. This is a view of the railroad station, facing northeast. There are two wagons and one car, a Ford Model T, *c.* 1915 at the railroad station awaiting a visit from the next scheduled train. By the way, folks can still catch a train here; they just have to purchase tickets on board.

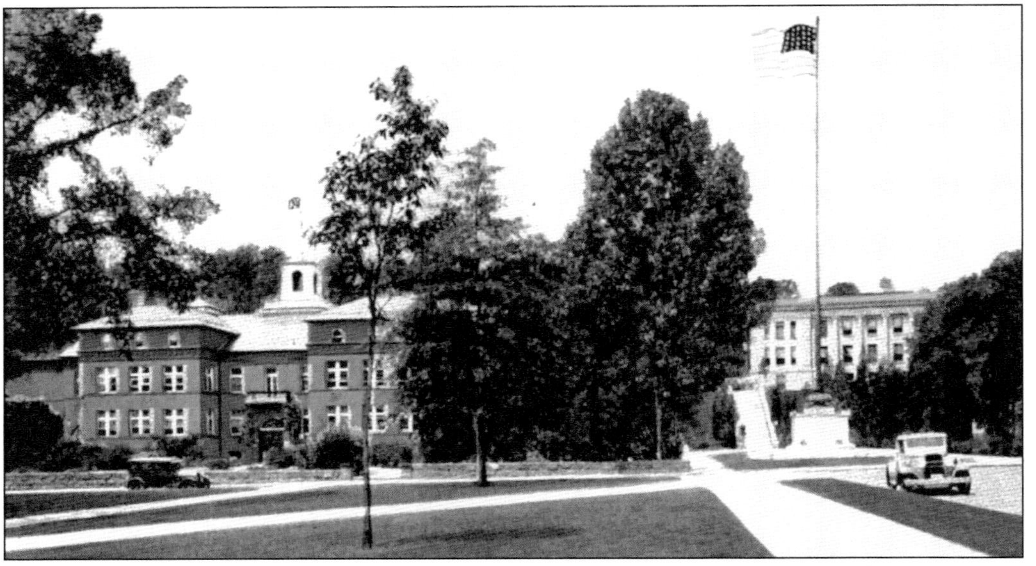

SALEM SCHOOL. Salem School, located west of the green, has been featured in numerous postcards over the years. The views on this page are seldom encountered. The Salem in the school's name comes from Salem Bridge, one of the early names of Naugatuck. The school was built in 1894 and is still in use today.

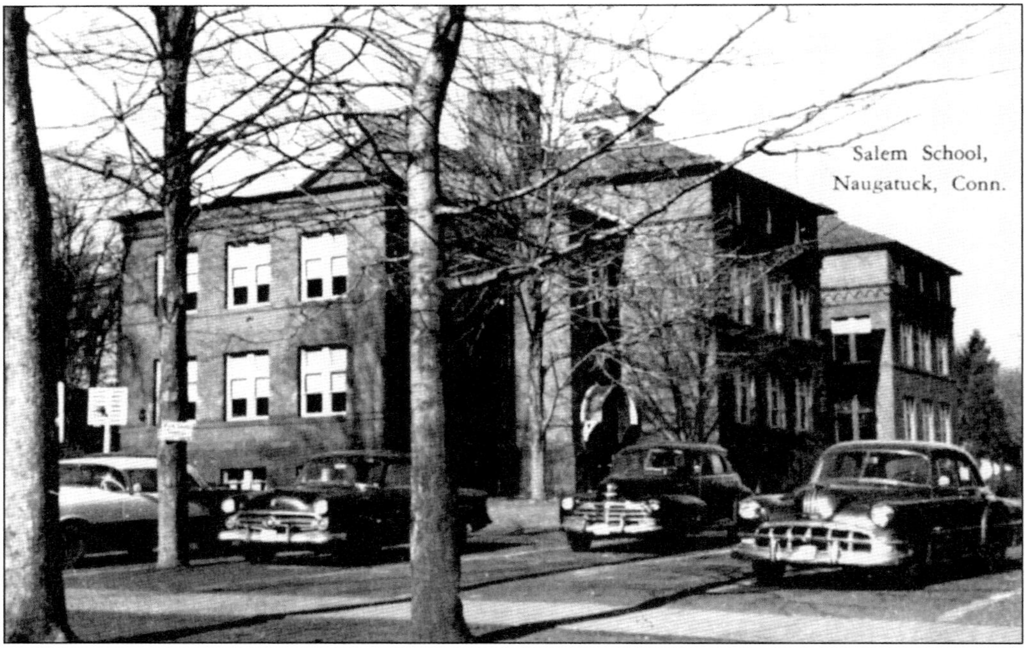

SALEM SCHOOL'S WITCH CONNECTION. There is no relationship between this school and the witches of Salem, Massachusetts. However, Salem School has a witch connection through one of its famous alumni, Gilbert Adrian. Adrian was the famed Hollywood designer for many movies, including *The Wizard of Oz*. His favorite pastime as a student was designing costumes for Frank Baum's Oz books. Amazingly, he was given his dream job and used his childhood notebooks to design the ruby slippers and the costumes for the movie, including the witches' costumes.

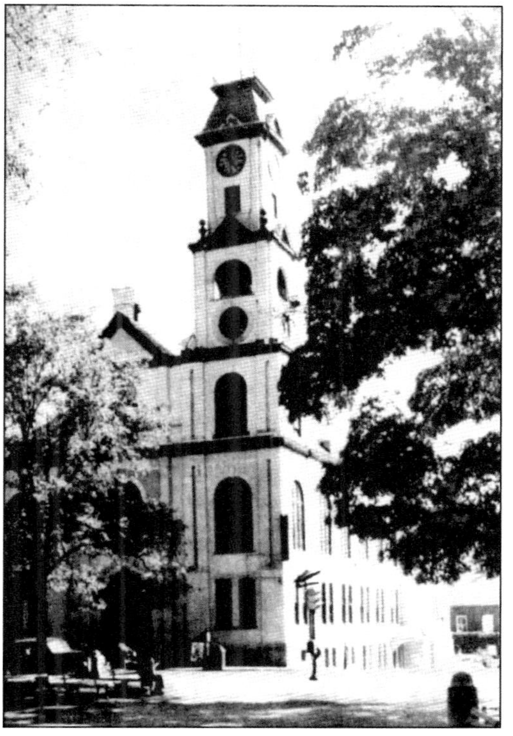

A Venerated Structure. Ralph Jankins of Waukegan, Illinois, probably collected town hall postcards and must have written Mayor Clark asking for one. Secretary Jayne Quint sent him this card with an arrow pointing to what may have been the mayor's office. Historians really enjoy postcards that have a story. This card, sent to Wisconsin on June 28, 1956, somehow found its way back East into the author's collection.

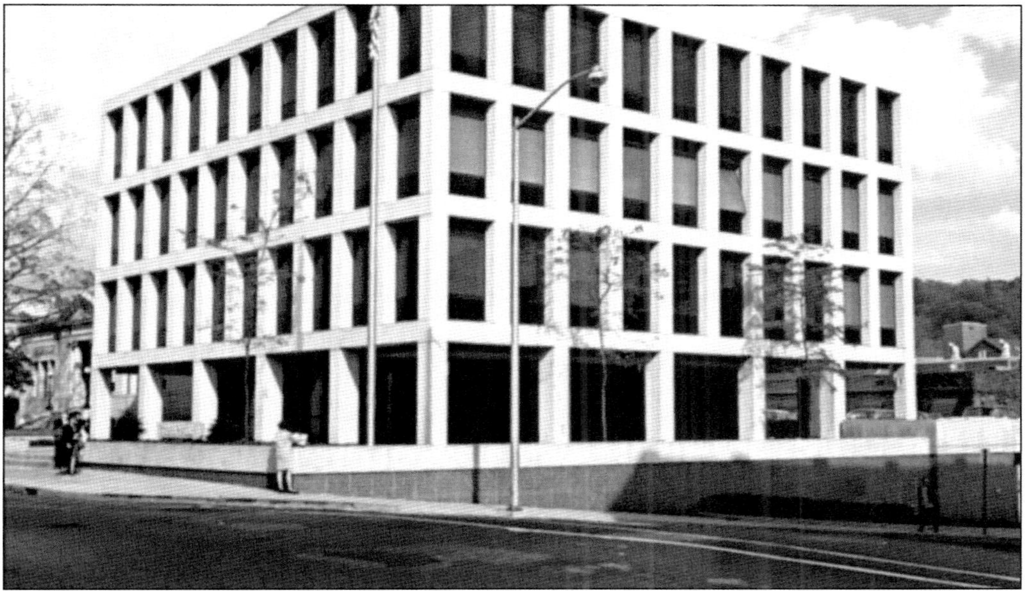

The Box Replaces the Tower. In many situations, this structure would have been hailed as an architectural jewel. The former town hall was demolished in 1964, and when this modern building replaced it, residents greeted it with mixed reviews. Many citizens still wonder how the one designed by L. B. Valk and dedicated on July 24, 1882, was ever permitted to be destroyed. A large model of the old town hall, made by Andy and Mary Doback, resides at the Naugatuck Historical Society Museum.

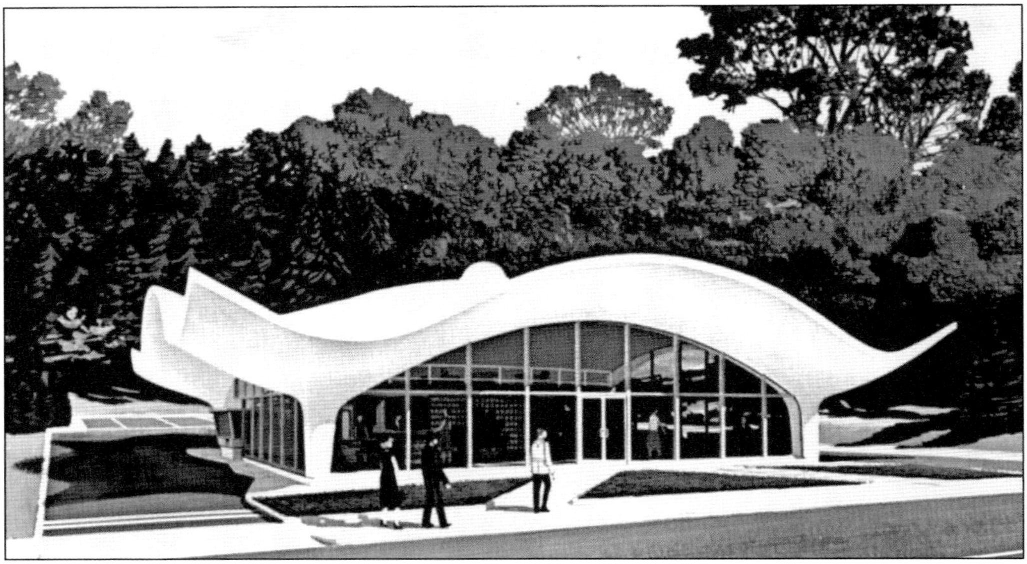

The Flying Nun Building. The Waterbury National Bank building is nicknamed "the flying nun building" after the habit Sally Fields wore in the 1960s television show of the same name. The building's roof was poured in just one day. This planar form consists of 675 tons of lightweight aggregate concrete reinforced with 37 tons of steel. The building is located at 198 Meadow Street. The bank opened on April 11, 1964; the building now houses the Horgan School for Irish Dancing.

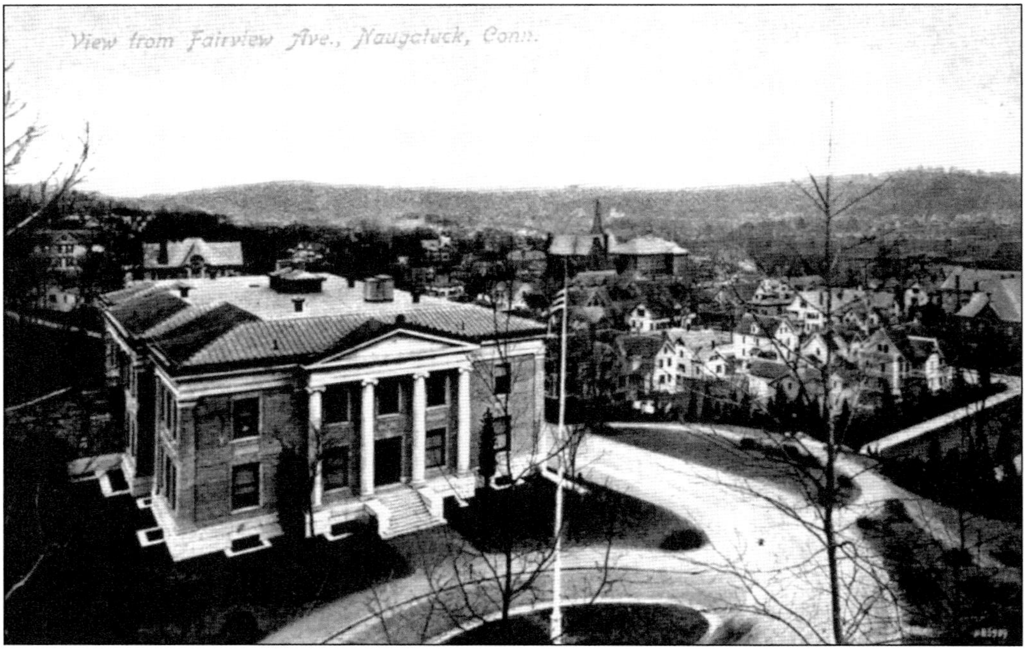

A Fair View from Fairview. Elizabeth Edwards of 487 North Church Street in Naugatuck received this postcard on February 25, 1913. Naugatuck High School, now the Hillside Middle School, dominates this northeast-facing view of the borough.

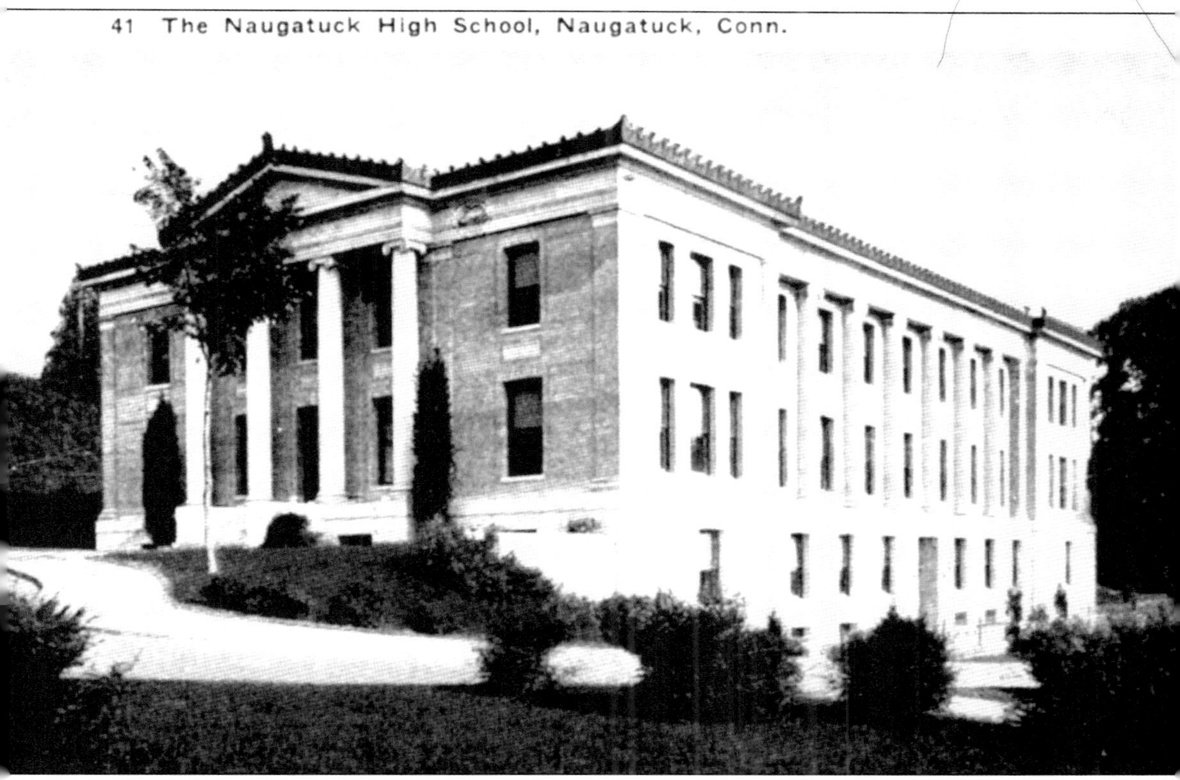

ANOTHER GEM FROM MCKIM, MEAD AND WHITE. This "jewel on a hill" was a gift from John H. Whittemore and was designed by his favorite architectural firm. It was completed in 1905 and was considered state of the art for its era. Hillside Avenue wraps around three sides of the building. This feature gave the building a unique distinction that once placed Naugatuck in the national eye. The high school, now a middle school, appeared in a 1933 *Ripley's Believe It or Not* feature. It has three floors, each with an entrance or exit onto the same street.

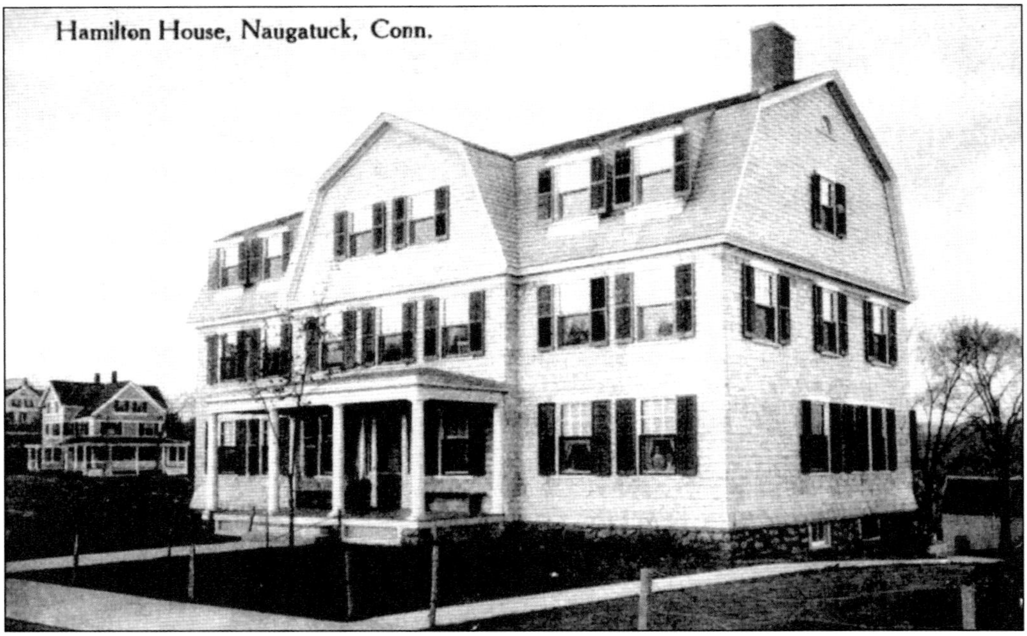

A House Can Be a Home. Hamilton House was paid for in 1907 by Gertrude Whittemore to serve as a home for working women who came to Naugatuck but had no place to stay. Eventually it became a regular boardinghouse. Immigrants and new employees in the factories stayed here until they could earn enough money to move to permanent housing. The house no longer exists, having succumbed to fire.

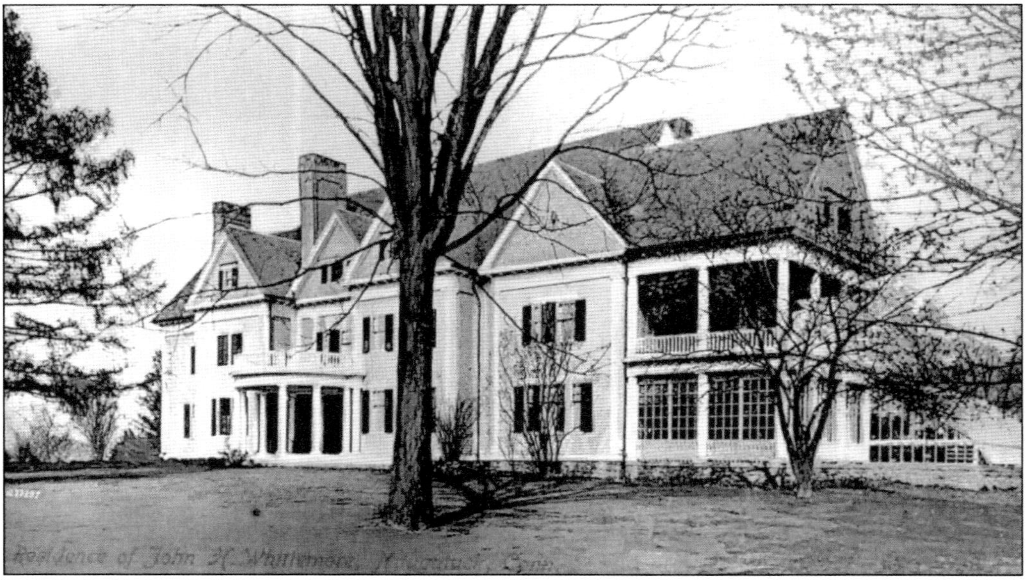

The Anchorage. John Howard Whittemore was one of Naugatuck's wealthiest citizens. He made his money as one of the partners in the Eastern Malleable Iron Company and through other ventures. This mansion, called the Anchorage, was designed in the 1880s by the firm of McKim, Mead and White. It is an example of a transitional style from Queen Anne to Colonial Revival. This home was also lost to fire.

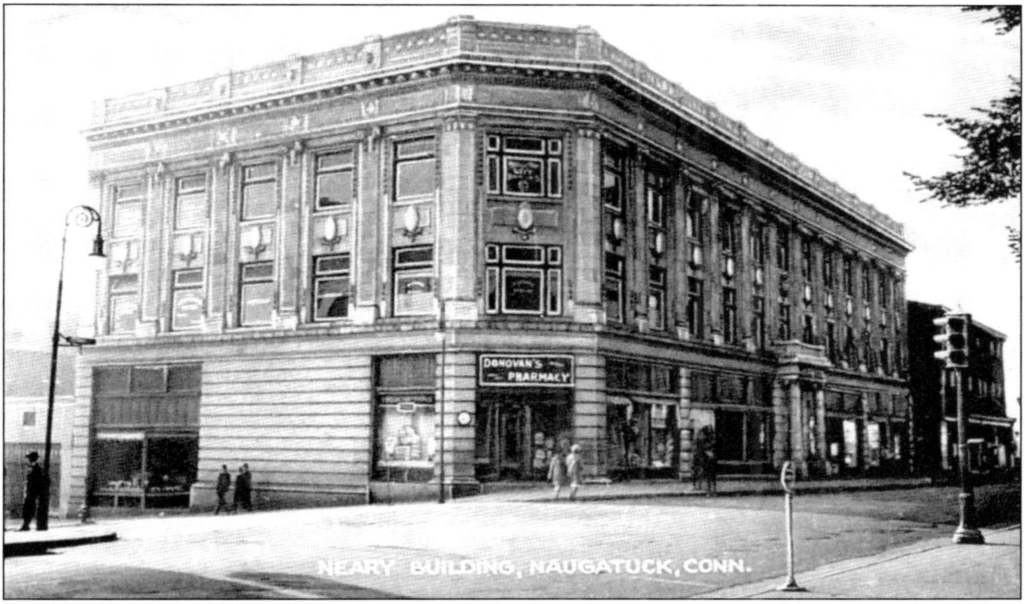

THE THOMAS NEARY BUILDING. The Thomas Neary Building, an imposing edifice on the corner of Maple and Church Streets, was completed between 1909 and 1911, depending on which source one consults. It has dominated the corner in numerous postcards and has housed a variety of stores and professional offices, including the office of its namesake, Thomas Neary, a local businessman and landlord.

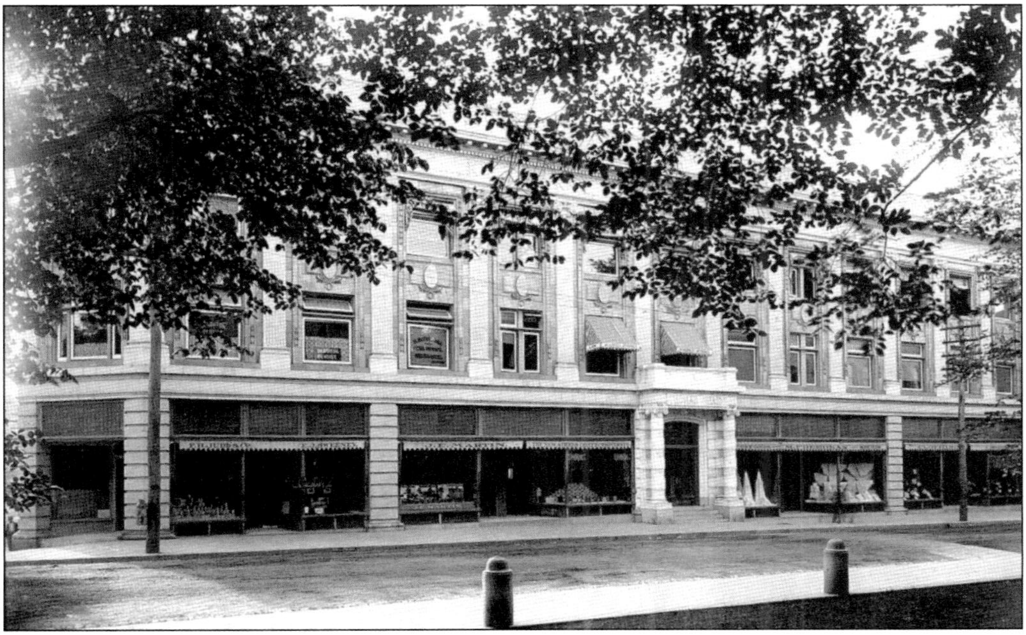

A CLOSEUP ON THE CORNER. A closer view of the west-facing Church Street side of the Neary Building reveals its detailed facade and some professional offices, including a dentist's office. The Waldorf was located on the second floor, and the building contained a large hall that was used for meetings, dances, and ceremonies.

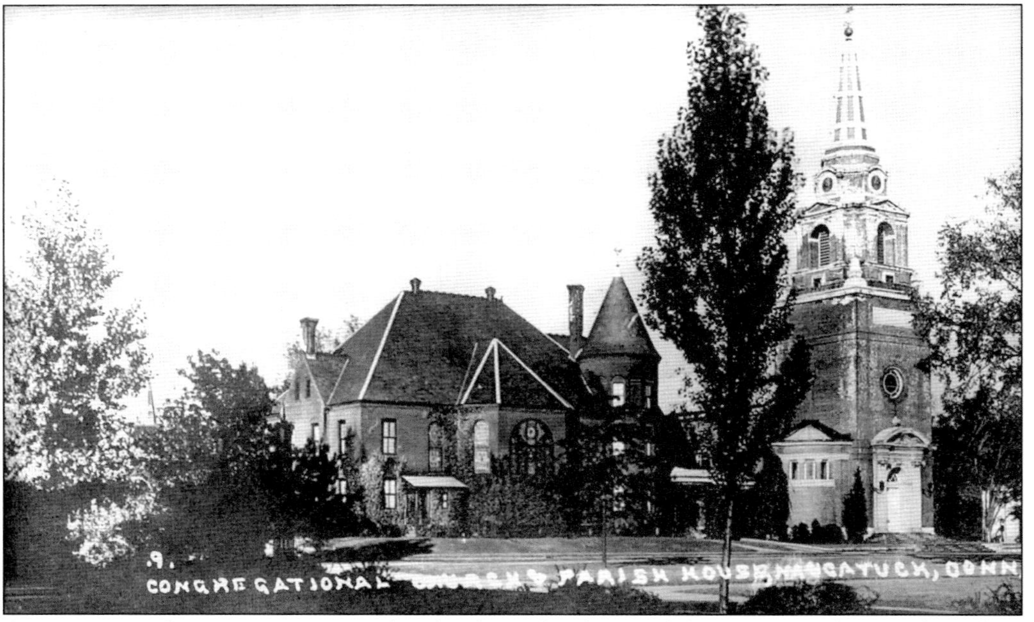

An Inspiring Spire. McKim, Mead and White also designed this imposing house of worship. It was yet another gift from John H. Whittemore and was dedicated on May 20, 1903. Its distinctive spire is a visible landmark as one approaches Naugatuck, and it marks the third site of the church. The members of this church were the parishioners who originally petitioned to be set off from Waterbury and became the Salem Society in 1773.

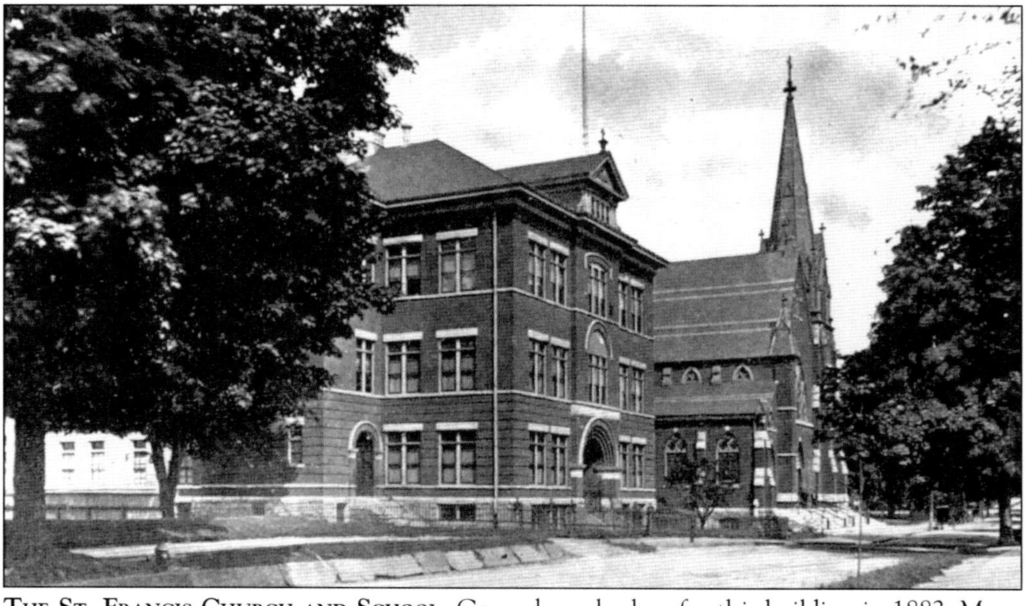

The St. Francis Church and School. Ground was broken for this building in 1882. Many Irish families attended mass here. The plans called for the basement to be completed first, in 1883. It served as the church until the full structure was completed on November 3, 1890. James Murphy of Providence, Rhode Island, was the architect. A new rectory was added in 1903.

The Methodist Church. The Methodist Episcopal Conference determined the "class" in Naugatuck was significant enough to grant it a "circuit rider," and it received its own pastor in 1849. In 1851, Rev. W. H. Bangs initiated a small frame church on Water Street; in 1868, the church moved to the corner of Maple and Church Streets. This church was built after the congregation outgrew its second home.

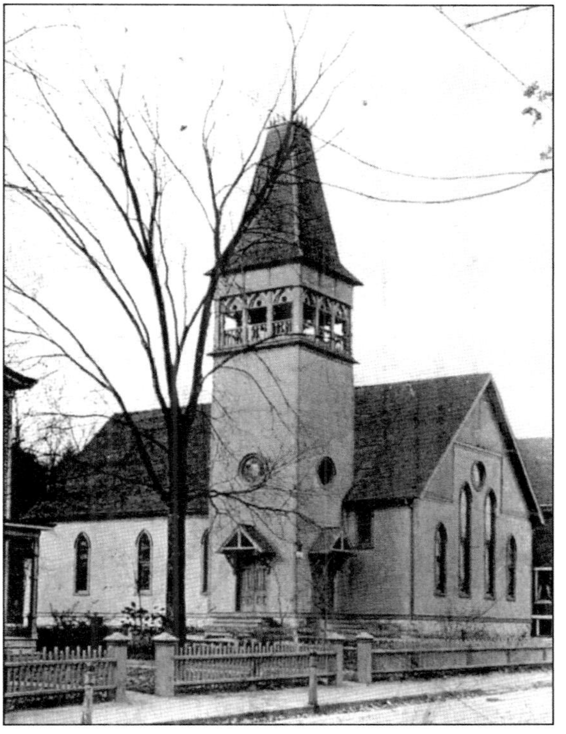

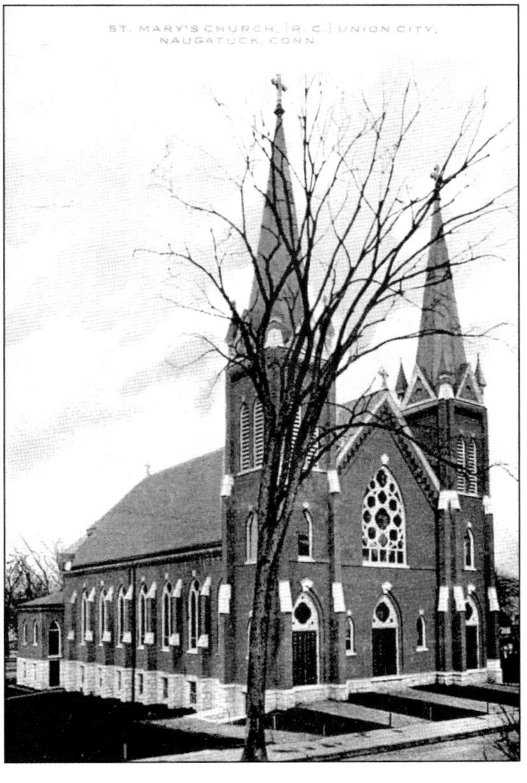

St. Mary's Church. An example of the Gothic style, St. Mary's was partially finished by Michael Donahue of Hartford. Lewis Walsh of Waterbury then took charge of the project until its completion in 1923. St. Mary's was predominately a Polish parish.

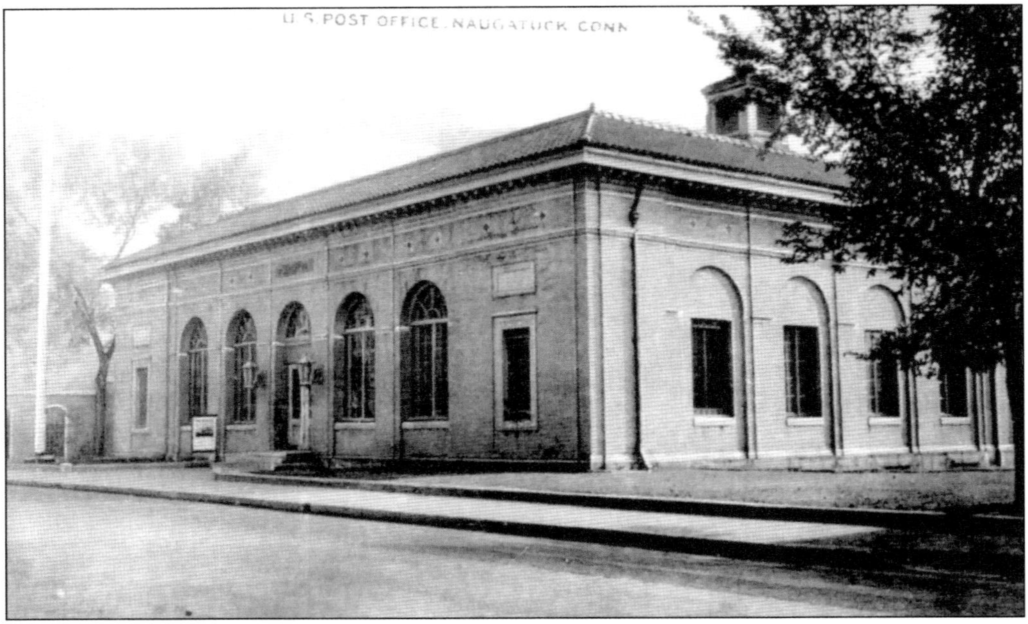

THE POST OFFICE. This building was designed by James Wetmore, an architect for the federal government. It was built in 1915 and served as Naugatuck's post office until 2000, when the new post office, located on Water Street, came into service.

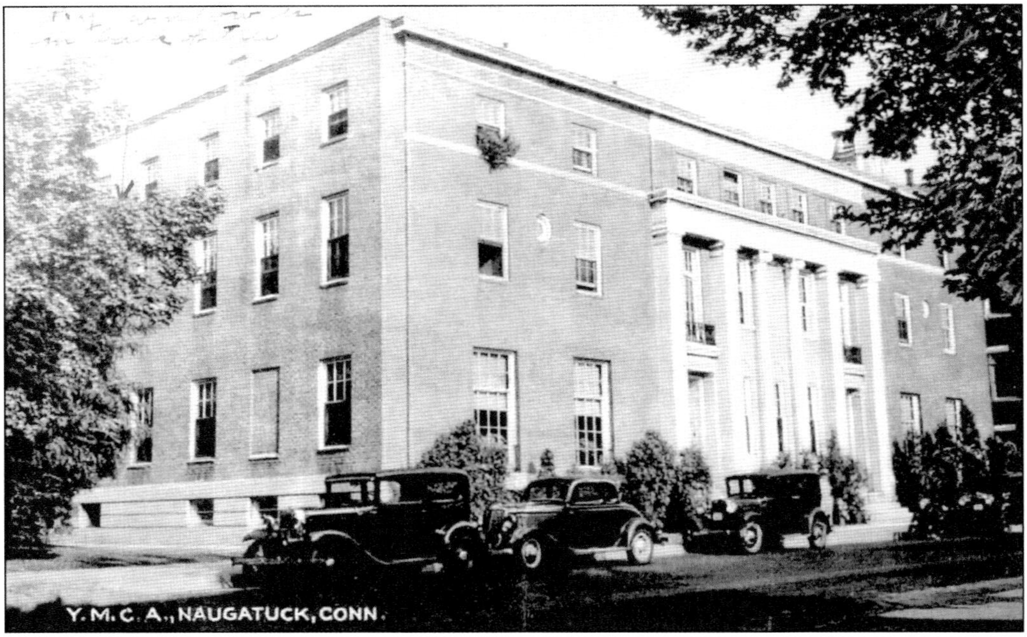

THE YMCA. The YMCA building, located on Church Street, was designed by Jallade, Lindsay and Warren in 1922. In addition to providing sports and educational activities, it serves as a place for temporary lodging. This postcard was written by a father to his family. He drew an arrow to point out the window to his room. The cars parked in front of the building are from the 1930s.

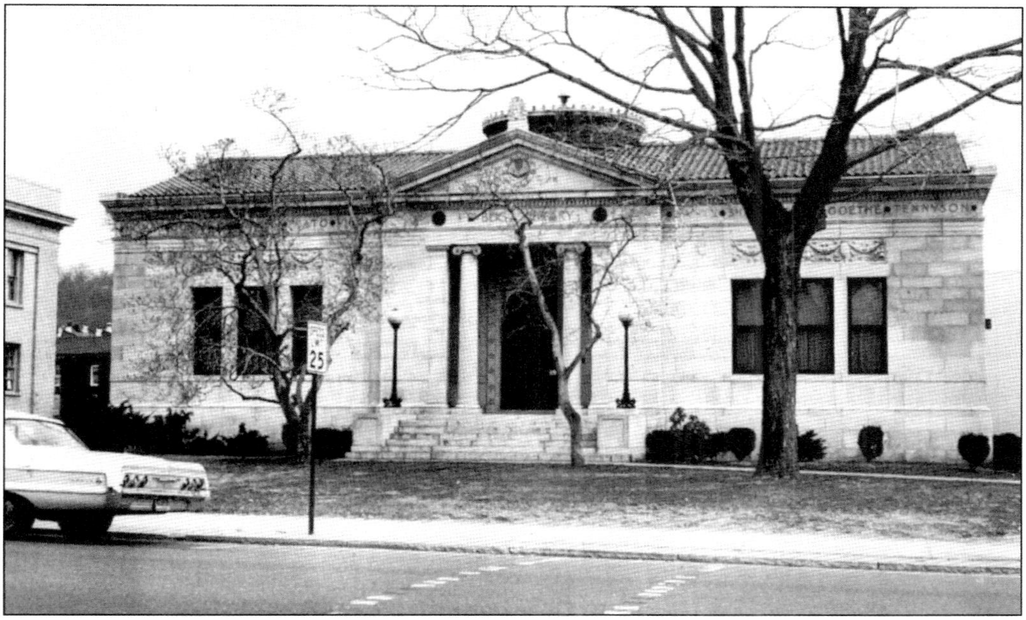

THE HOWARD WHITTEMORE MEMORIAL LIBRARY. This building is not only a memorial but also truly memorable. It was funded by John H. Whittemore and his wife to memorialize their son who had died in 1880 at the age of 15. McKim, Mead and White designed the building, which was erected in 1894. This photograph was taken in the 1960s. One of the building's most memorable features is the names of famous men of history that are carved around it.

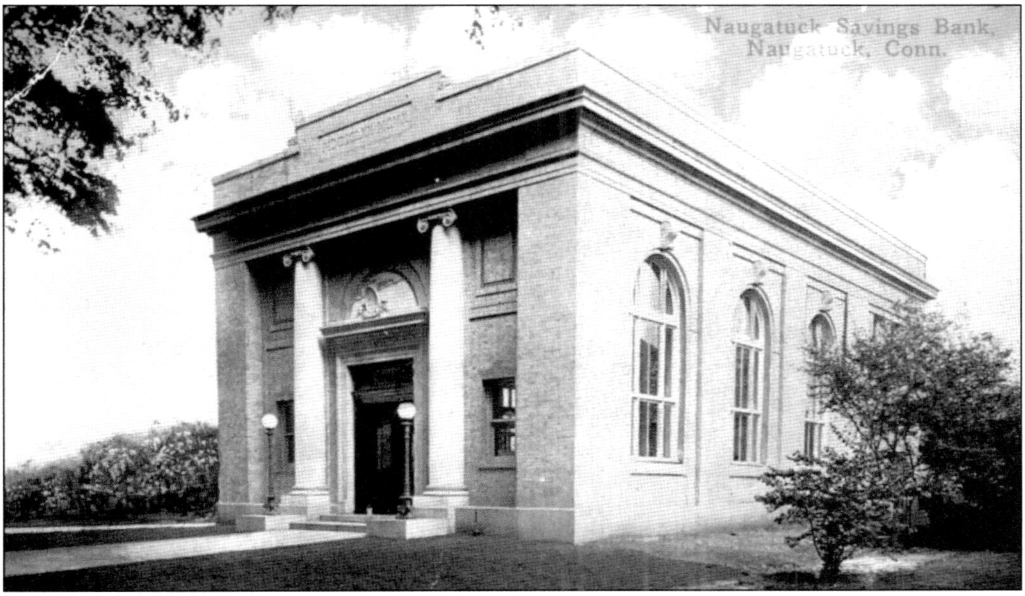

A SAFE PLACE FOR YOUR MONEY. This Naugatuck Savings Bank building, located on Church Street, was completed in 1910 and was designed by the firm of Crowe, Lewis and Wickenhofer of New York. The bank still exists today and has numerous branches in Naugatuck and surrounding communities, including Waterbury and Cheshire. This building is now the corporate office.

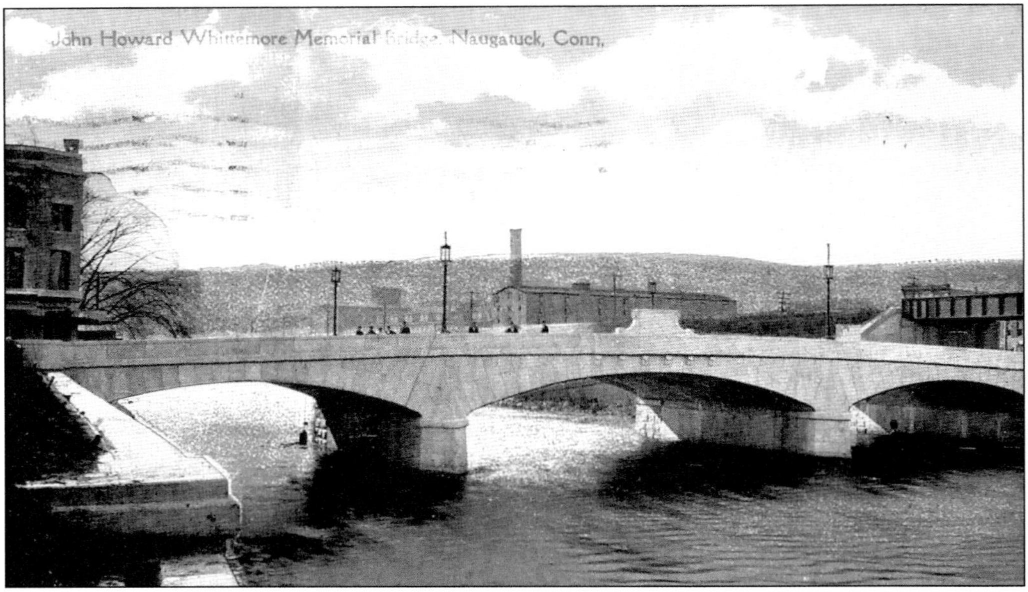

Pennies from Children. The John H. Whittemore Memorial Bridge honors one of Naugatuck's major benefactors. An industrialist, entrepreneur, and philanthropist, Whittemore died in 1910. The community wanted to honor him by building a bridge, and even children added their pennies to the fund to pay for its construction. It was sound enough to survive the flood of 1955, only losing its side panels and the memorial plaque. A new plaque was installed nearby.

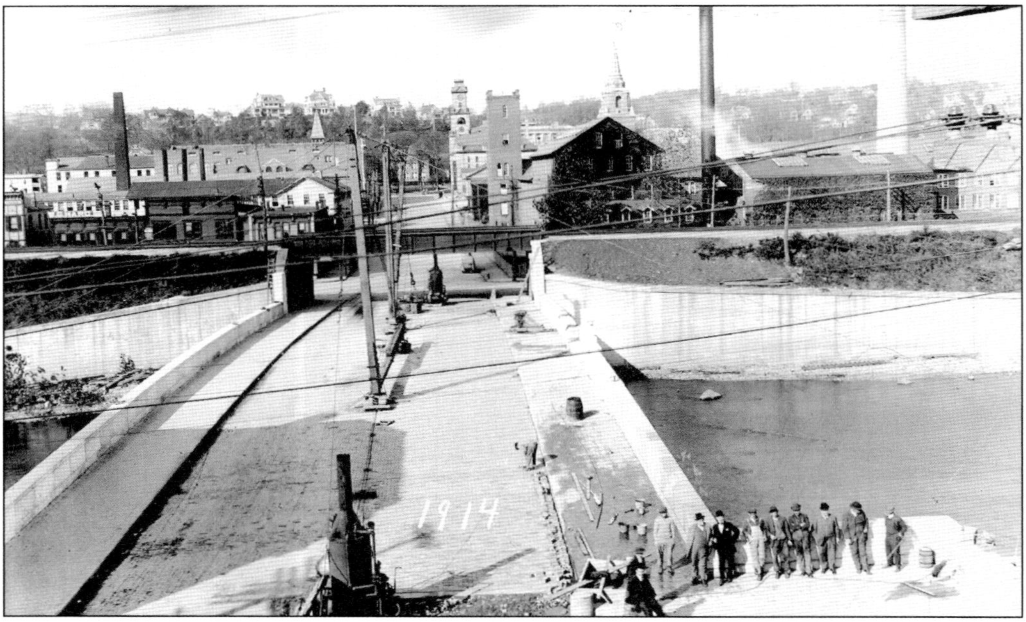

A Bridge over Troubled Waters. It is not as long as the Verazzano Narrows Bridge, nor as storied as the Golden Gate Bridge, nor as famous as the Brooklyn Bridge, but Naugatuck's John H. Whittemore Memorial Bridge has withstood the tests of time and torrent. It still stands as a community's tribute to a fine man. It was designed by Henry Bacon and completed in 1914. This view shows it during construction.

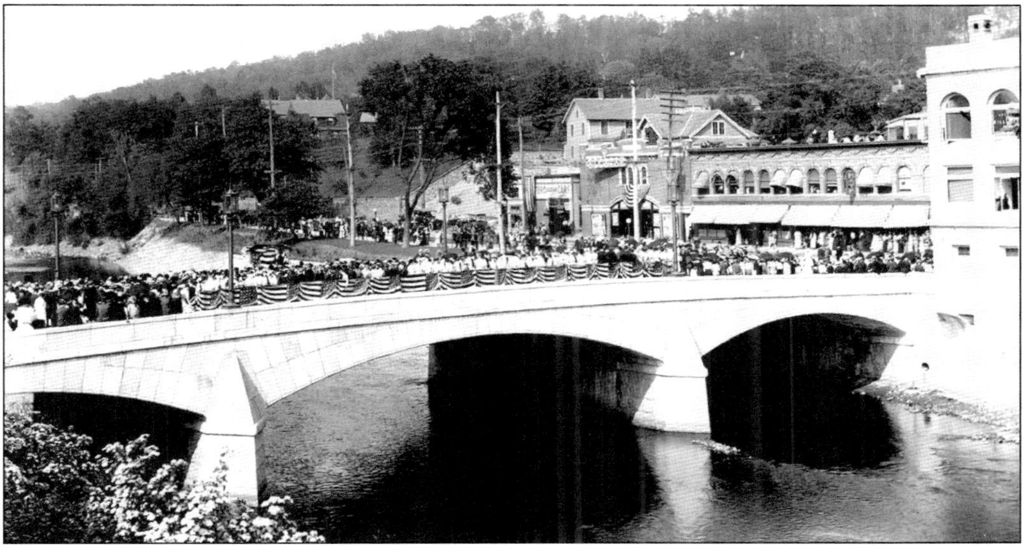

DEDICATION DAY. It was a clear day on May 30, 1914. The weather was perfect for the dedication of the John H. Whittemore Memorial Bridge. If you had traveled down to the Naugatuck River for a look-see, this is the scene that would have greeted you as you gazed southward. The solid structure is bedecked with bunting, and throngs of excited residents and luminaries are already assembling on and near the bridge.

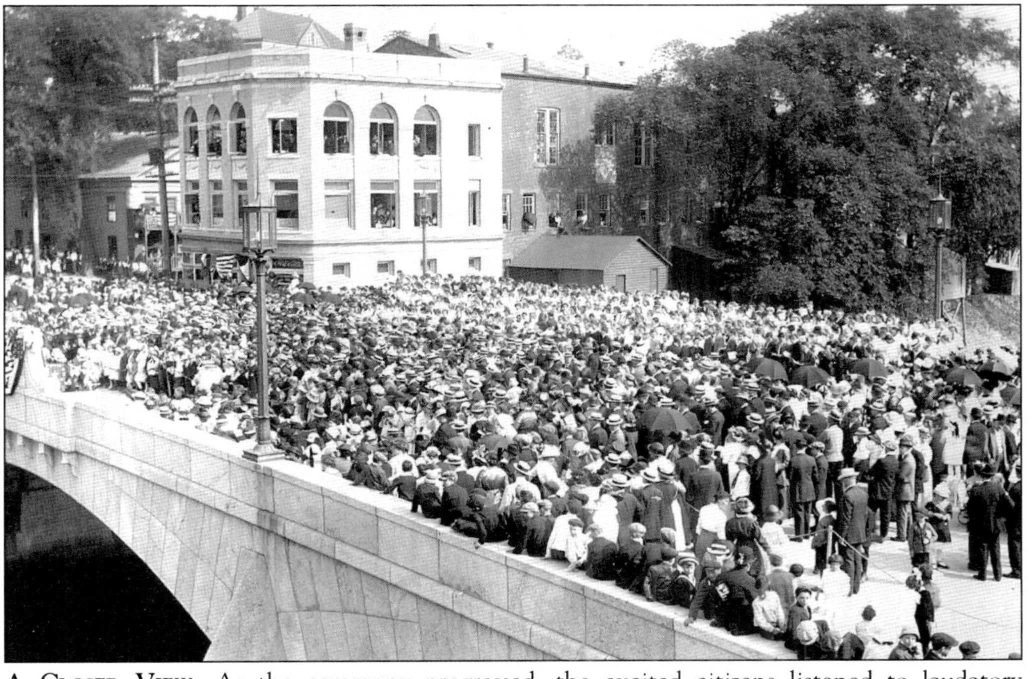

A CLOSER VIEW. As the ceremony progressed, the excited citizens listened to laudatory dedication speeches by many dignitaries. After the ceremony, they had the opportunity to stroll back and forth across their brand-new bridge. Notice the large number of distinctive hats on many of the gentlemen. Just as bowlers and fedoras characterized their respective eras, skimmers were often the hat of choice for the dapper dressers of this era.

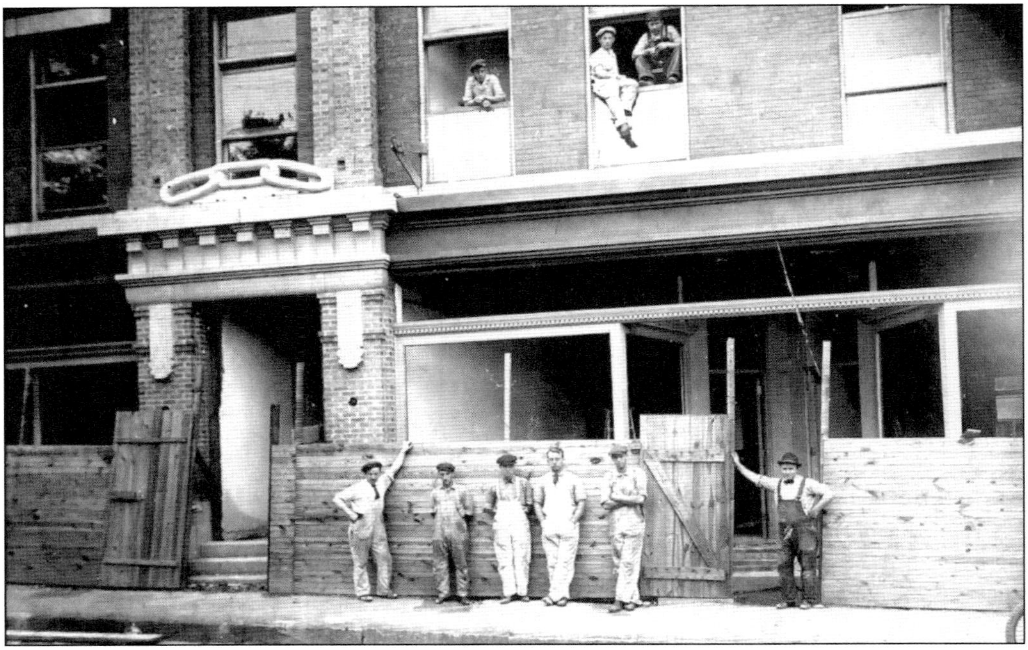

CONSTRUCTING THE ODD FELLOWS BUILDING. These unidentified workmen are taking a rest during the completion of the Odd Fellows building, still located east of the Route 8 underpass on Maple Street. The building became the home of the Independent Order of Odd Fellows c. 1913; it now houses a furniture store. The unique sculpture of the three chain links, now missing, was an identifying feature of this building for many years.

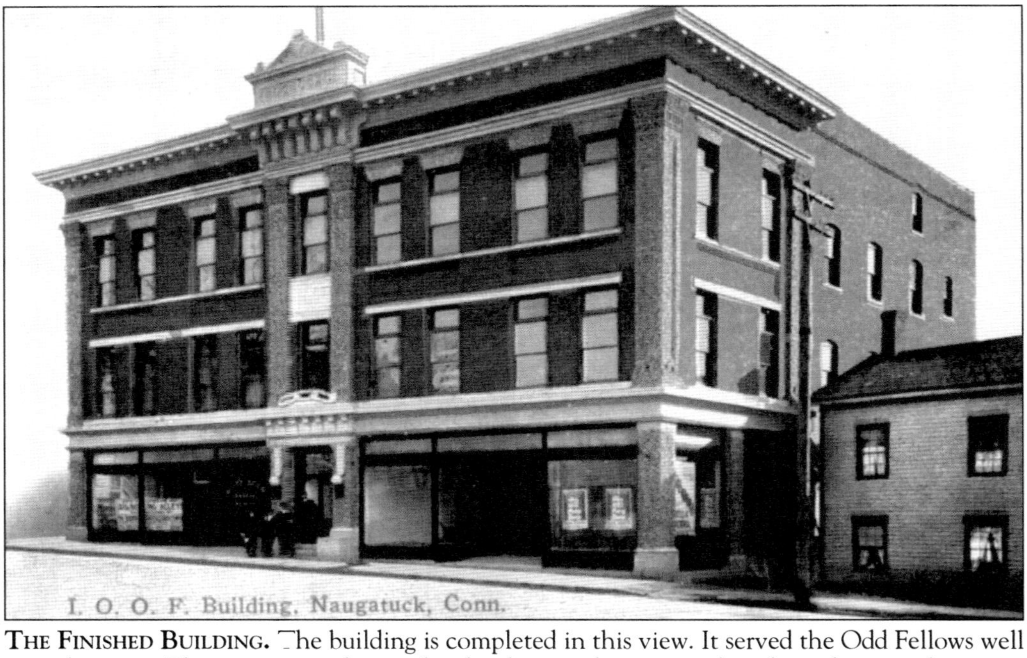

THE FINISHED BUILDING. The building is completed in this view. It served the Odd Fellows well over the years. Their group is a fraternal order that emphasizes good works and camaraderie.

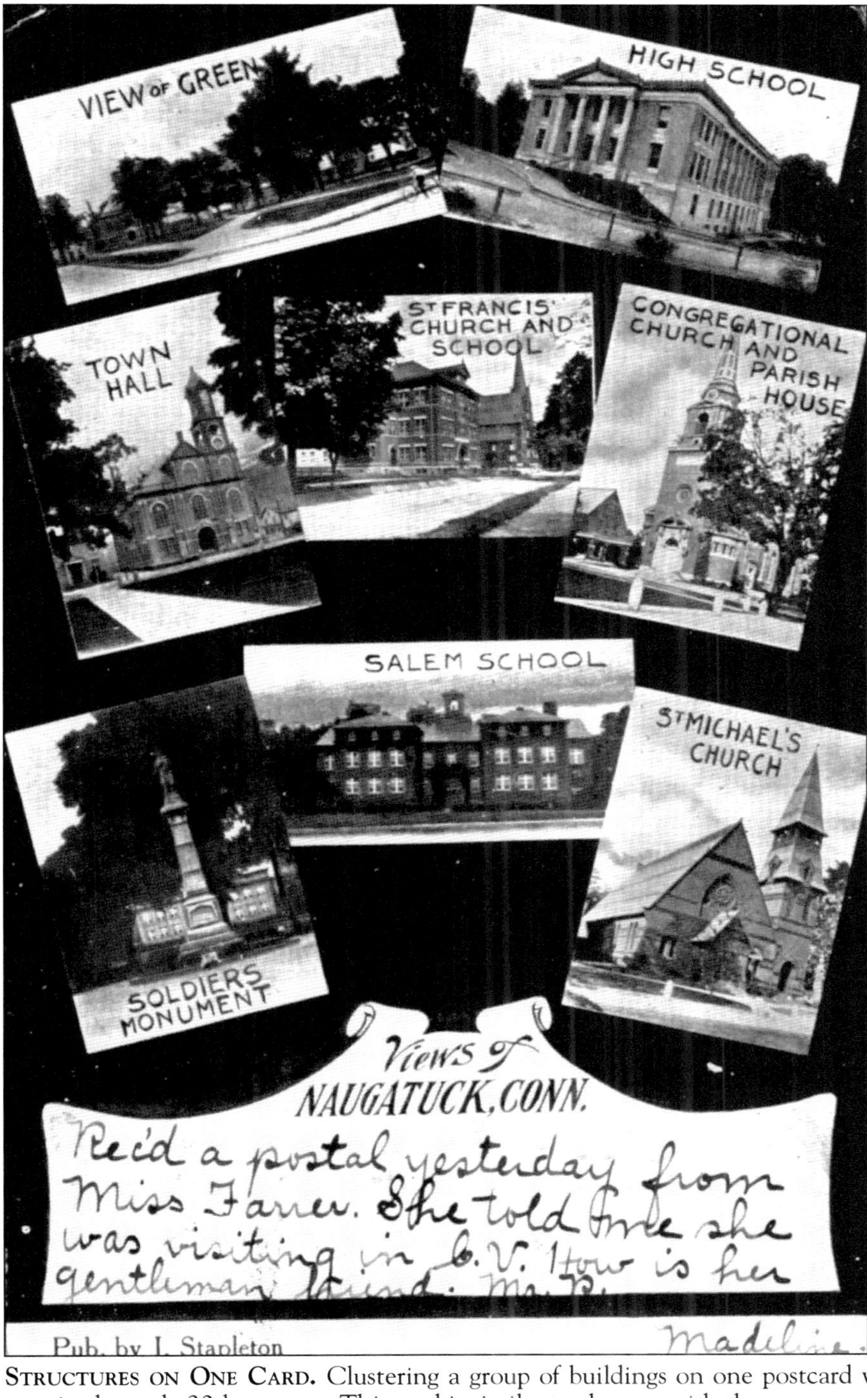

SEVEN STRUCTURES ON ONE CARD. Clustering a group of buildings on one postcard was not uncommon in the early 20th century. This card is similar to the one with the pansy on page 8. This style of card gave the recipient a quick tour of some of a community's architectural history. Because of the philanthropy of J. H. Whittemore and the prosperity that required the building of new structures, Naugatuck has a rich architectural heritage.

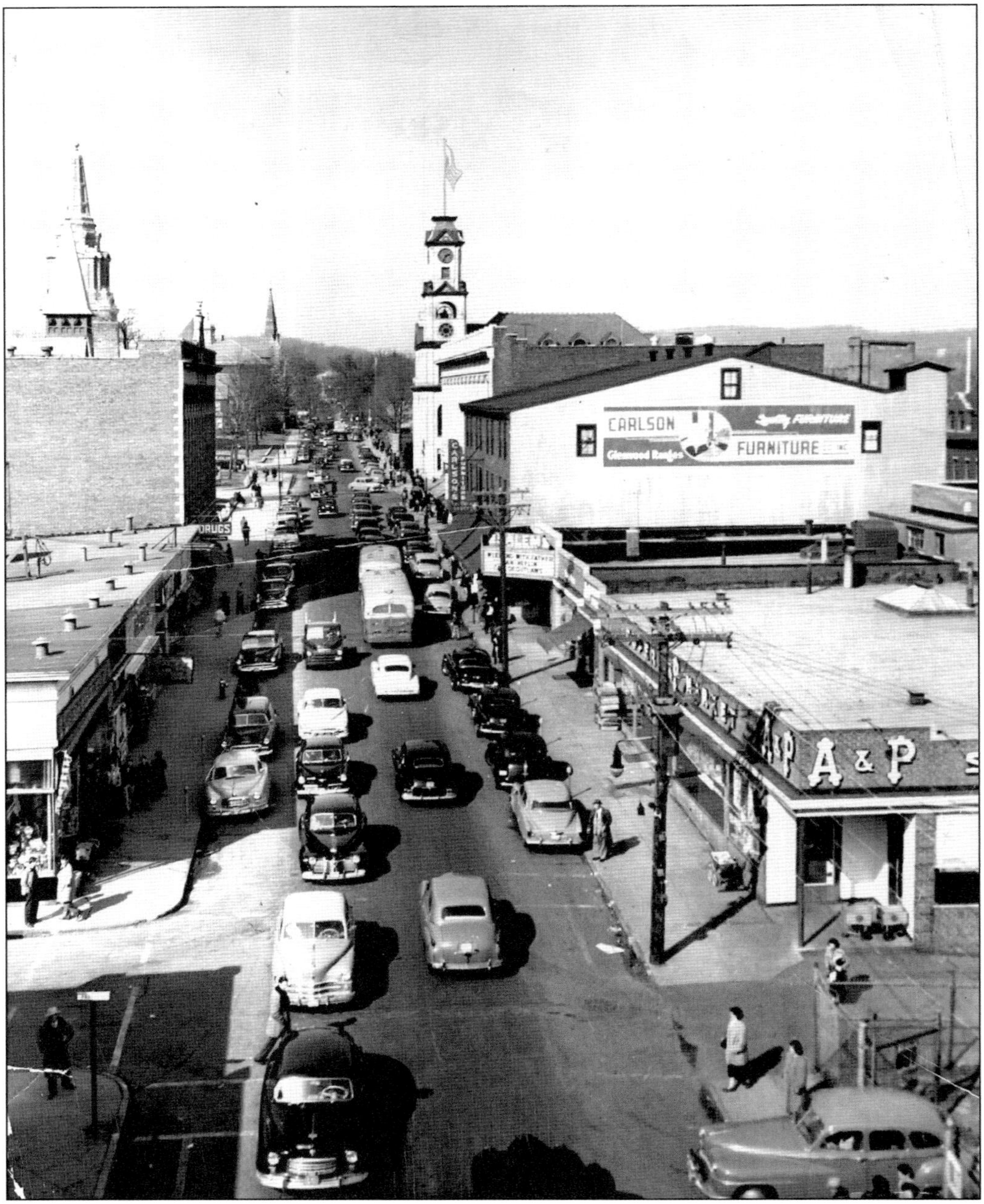

Looking North on Church Street during the 1950s. A portrait of a small New England community, this view of Naugatuck's downtown area could be a Rockwellian poster for prosperity. Cars with names like Studebaker, Dodge, Chrysler, and Nash fill the streets, and shoppers crowd onto the bus. Strolling through town in this era, you could learn who was in the new feature at the Salem Playhouse, discover what was on sale at the A&P, and pick up some of the latest gossip being exchanged on the corner.

Eight

Events, Parades, and Performances

Naugatuck has hosted some swinging parties in the more than 300 years of its existence, including parades, parties, theatrical events, recitals, dedications, graduations, and banquets. Its numerous organizations have held hundreds of fundraisers, awards presentations, and inductions of officers. The borough has also had its share of visits from prominent politicians, sports figures, and actors. Ella T. Grasso visited Uniroyal while she was governor of Connecticut. Sen. John F. Kennedy made a memorable campaign stop off Route 8 in the predawn hours of November 7, 1960. Many famous athletes have attended Naugatuck's annual Hall of Fame dinners, including Boston Red Sox third baseman Wade Boggs and New York Yankees Chris Chambliss, Roy White, Mike Pagliarulo, and Lou Piniella.

Some of the more recognizable and memorable activities and a few of the lesser-known events are included in this chapter. Other memorable events that were unfortunately not recorded on film include the visits of actor Clark Gable, who once got off the train here only to learn he was at the wrong stop, and of Hermione Baddeley, the actress who played Mrs. Nell Naugatuck on Norman Lear's hit television show *Maude* in the 1970s and who made a personal appearance at the green in that time period.

You are invited on a tour through the ages. The only ticket you will need is a turn of the page.

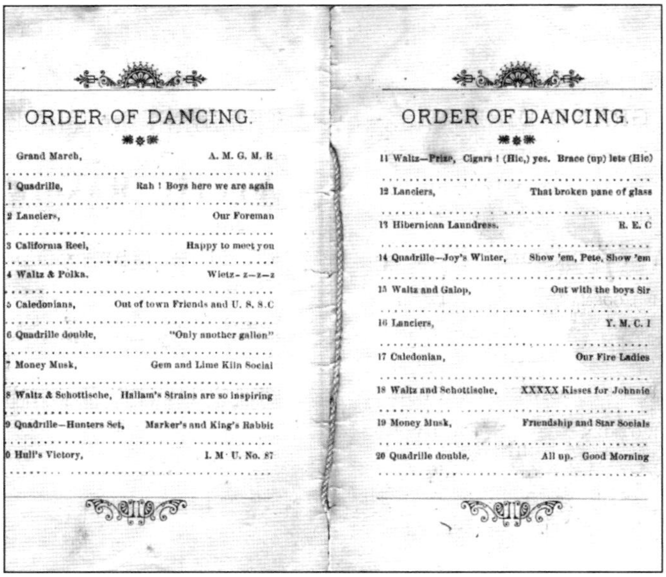

ORDER OF DANCING.

Grand March, A. M. G. M. R

1 Quadrille, Rah ! Boys here we are again

2 Lanciers, Our Foreman

3 California Reel, Happy to meet you

4 Waltz & Polka. Wietz-z-z-z

5 Caledonians, Out of town Friends and U. S. S. C

6 Quadrille double, "Only another gallon"

7 Money Musk, Gem and Lime Kiln Social

8 Waltz & Schottische, Hallam's Strains are so inspiring

9 Quadrille—Hunters Set, Marker's and King's Rabbit

10 Hull's Victory, I. M. U. No. 87

ORDER OF DANCING.

11 Waltz—Prize, Cigars ! (Hic,) yes. Brace (up) lets (Hic)

12 Lanciers, That broken pane of glass

13 Hibernican Laundress. R. E. C

14 Quadrille—Joy's Winter, Show 'em, Pete, Show 'em

15 Waltz and Galop, Out with the boys Sir

16 Lanciers, Y. M. C. I

17 Caledonian, Our Fire Ladies

18 Waltz and Schottische, XXXXX Kisses for Johnnie

19 Money Musk, Friendship and Star Socials

20 Quadrille double, All up. Good Morning

A Real Soiree. The Arctic Makers of the Goodyear Metallic Rubber Shoe Company used this ornate invitation to announce their third annual soiree, held Thursday evening, January 22, 1885, in the Gem Opera House. A casual first-time visitor to the venue might not have known it was located in town hall. Dances, including quadrilles, lancers, and Caledonians, were listed on the inside of the invitation. The names of groups and attendees were also listed, possibly as dedications.

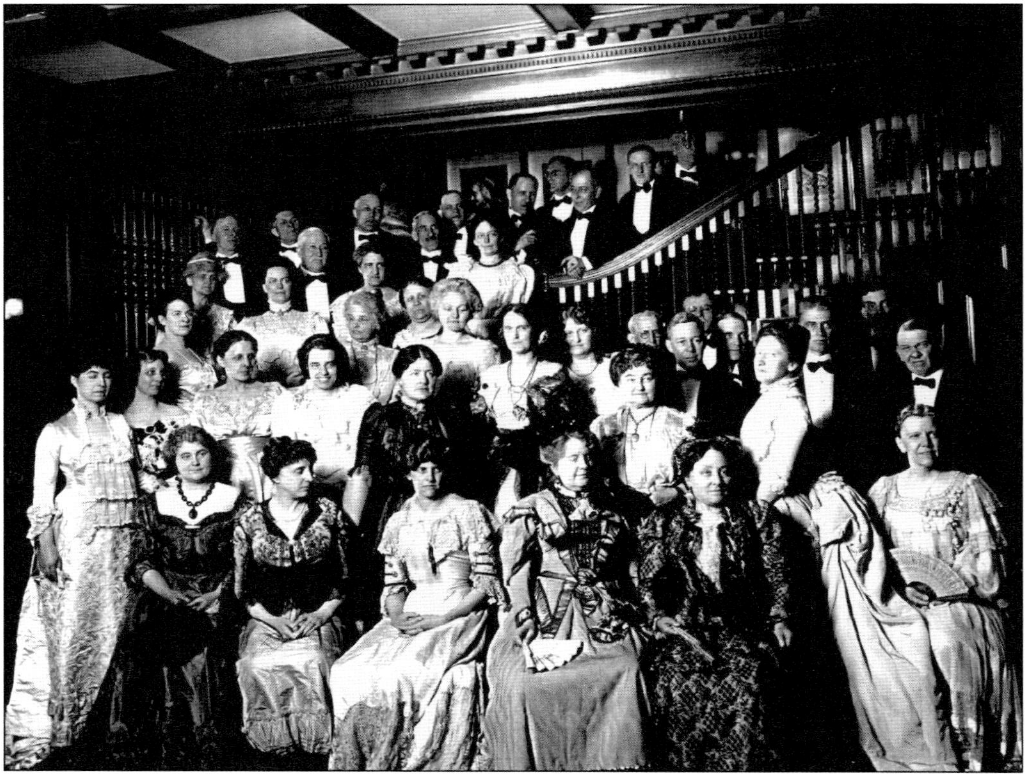

Vintage Visitors. Gertrude Whittemore was a member of Naugatuck's "landed gentry." This well-attended party of well-dressed members of the area's elite took place at her Church Street home on Columbus Day 1922. Some of the more notable guests are Wilbur Squires, Howard B. Tuttle, and Harris Whittemore. Gertrude was responsible for transforming the Naugatuck National Bank into the Children's Library in 1930.

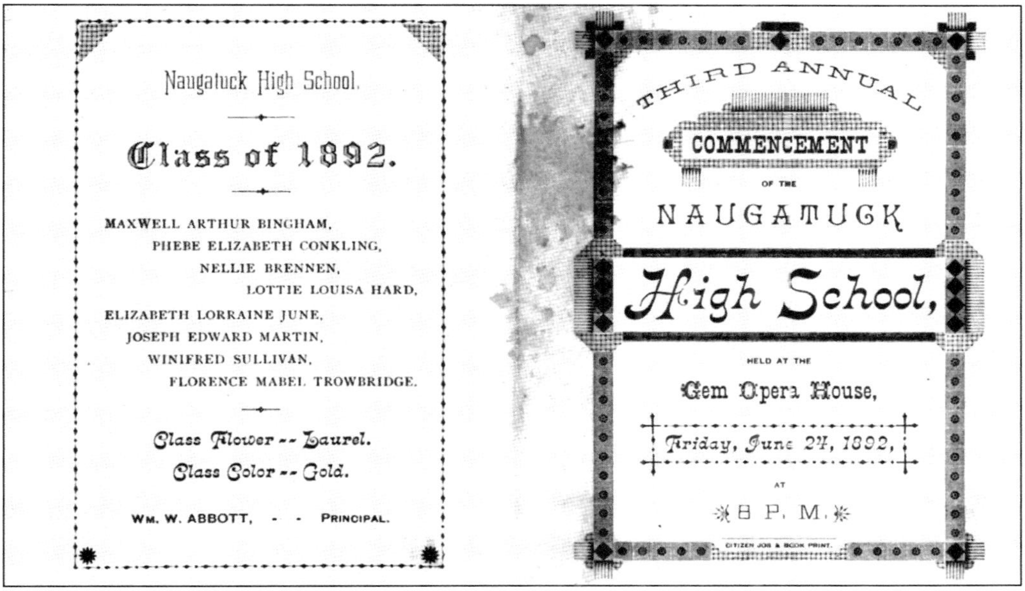

Naugatuck High School.

Class of 1892.

MAXWELL ARTHUR BINGHAM,
PHEBE ELIZABETH CONKLING,
NELLIE BRENNEN,
LOTTIE LOUISA HARD,
ELIZABETH LORRAINE JUNE,
JOSEPH EDWARD MARTIN,
WINIFRED SULLIVAN,
FLORENCE MABEL TROWBRIDGE.

Class Flower -- Laurel.
Class Color -- Gold.

WM. W. ABBOTT, - - PRINCIPAL.

THIRD ANNUAL
COMMENCEMENT
OF THE
NAUGATUCK
High School,
HELD AT THE
Gem Opera House,
Friday, June 24, 1892,
AT
8 P. M.

CITIZEN JOB & BOOK PRINT.

YOU'RE INVITED. Friday, June 24, 1892, was the third annual commencement of the Naugatuck High School. The ceremony was held at the Gem Opera House and began at 8:00 p.m. The members of the class were prominently featured on the invitation.

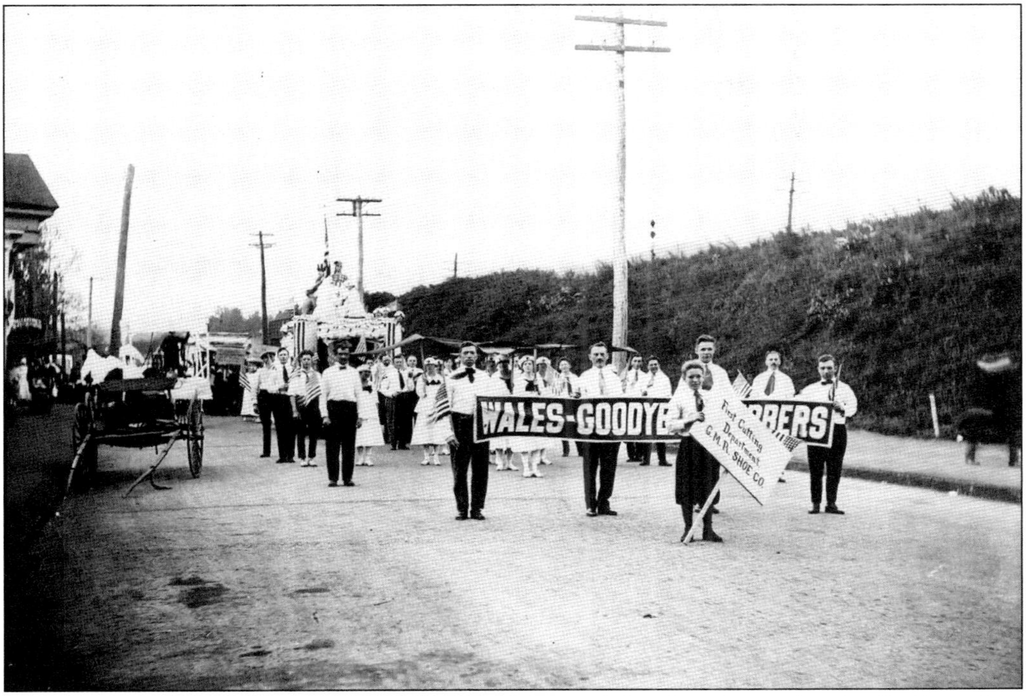

WHATEVER FLOATS YOUR FLOAT. These employees of the Goodyear Metallic Rubber Shoe Company, representing the First Cutting Department, are taking part in the Independence Day parade on July 4, 1919. They paused to have their photograph taken while marching along the parade route.

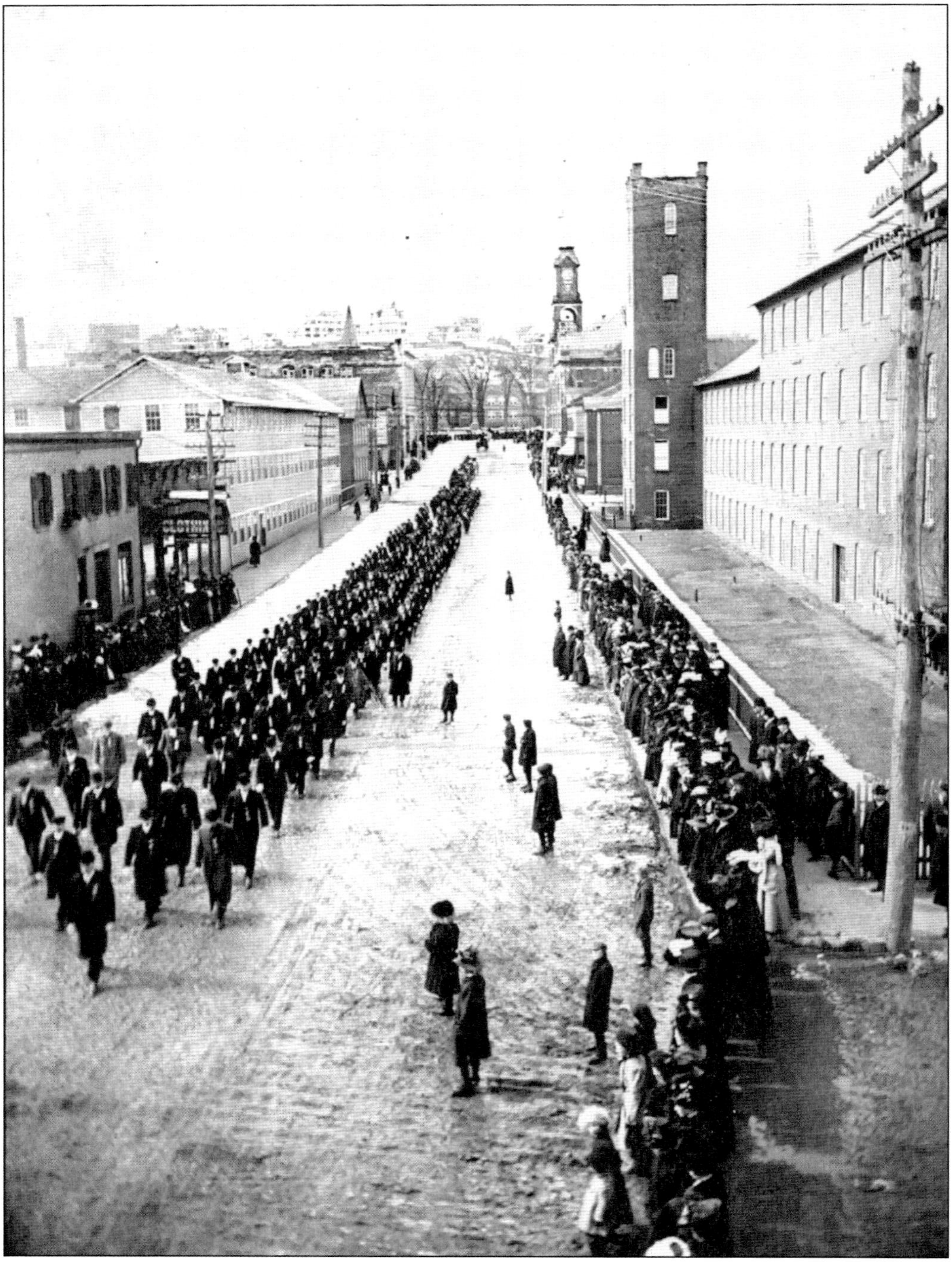

Somber Marchers. In this B. Benander photograph, a long column of men proceeds east down Maple Street. No date is given, but the Salem School can be seen in center area, so the photograph had to have been taken in the late 1800s or in the early part of the 20th century. It is difficult to say with certainty, but this might be a funeral procession of a fraternal organization. There appears to be a hearse toward the end of the line.

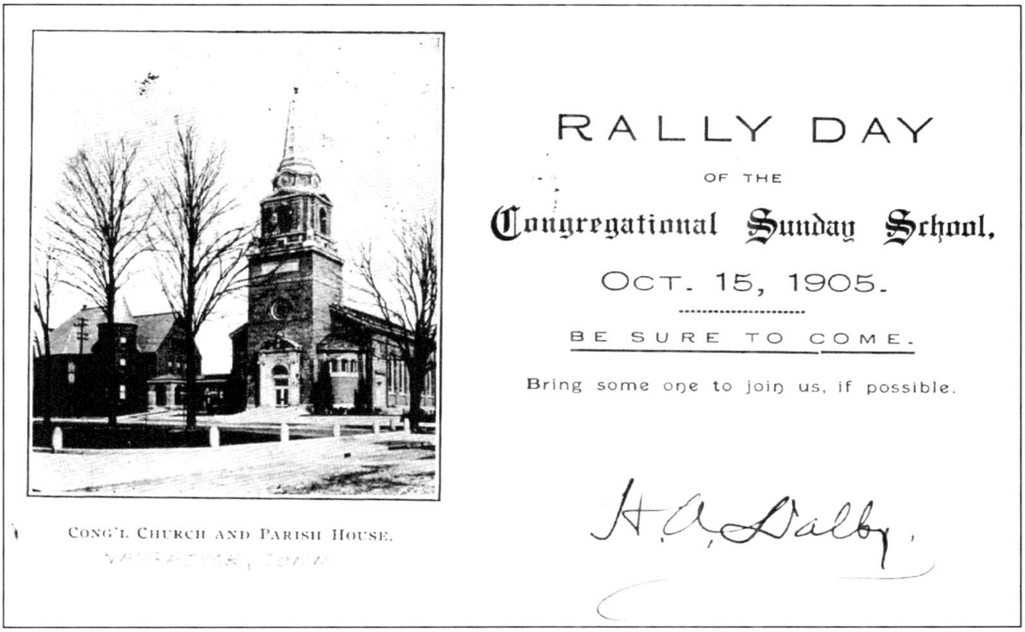

RALLY DAY

OF THE

Congregational Sunday School.

OCT. 15, 1905.

BE SURE TO COME.

Bring some one to join us, if possible.

H. A. Dalby.

CONG'L CHURCH AND PARISH HOUSE.

A RALLY 'ROUND RELIGION. A Rally Day reminder from October 15, 1905, included a photograph of the Congregational church and parish house. It was signed by H. A. Dalby and entreated a potential religious learner to attend the start of Sunday school.

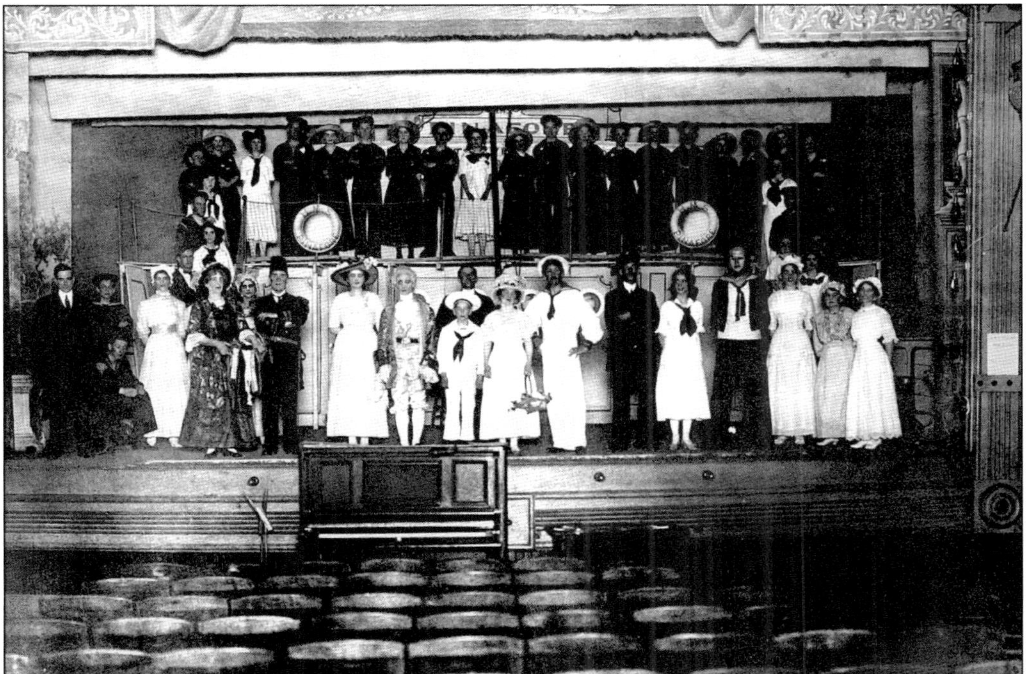

GILBERT AND SULLIVAN SAIL IN. The comic opera classic *H.M.S. Pinafore* was staged in 1912. It may have been a traveling company's production or a local effort, but culture had definitely arrived in Naugatuck. The show was presented in the Gem Opera House.

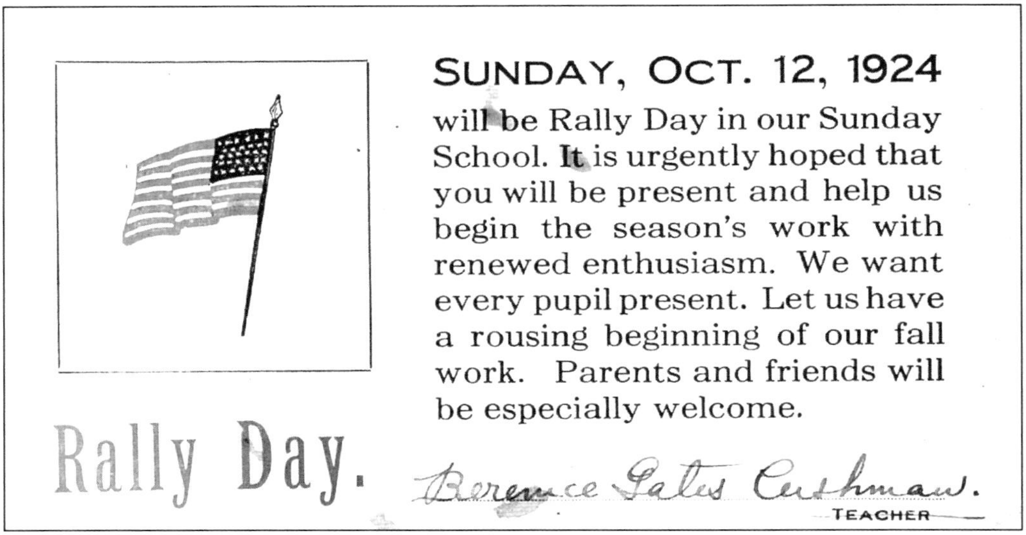

SUNDAY, OCT. 12, 1924

will be Rally Day in our Sunday School. It is urgently hoped that you will be present and help us begin the season's work with renewed enthusiasm. We want every pupil present. Let us have a rousing beginning of our fall work. Parents and friends will be especially welcome.

Rally Day.

Berenice Gates Cushman.

TEACHER

A Rousing Beginning. Myrtle Wooster was invited to attend her church's Rally Day on October 12, 1924. Apparently, Berenice Gates Cashman, the Sunday school teacher, had sent a postcard to each of her students, inviting them, their parents, and their friends to attend the kickoff event for the fall's Sunday school session.

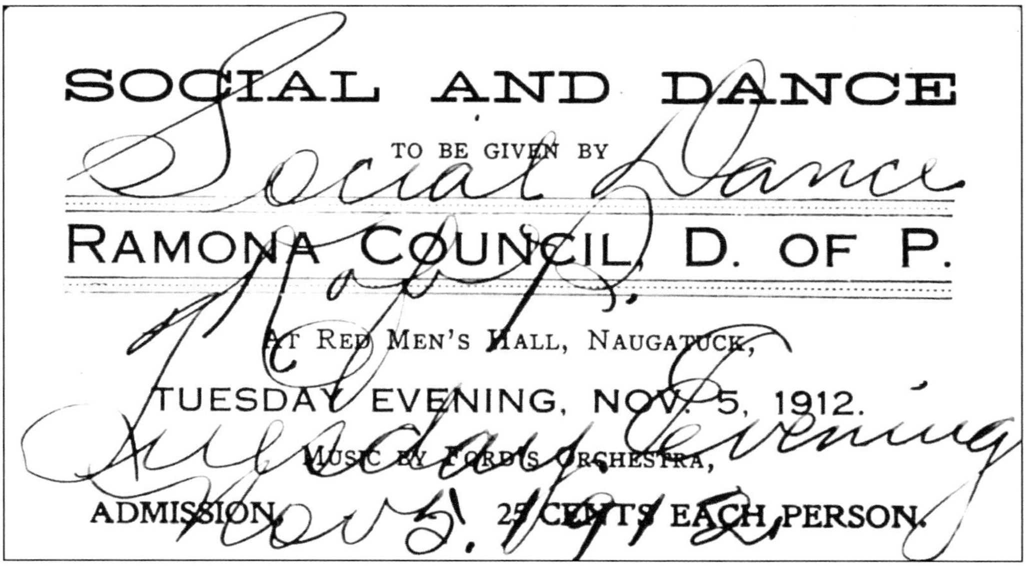

SOCIAL AND DANCE

TO BE GIVEN BY

RAMONA COUNCIL, D. OF P.

AT RED MEN'S HALL, NAUGATUCK,

TUESDAY EVENING, NOV. 5, 1912.

MUSIC BY FORD'S ORCHESTRA,

ADMISSION, 25 CENTS EACH PERSON.

Dancin' Up a Storm at Red Men's Hall. The Ramona Council held a dance on Tuesday evening, November 5, 1912. The cost was 25¢ per person to gain admission to Red Men's Hall. The name of the hall would be considered politically incorrect today. Ford's orchestra was listed as the musical group.

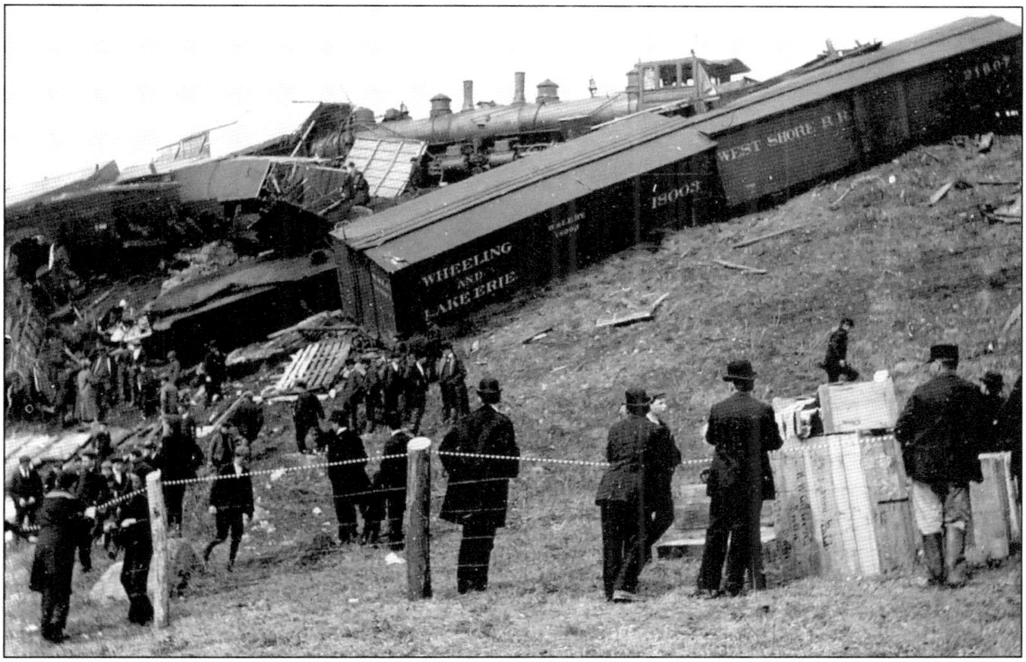

A Train Accident. "Old New England Road, Gunntown," is all that appears on this image of a train crash. It may have occurred in Millville near the trolley. The attire of the assembled crowd indicates that the mishap probably occurred prior to the 1930s.

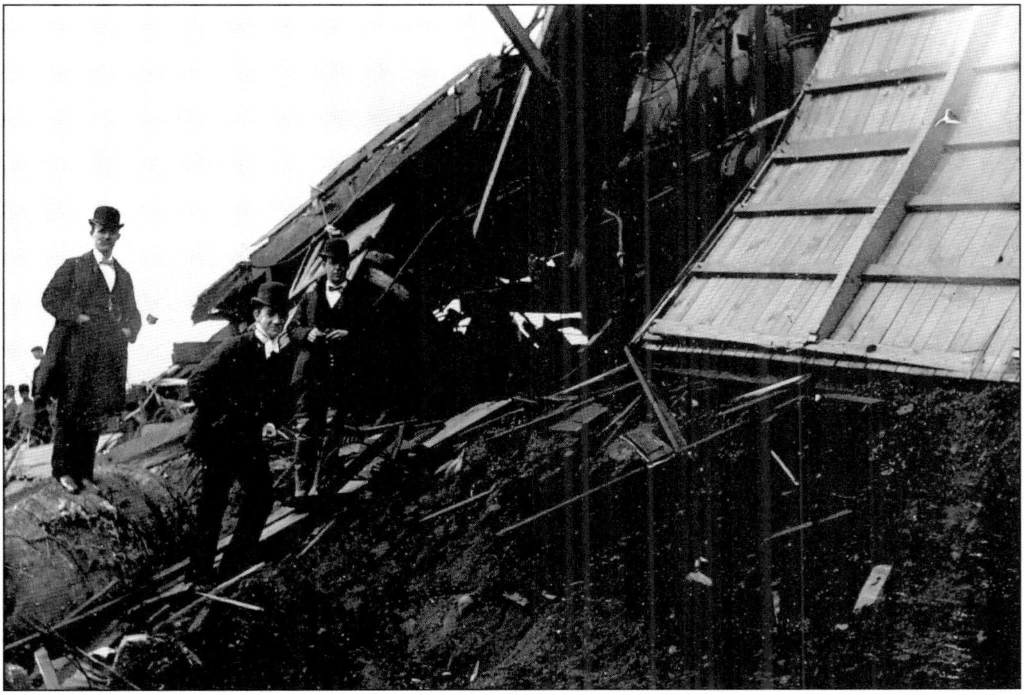

Dependable Witnesses. These three gentlemen seem quite pleased to have witnessed this major accident. At least they got close enough to view the aftermath.

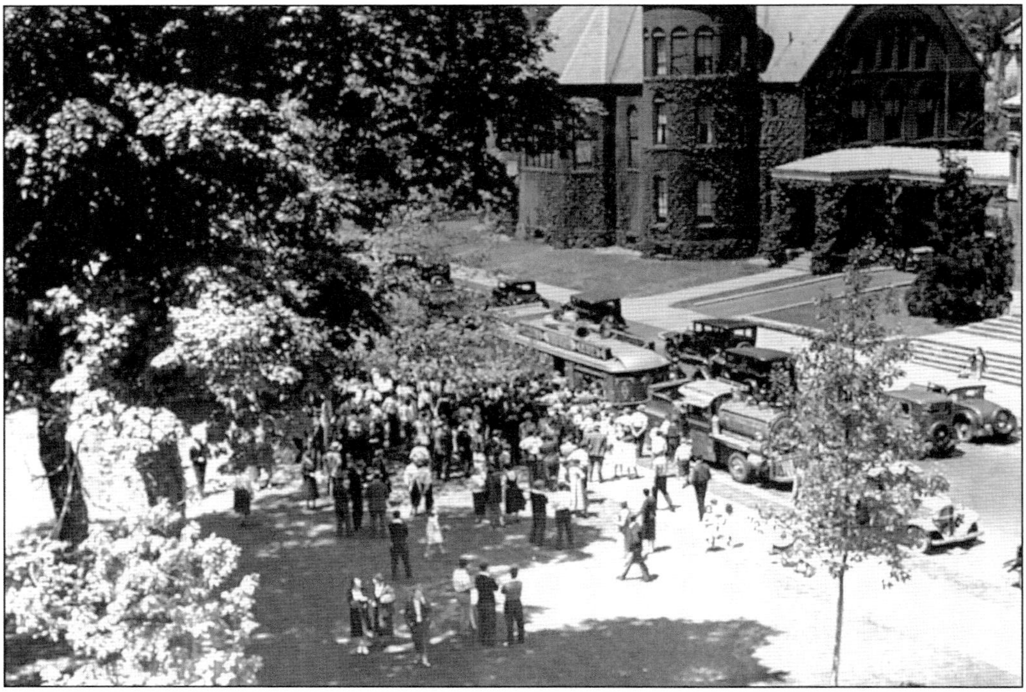

Hollywood in the Hills of Naugatuck. It was a special day in Naugatuck when the MGM Talking Picture Globetrotter World Tour arrived. Judging by the vehicles parked on Division Street, this photograph was taken sometime in the 1930s. Movies were an important recreational pastime then, as they are now. Television, computers, and video games had not been invented, so movies, radio, and theater were the only available entertainment.

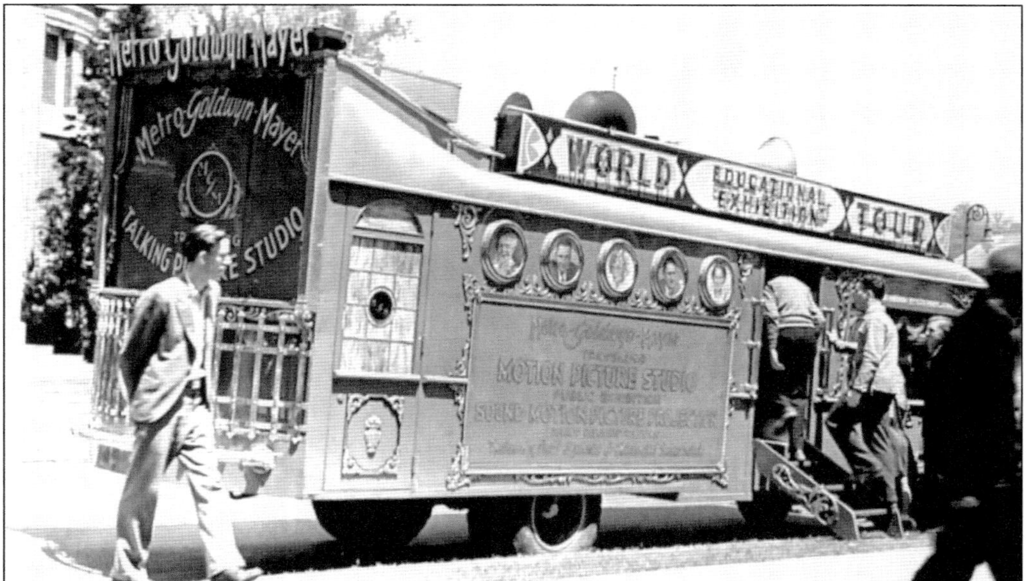

Stars on the Street. This closeup of the side of the traveling exhibit features photographs of stars of the silver screen under contract to MGM.

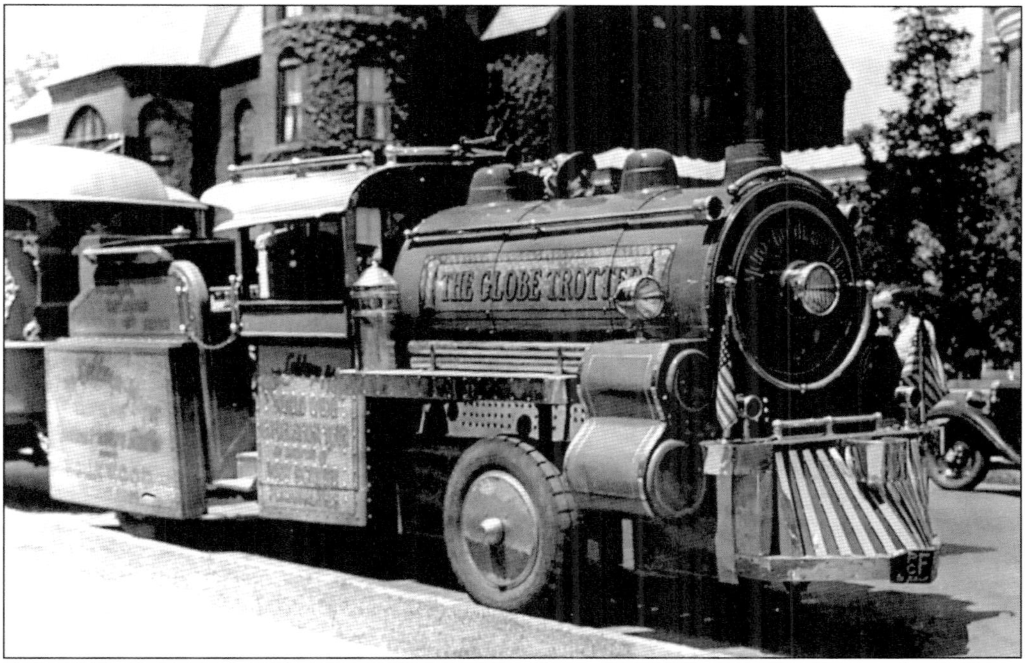

A LOCO MOTIVE. The mock train engine must have driven local residents crazy, as it surely created quite a stir as it pulled up to park in "Anytown, U.S.A." Naugatuck was no different than any other town; the exhibit attracted a large crowd on a pleasant day.

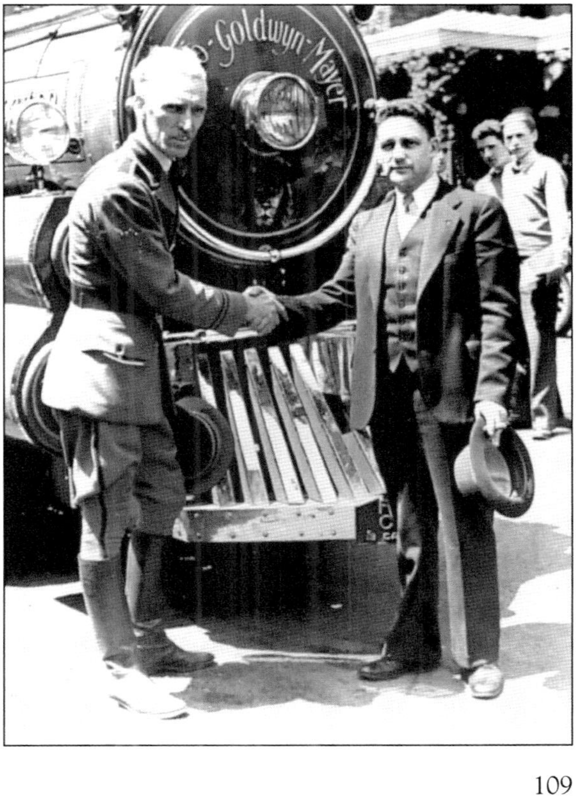

THE ENGINEER. This man, apparently the driver and manager of this traveling show, had an impressive uniform. It is believed that he is shaking hands with Mr. Pasho, manager of the Salem Playhouse.

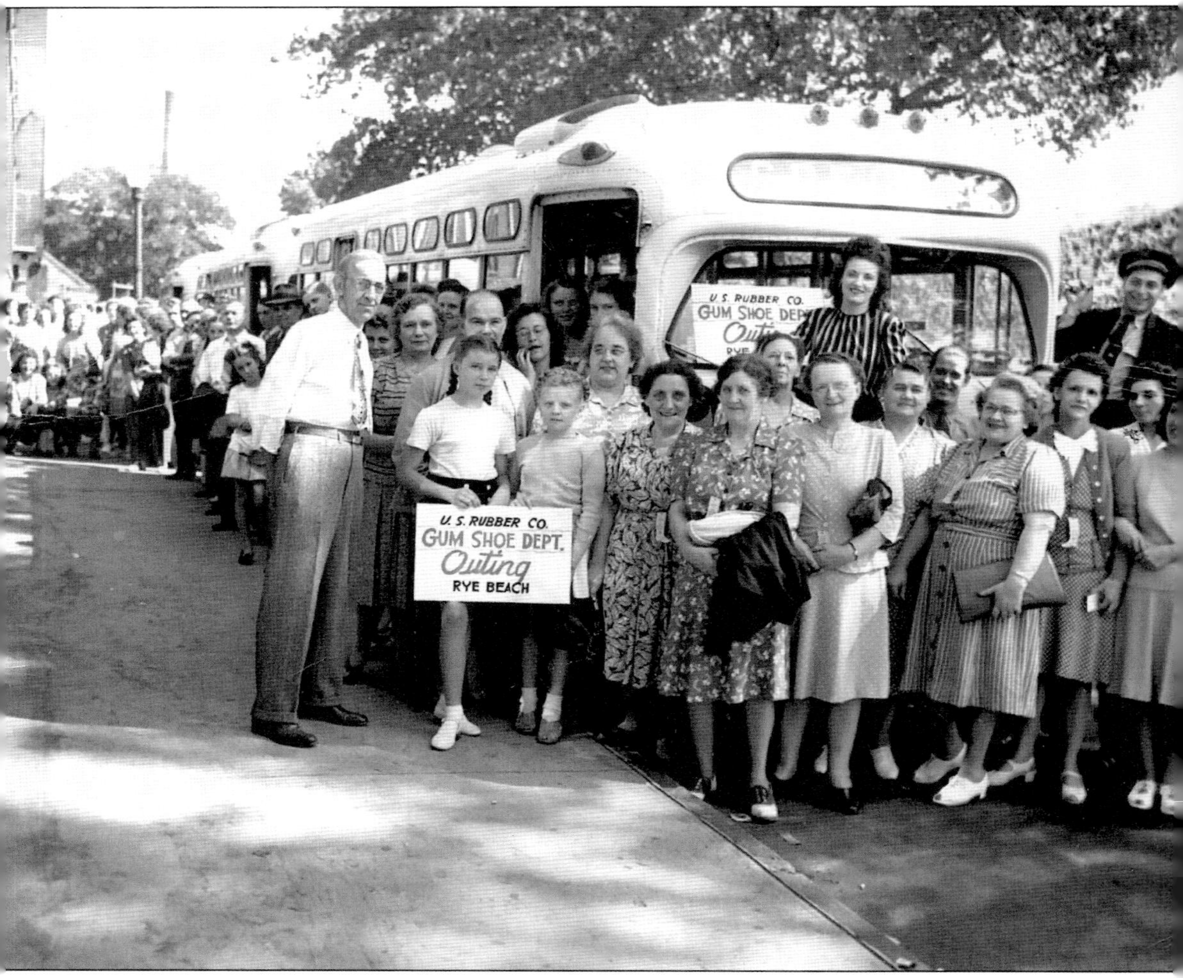

RYE IN THE FUTURE. The employees of U.S. Rubber (later Uniroyal) and their families were occasionally treated to trips to area amusement parks. This group is about to leave for a day of frolic and fun at Rye Beach in Rye, New York. The names of the participants do not appear anywhere on the print, but the tall gentleman near the door of the bus may be one of the plant supervisors. This trip probably took place in the 1950s.

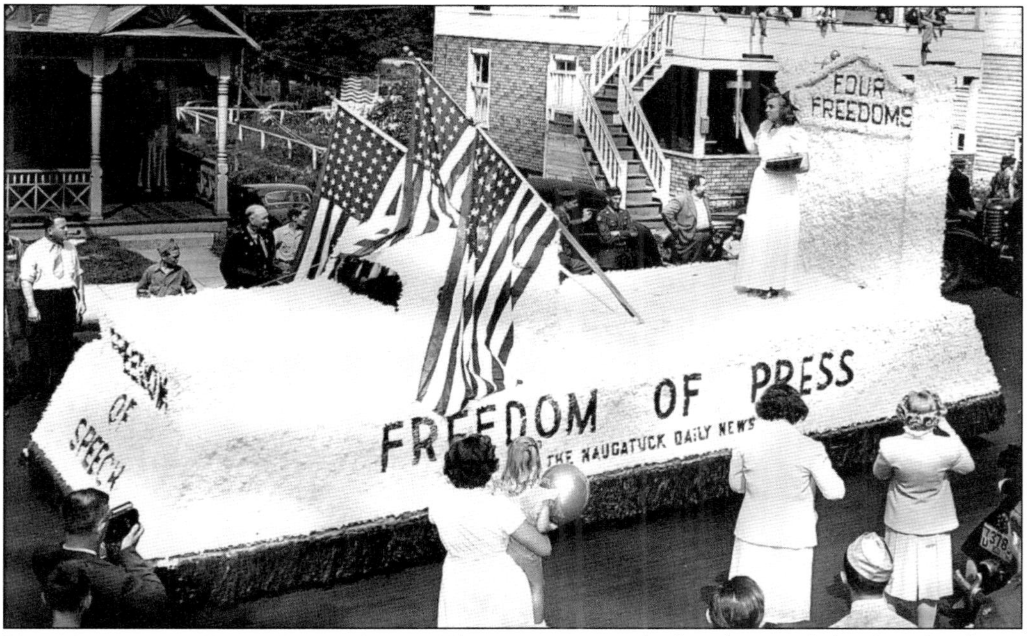

The Naugatuck Daily News Float. This postwar parade float honored the four freedoms: freedom of speech, freedom to worship God, freedom from want, and freedom from fear. These freedoms were emphasized in Pres. Franklin D. Roosevelt's State of the Union address on January 6, 1941. Artist Norman Rockwell was inspired by the speech and painted the four freedoms in a celebrated series of paintings that appeared in the *Saturday Evening Post*.

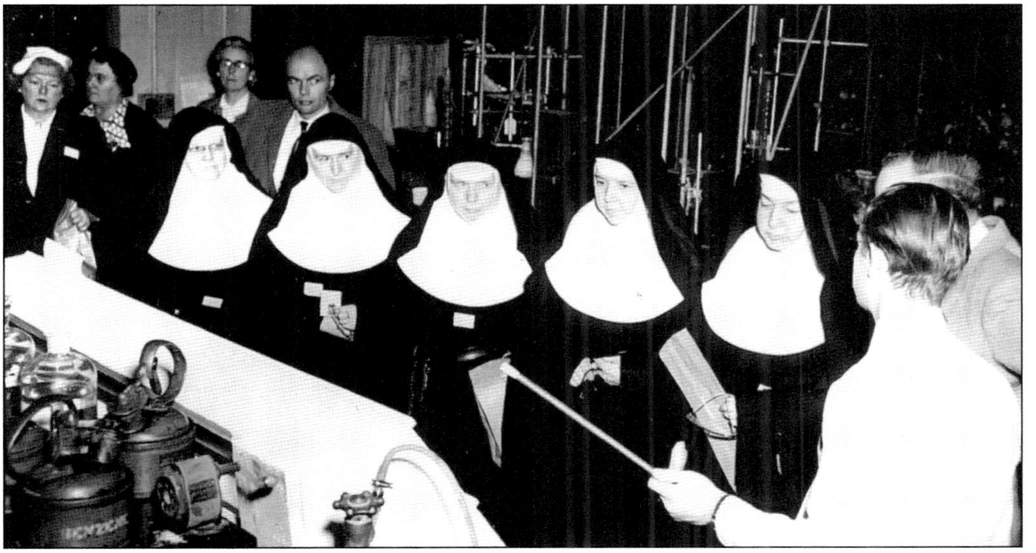

Religiously Studying Chemistry. The Naugatuck Chemical Plant was the site of a tour for area schools' staff and teachers on December 2, 1952. Visitors were treated to an informative view of plant procedures and products. Pictured are Dorothy Moss of Naugatuck High School, Catherine Brooks of Salem School, Marie Daly of Prospect School, guide R. Van Allen, and Sisters Mary Hilda, Mary Joseph, Mary Madelina, Mary Ernestine, and Mary Gertrude Claire, possibly from St. Francis School.

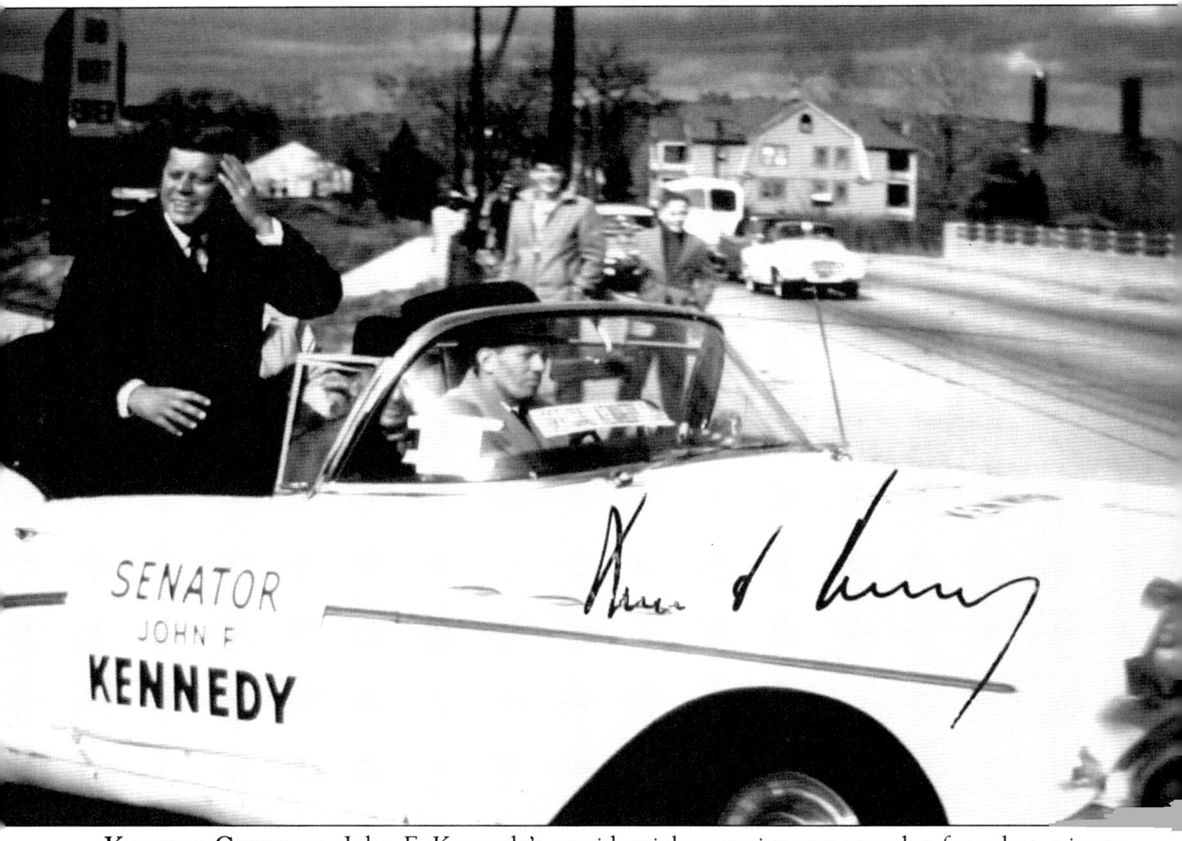

Kennedy Charisma. John F. Kennedy's presidential campaign was overdue for a last-minute stop in Naugatuck. Hundreds waited for this charismatic leader until his caravan pulled off Route 8 in the predawn hours of November 7, 1960, on the way to Waterbury. Residents John McKee and his sister Linda recall how well Kennedy pronounced "Naugatuck." This recently discovered photograph was taken the next day in Waterbury and was lent by its owner, Ron Guerrera of Mattatuck Antiques.

Nine

Groups and Organizations

Naugatuck has been fortunate enough to have been home to a panoply of organizations, both sectarian and nonsectarian. Some groups represented in the next few pages are well known and even international in scope, like the Red Cross and the Little League. Some, like the St. Francis Church Temperance and Abstinence Brotherhood, are lesser known and have disbanded or have faded into history.

Over the years, these organizations have promoted brotherhood, industry, religion, and ethnic camaraderie. Their members have contributed countless hours to their causes and to the betterment of their community and the world. They have provided a model for today's citizens, especially our younger citizens, to follow.

Peruse the following pages carefully; you may find a relative who was once a valued member of one of these groups. You may even be able to provide information about or a definitive identification for an anonymous group or unknown person. Perhaps you may encounter your own cherished group, the one to which you devote your time and energy.

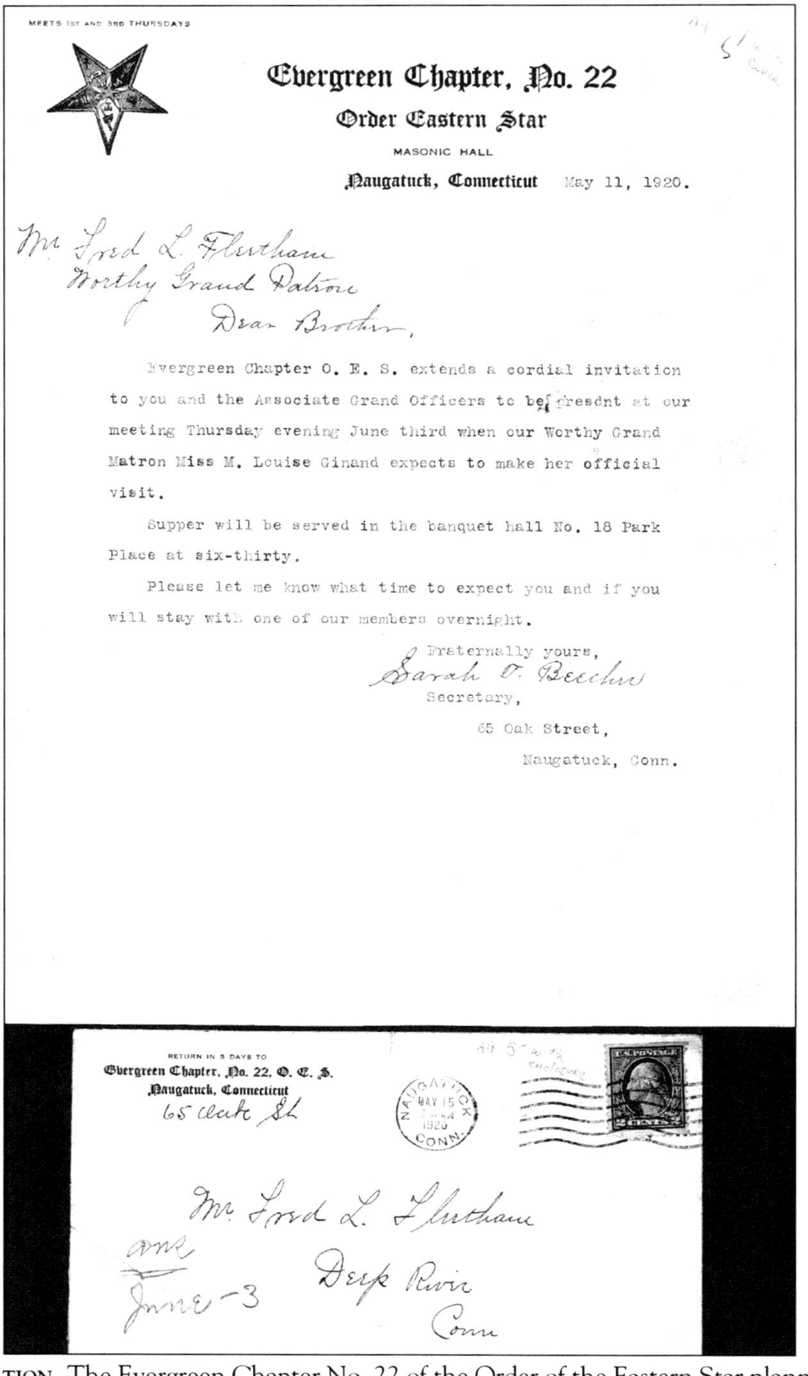

MEETS 1ST AND 3RD THURSDAYS

Evergreen Chapter, No. 22
Order Eastern Star
MASONIC HALL
Naugatuck, Connecticut May 11, 1920.

Mr Fred L. Flertham
Worthy Grand Patron
Dear Brother,

Evergreen Chapter O. E. S. extends a cordial invitation to you and the Associate Grand Officers to be present at our meeting Thursday evening June third when our Worthy Grand Matron Miss M. Louise Ginand expects to make her official visit.

Supper will be served in the banquet hall No. 18 Park Place at six-thirty.

Please let me know what time to expect you and if you will stay with one of our members overnight.

Fraternally yours,
Sarah O. Beecher
Secretary,
65 Oak Street,
Naugatuck, Conn.

RETURN IN 5 DAYS TO
Evergreen Chapter, No. 22, O. E. S.
Naugatuck, Connecticut
65 Oak St

NAUGATUCK CONN. MAY 15 1920

Mr Fred L. Flertham
Deep River
Conn

Ans
June-3

AN INVITATION. The Evergreen Chapter No. 22 of the Order of the Eastern Star planned a get-together for June 3, 1920. Sarah Beecher, secretary of the female counterpart of Naugatuck's Masons, invited guests from all areas of the state to attend. The travel involved must have been a consideration for the guests, for Beecher is offering Ford Flertham of Deep River the possibility of accommodations at a local member's home.

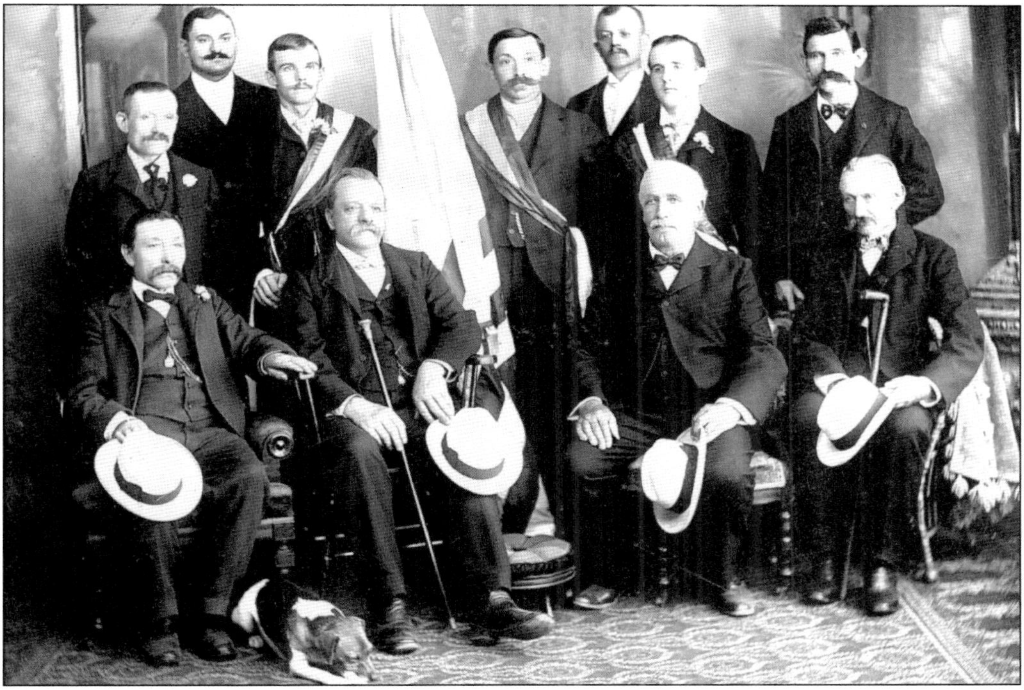

DISTINGUISHED MEN. These 11 men gathered for a formal portrait of their group, possibly early in the 20th century. Unfortunately, neither they nor their organization were identified on the photograph. The flag in the center may be the flag of a country, but not enough of it is visible to state with certainty what country or group the flag represents. Apparently, white hats, moustaches, and bow ties were popular, while corsages were optional.

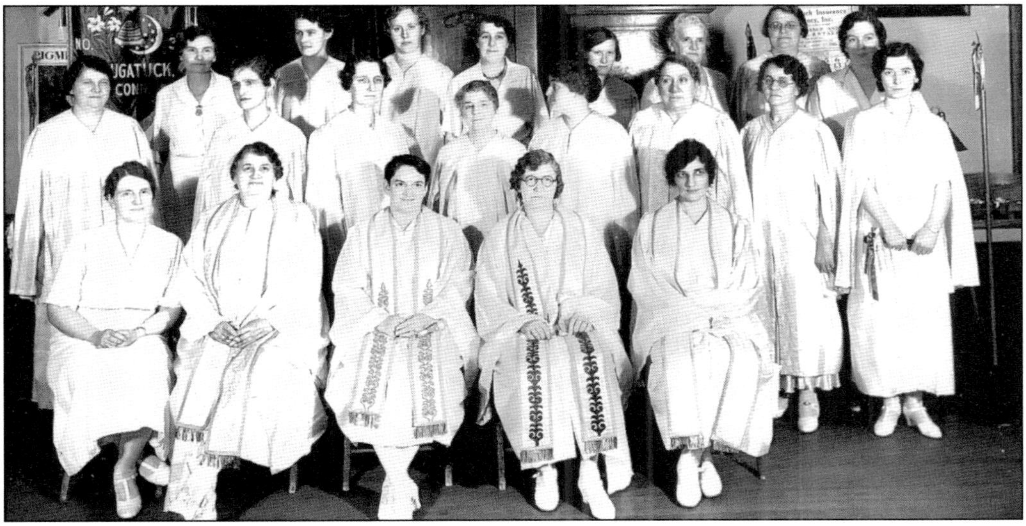

THE LADIES OF THE REBEKAH LODGE. It was a special night when these 21 ladies of the Columbian Rebekah Lodge dressed in their finest attire, ready to celebrate. Perhaps the occasion was an installation of officers. The richly ornate sashes may indicate status or position. The Rebekah Lodge is the female counterpart of the Independent Order of Odd Fellows, an organization with international ties that promotes fellowship.

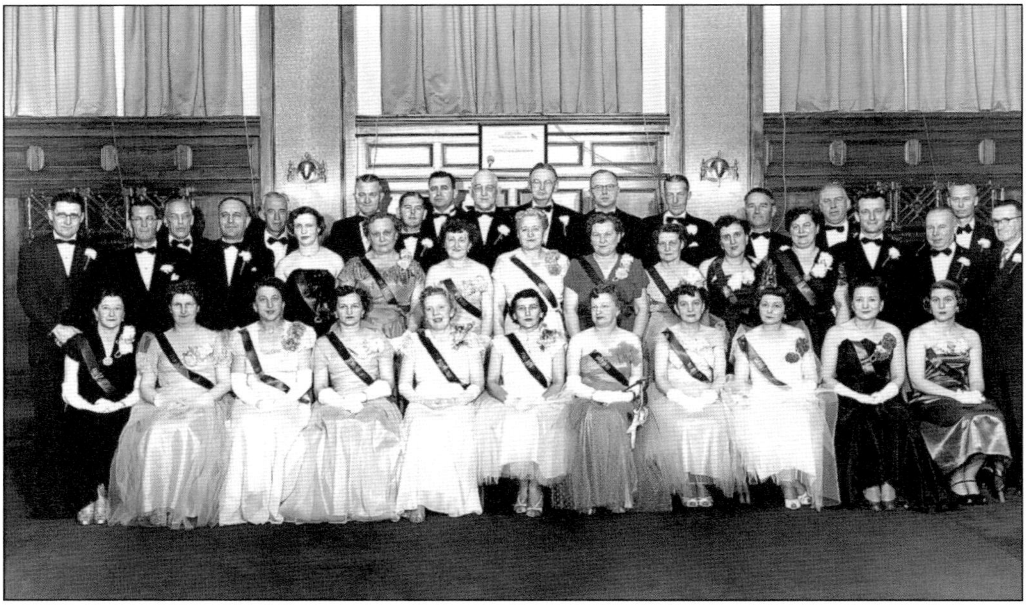

A NIGHT TO REMEMBER. This pre-1955 photograph features the Emblem Club at one of its major meetings on the second floor of the Neary Building, which is often seen in exterior views but is rarely glimpsed inside. Emblem Clubs were originally chartered in 1917, when a group of Elks ladies began meeting to wrap bandages for medical use during World War I. The Elks are officially known as the Benevolent and Protective Order of Elks.

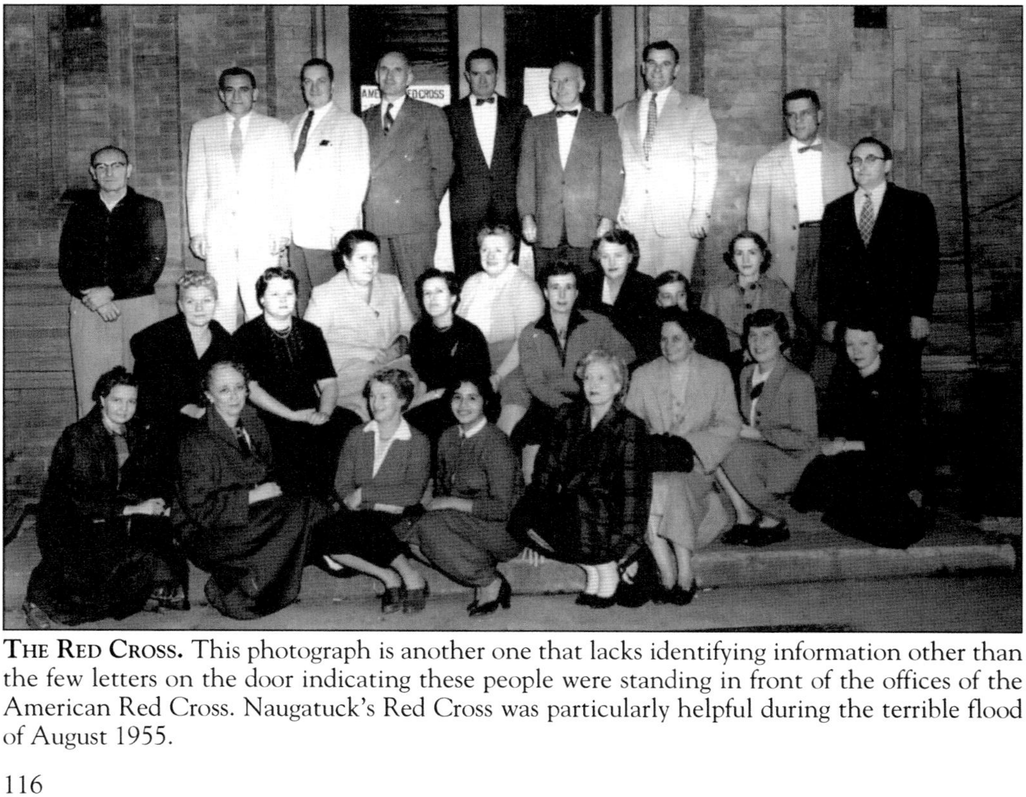

THE RED CROSS. This photograph is another one that lacks identifying information other than the few letters on the door indicating these people were standing in front of the offices of the American Red Cross. Naugatuck's Red Cross was particularly helpful during the terrible flood of August 1955.

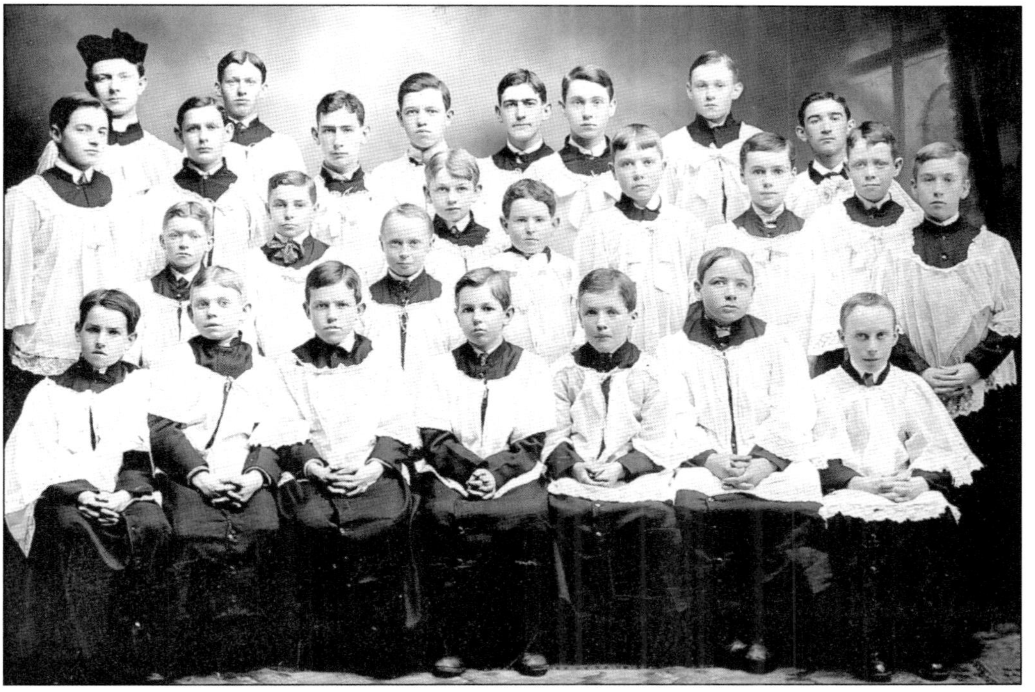

ALTAR BOYS WITH THEIR MENTOR. These angelic altar boys, with hands folded and stern faces, may be looking forward to the next mass in which they will participate. On the other hand, they may also be lamenting having to dress up in white lace to pose for the photographer and thinking about escaping to the local playground. The church and the identities of the boys and their mentor are not written on the photograph.

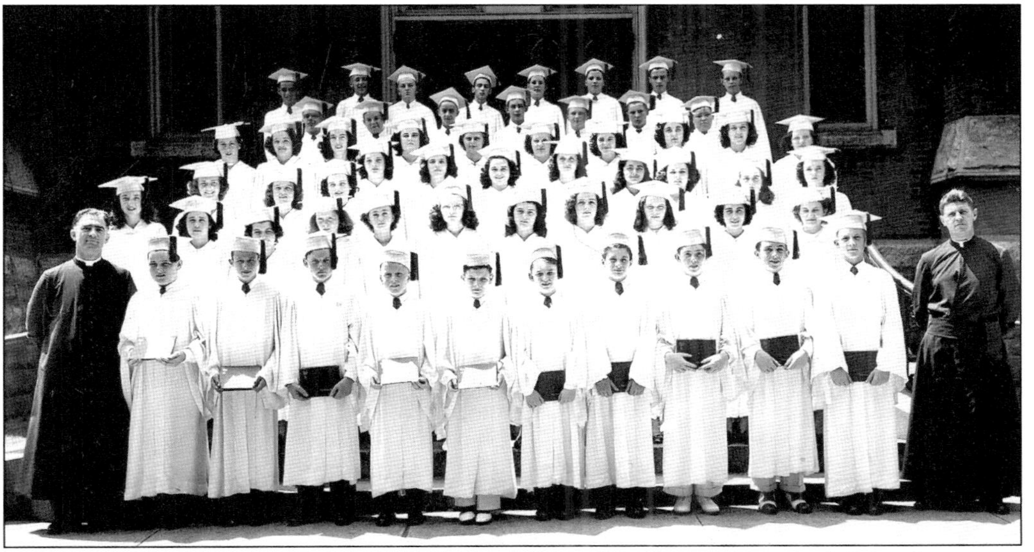

GRADUATES ON DISPLAY. The 1945 graduating class of St. Francis Parochial School poses on the steps of the church with Rev. Albert Taylor and Rev. George Dunn. Some display their diplomas. Sandra Klonoski Clark, a member of the Naugatuck Historical Society and an adviser to the author on this book, is the seventh girl from the left in the third row.

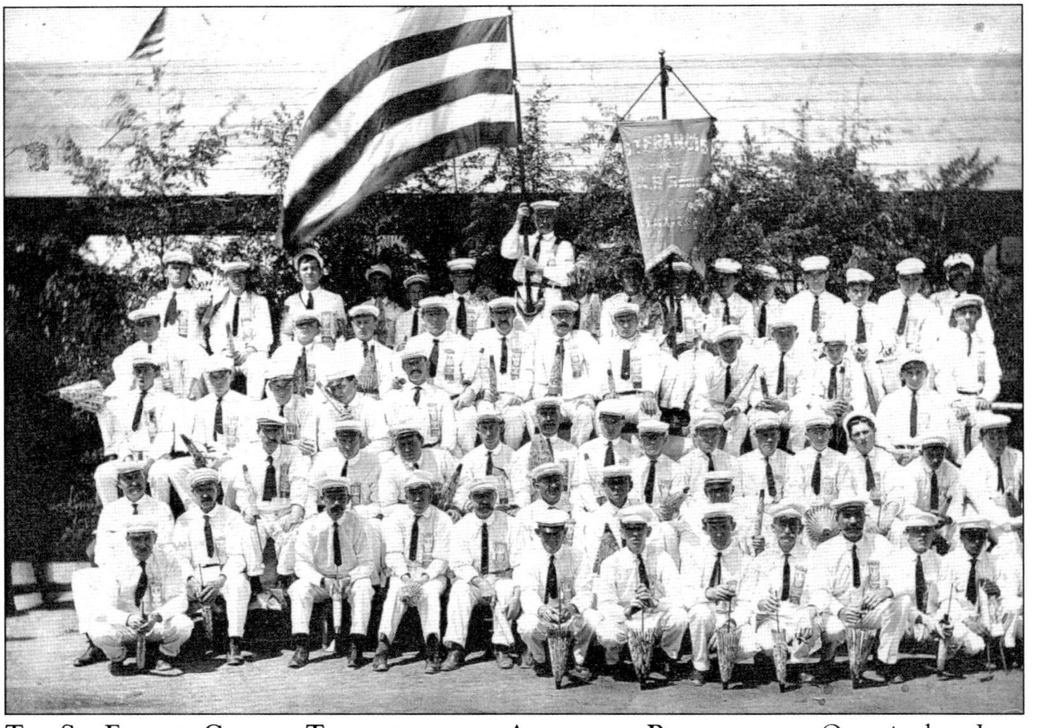

The St. Francis Church Temperance and Abstinence Brotherhood. Organized on June 24, 1899, the St. Francis Church Temperance and Abstinence Brotherhood pledged total abstinence from alcoholic beverages. The meaning of the umbrellas is unknown. There was also a female counterpart to the society. This picture was probably taken in the early 20th century.

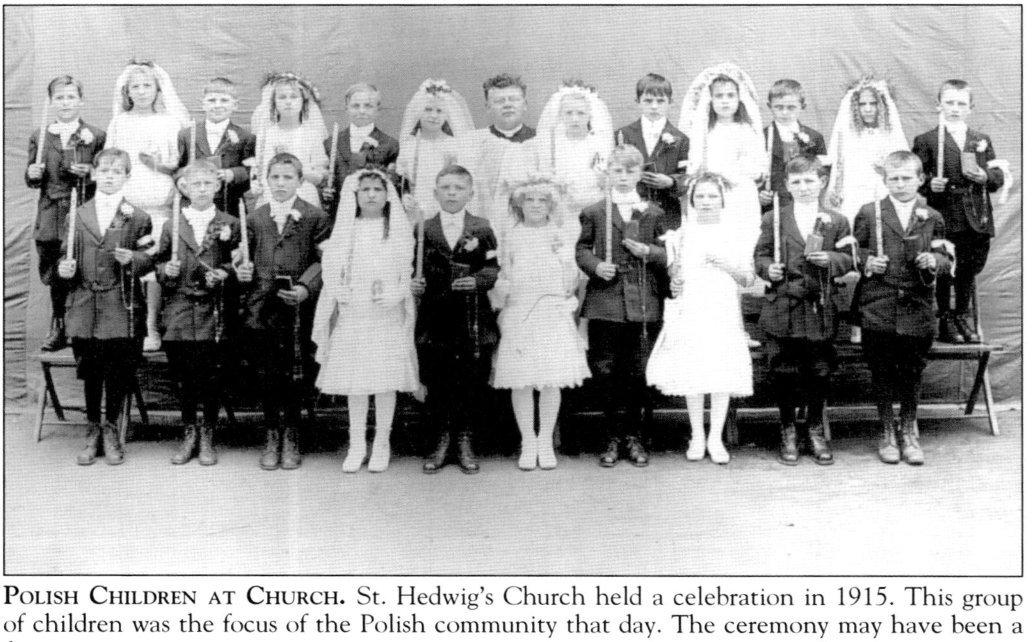

Polish Children at Church. St. Hedwig's Church held a celebration in 1915. This group of children was the focus of the Polish community that day. The ceremony may have been a first communion.

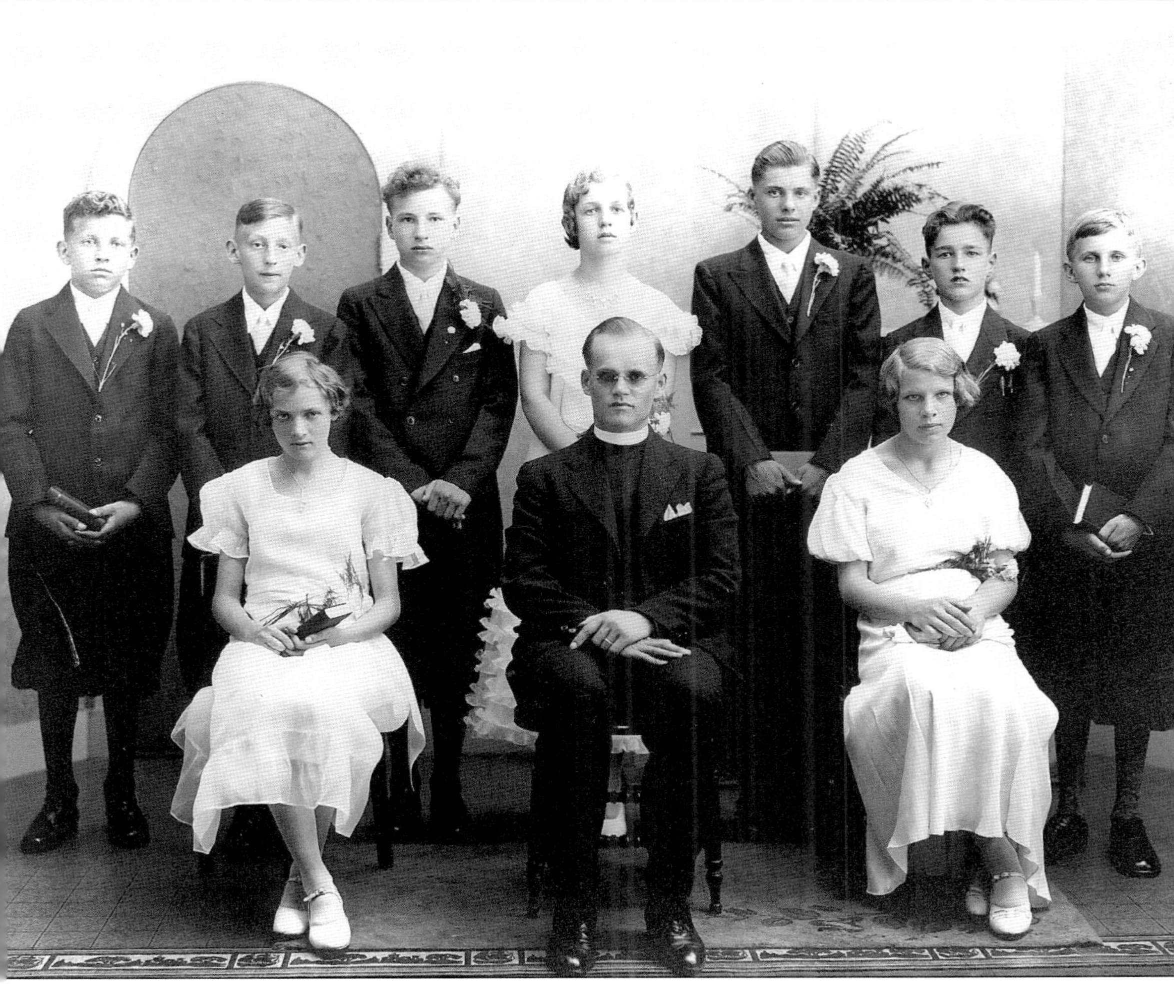

THE IMMANUEL EVANGELICAL LUTHERAN CHURCH. Organized by 14 German-born men on June 3, 1901, the Immanuel Evangelical Lutheran Church was originally located on Curtis Street. The congregation began work on the present building on High Street in November 1902. It was dedicated on July 13, 1903. In January 1934, Rev. John Frenssen (seen here in the front row) became pastor. He resigned in July 1934.

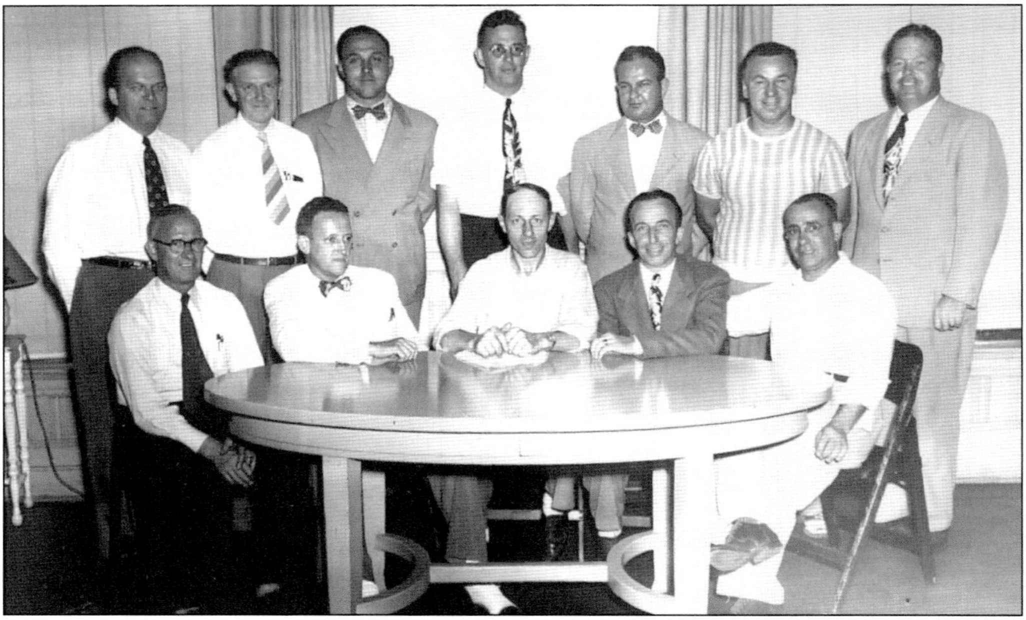

LITTLE LEAGUE BIGWIGS. This is the original board of directors of the Peter J. Foley Little League. Ralph Stotz, seated second from the left in the first row, was the brother of Carl Stotz, the founder of the Little League in Williamsport, Pennsylvania. Ralph helped Carl construct the first field in Williamsport. His founding of the Little League here made Naugatuck the first community in Connecticut to take part in what would become a worldwide phenomenon.

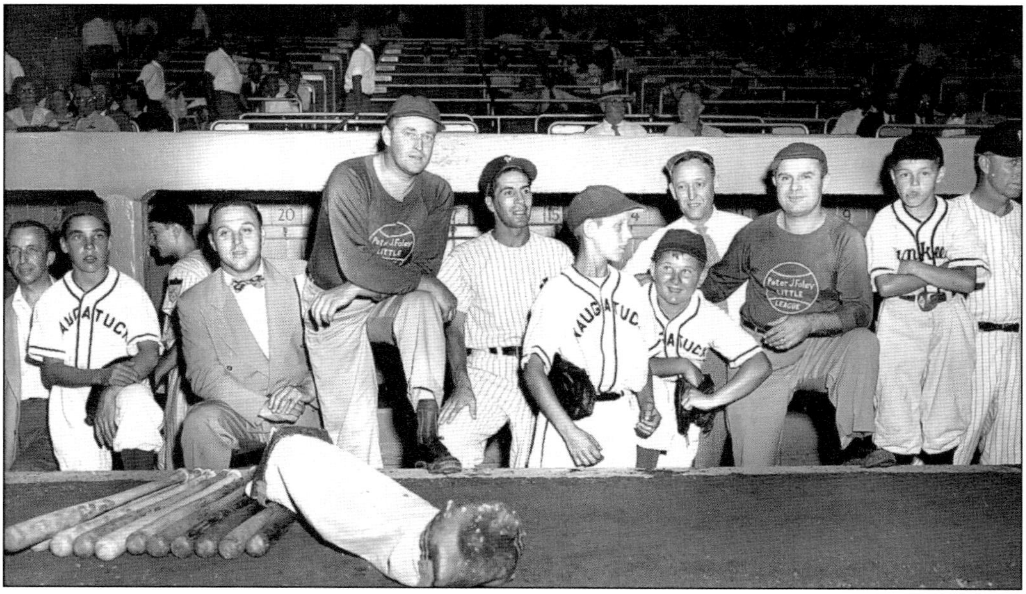

THE LITTLE LEAGUE IN THE BIG LEAGUES. One of a series of shots from the visit of the 1951 Little League All-Stars to Yankee Stadium, this image features Yankee great Phil Rizzuto surrounded by coaches and team members. The adults are, from left to right, Al Benz, Ed MacGrath, coach Dan Walsh, Phil Rizzuto, Ralph Stotz, coach Hootsie Marinello, and an unidentified Yankee (possibly Joe Collins).

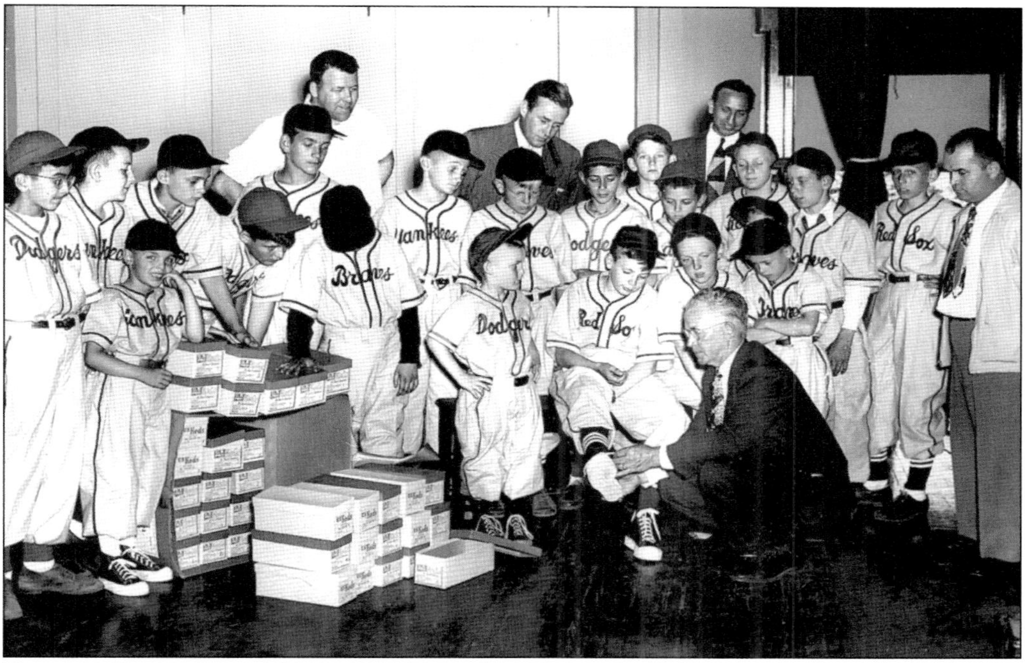

KEDS FOR KIDS. Some of the young athletes from the Naugatuck Little League gathered around a representative of U.S. Rubber to receive pairs of Keds sneakers. Keds were and still are a nationally known brand of sports footwear. They were undoubtedly given for free, probably at the start of the season, and may have been part of the company's wear-testing program.

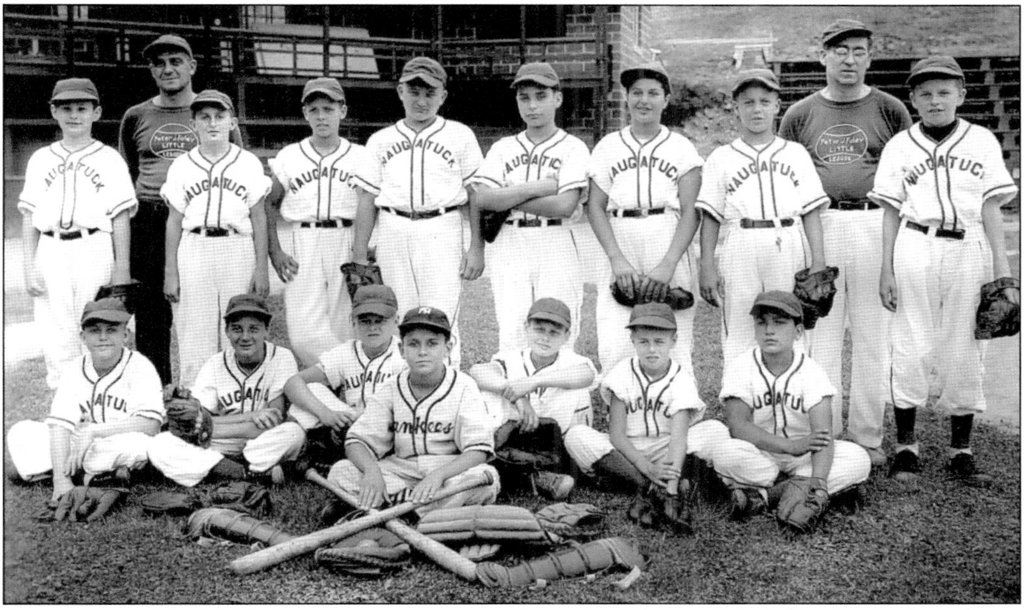

THE 1952 NAUGATUCK LITTLE LEAGUE RED SOX. In 1952, this group of all-stars was forged into a team by their coaches, including Joe Celello. Other names included Fenton, Gudauskas, Hyde, Holland, Haubrich, Kane, St. John, Slason, Olson, Oldakowski, Urashka, Weeks, Zettlemoyer, Posypanko, and Gibbs. Tom Curtin was the mascot.

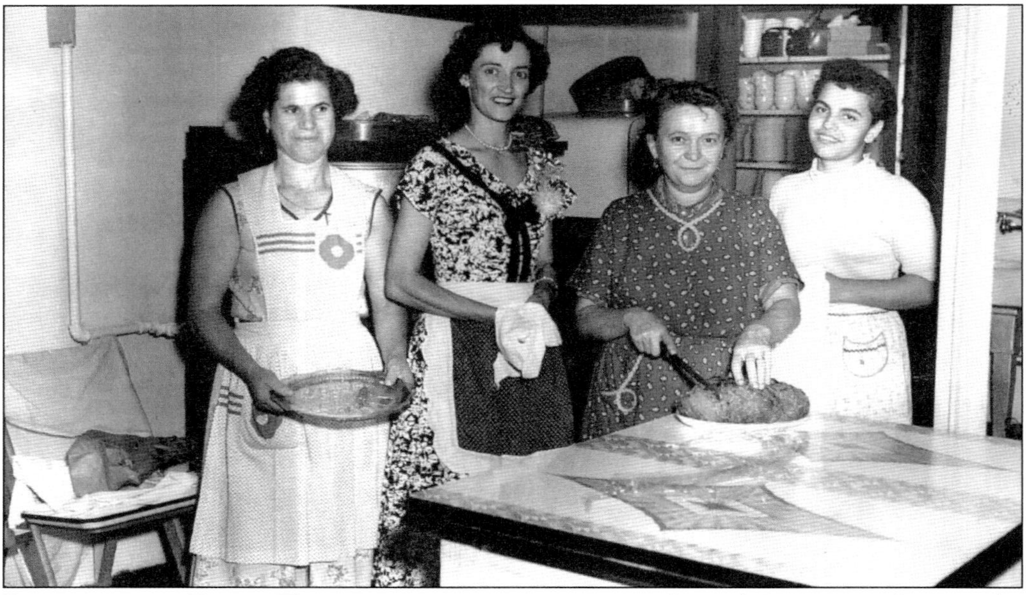

Preparing the Feast. These women are preparing a traditional Portuguese feast at the Portuguese Union Club on September 17, 1955. The club was originally housed in the Rubber Avenue School, where this photograph was taken. Their current club was later built on the site. Pictured are, from left to right, Maria Tavares, Sara Fortunato, Betty Fidalgo, and Dolores Fernandes Chepelo.

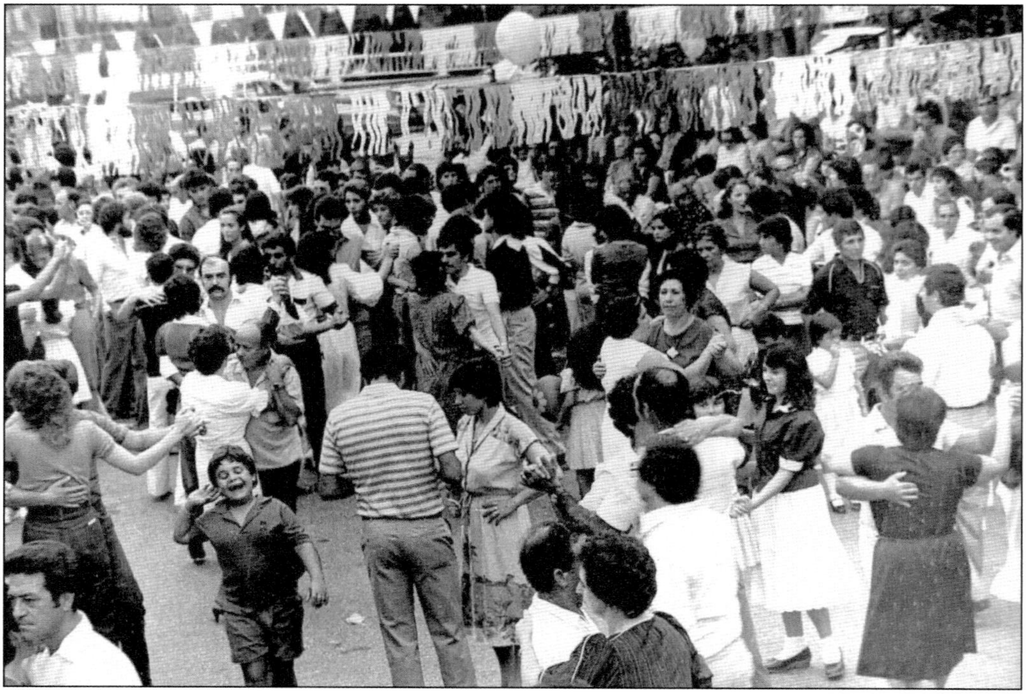

Celebration. Members of the Portuguese community are "dancing away the day" at this celebration, probably held at their club on Rubber Avenue.

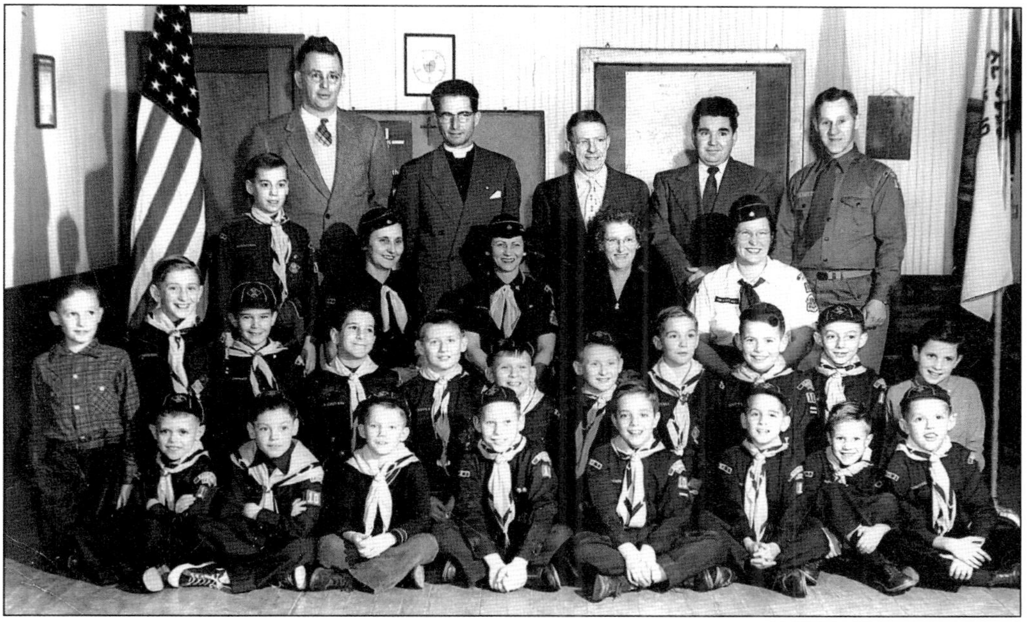

SCOUTING FOR SCOUTS. These unidentified Cub Scouts and their den fathers are seen here at a meeting at the Immanuel Lutheran Church. Perhaps a reader will be able to identify the people in this photograph.

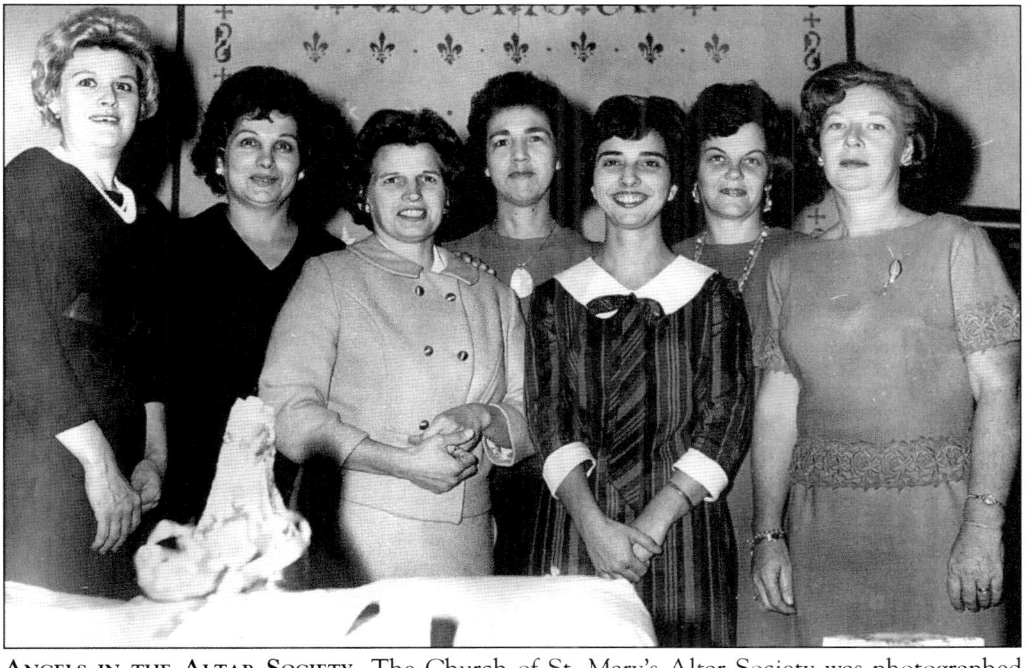

ANGELS IN THE ALTAR SOCIETY. The Church of St. Mary's Altar Society was photographed at one of its many events *c.* 1965. The group performed many valuable duties for the parish, including running fundraisers such as rummage and bake sales. The women who posed for this shot are, from left to right, Claire Harrington, Lucille Grella, "Sis" Vanasse, Lydia Schiller, Carol Suburry, Eleanor Braziel, and Eloise Gunnod.

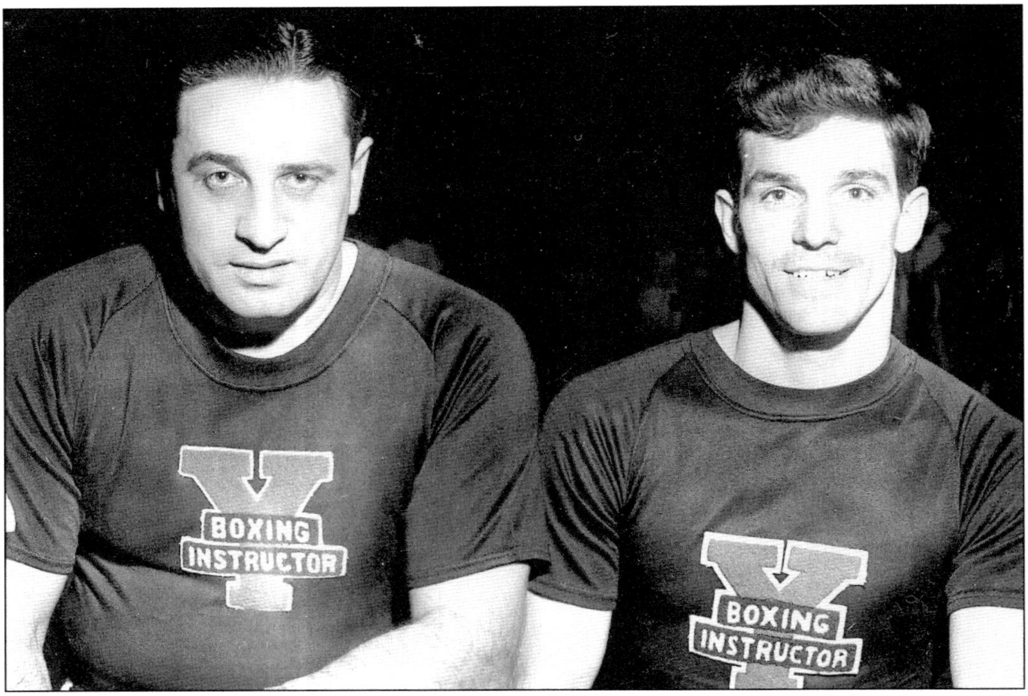

PULL NO PUNCHES. YMCAs traditionally offer many sports programs. One of the most popular ones used to be the boxing program, and it remains popular at many YMCAs. These men were the coaches for the Naugatuck program. They have been identified as Joe Triano and Eddie Martin.

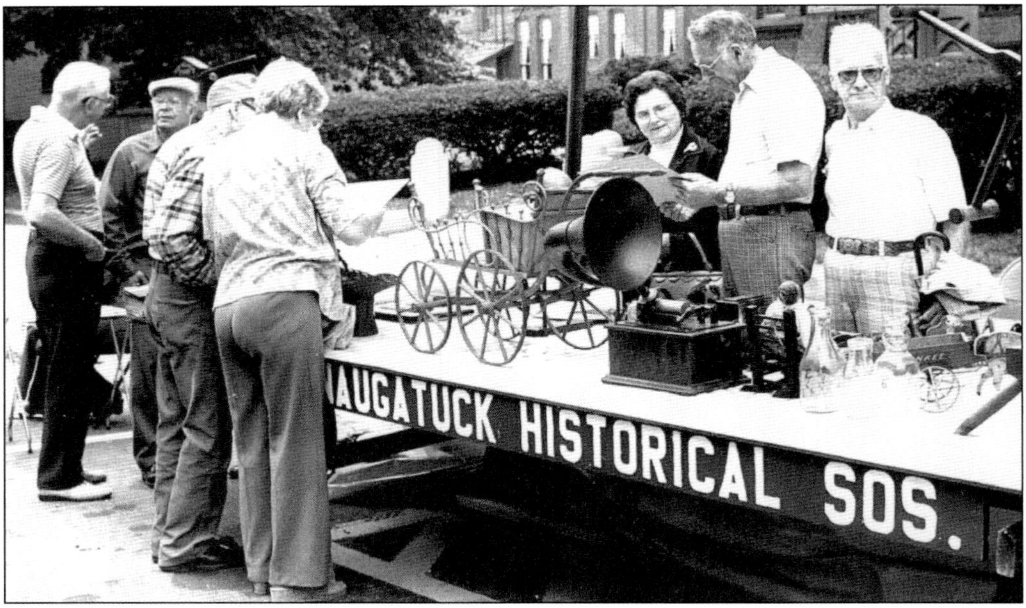

BROWSING THROUGH HISTORY. Members of the Naugatuck Historical Society gather around their booth at the 1984 Harvest Moon Festival on the green. Ann Simons, the current vice president of the society, is scrutinizing a document near the baby carriage. Nellie Kosko is the woman third from the right. Frank Kosko is the man second from the left.

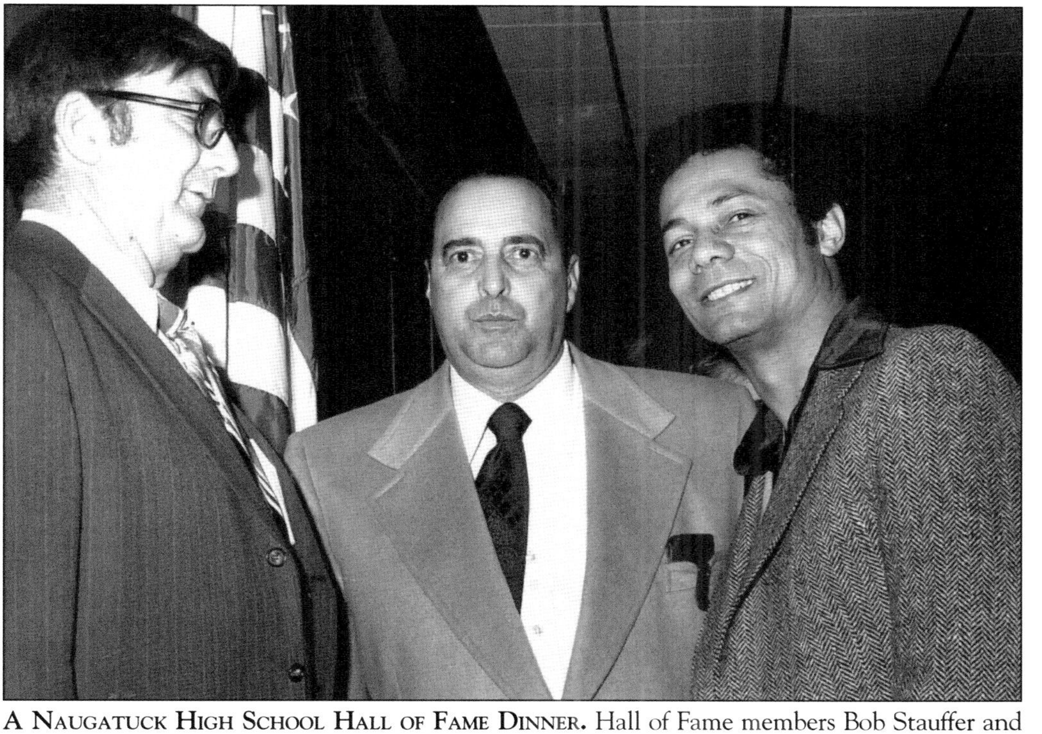

A Naugatuck High School Hall of Fame Dinner. Hall of Fame members Bob Stauffer and Manny Madeiros talk with guest speaker and New York Yankee Roy White at the 1978 dinner.

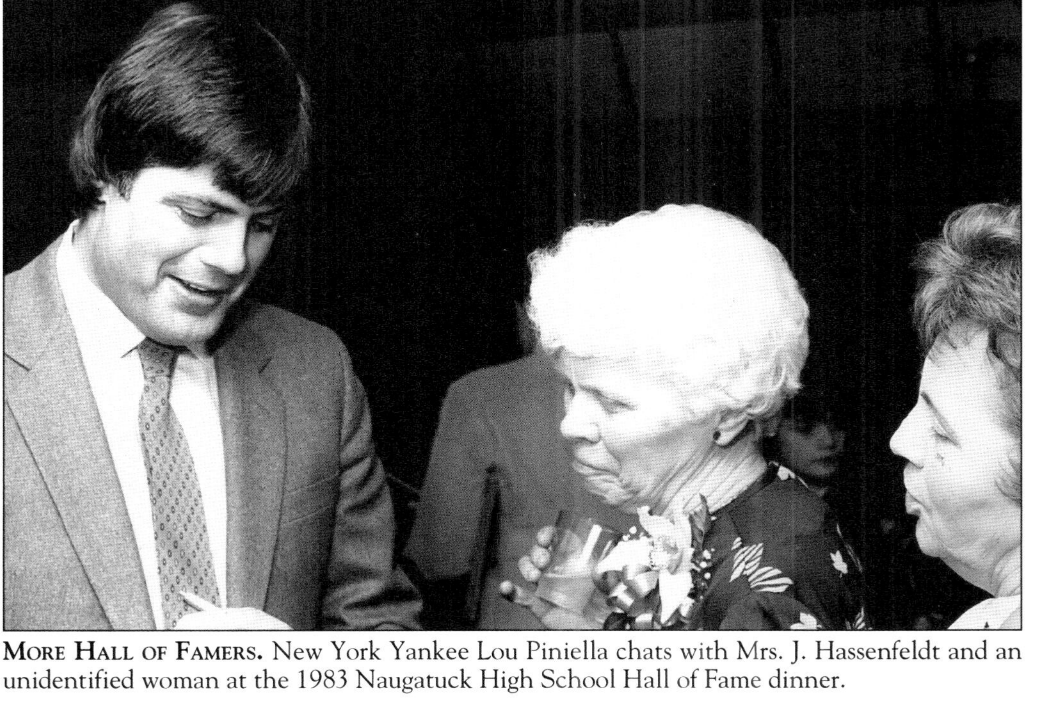

More Hall of Famers. New York Yankee Lou Piniella chats with Mrs. J. Hassenfeldt and an unidentified woman at the 1983 Naugatuck High School Hall of Fame dinner.

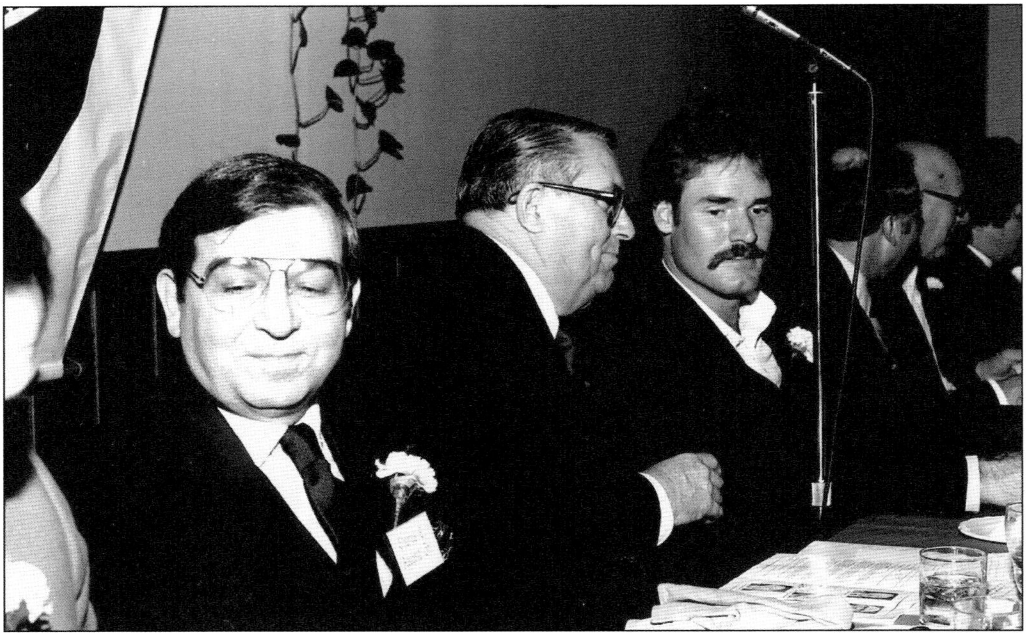

Male Bonding. Charles Aquavia Jr. sits next to former Yankee Frank "Spec" Shea and future Yankee Wade Boggs, Red Sox third baseman, in 1984.

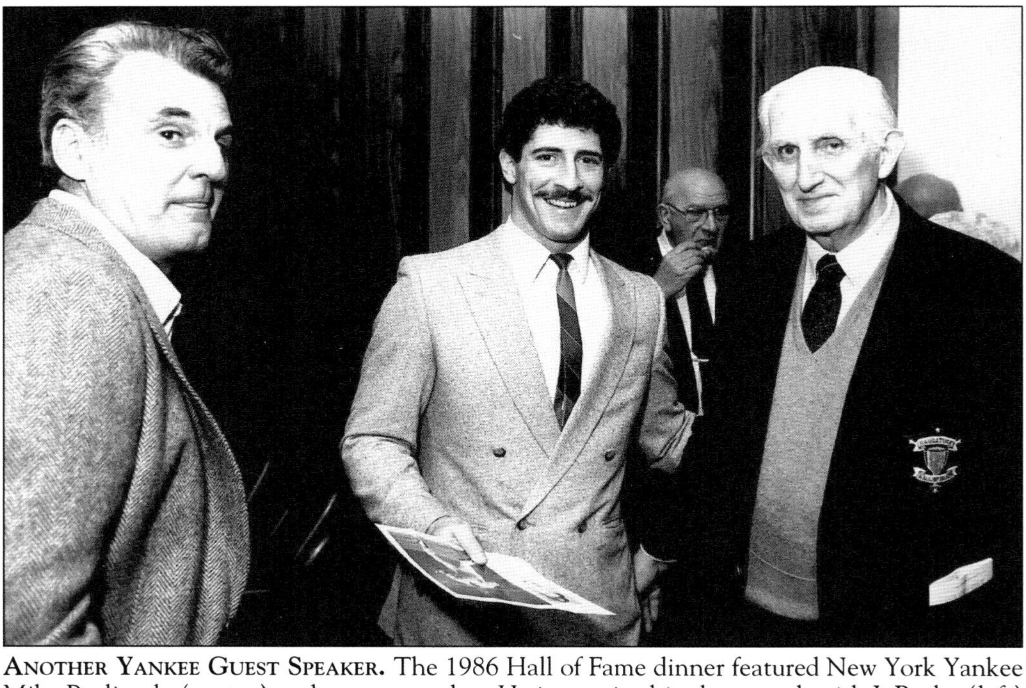

Another Yankee Guest Speaker. The 1986 Hall of Fame dinner featured New York Yankee Mike Pagliarulo (center) as the guest speaker. He is seen in this photograph with J. Butler (left) and Ray Goggin.

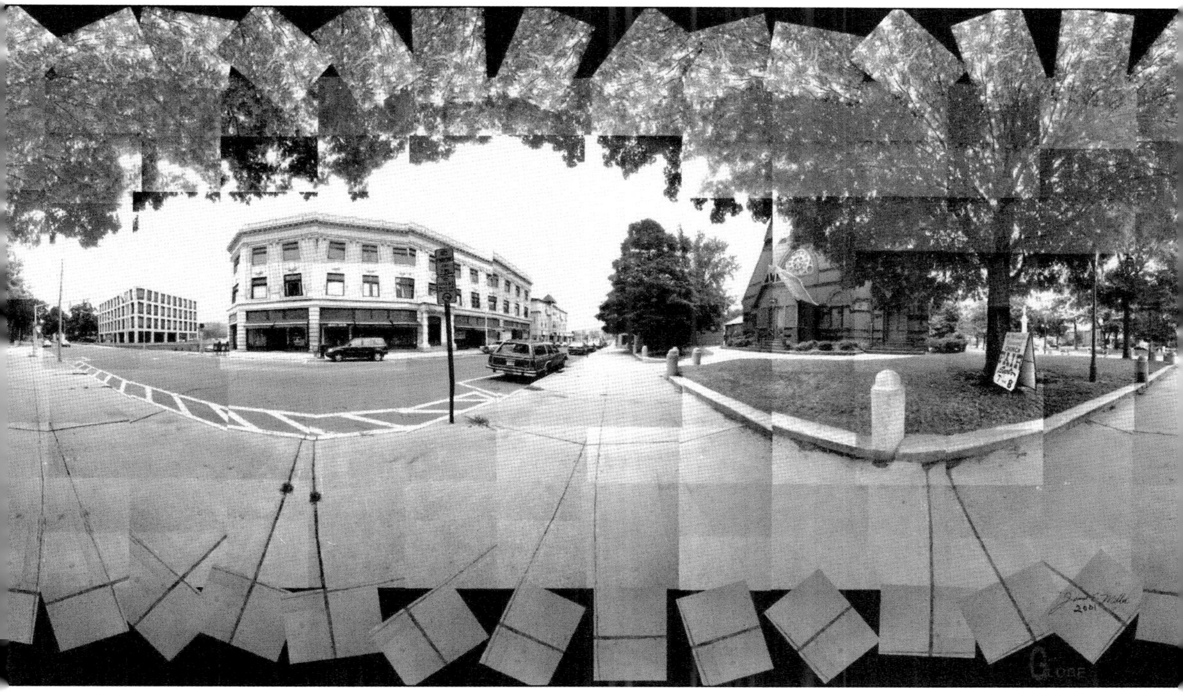

A UNIQUE VIEW OF NAUGATUCK'S CENTER. Jim Miller is a Naugatuck photographer with a one-of-a-kind eye. He takes a series of images of a scene and assembles them in a Mercator format to form a panoramic view of a particular scene. He calls them Photoglobes, and this one is a two-dimensional version. He also can transform them into a three-dimensional Photoglobe.

About the Author

Ron Gagliardi has wanted to be a writer ever since he wrote and illustrated his first children's book, *Peeblo Goes to Market*, in fourth grade. Arcadia Publishing gave him the opportunity to join the ranks of actual authors in 2001 with the publication of his first Arcadia book, *Cheshire*. That book, plus his historical background, convinced the board of directors of the Naugatuck Historical Society Museum to let him take up the banner from Dana Blackwell and crew (who wrote the first Arcadia book on Naugatuck) and to try his hand at the next installment. It also helped that Gagliardi had more than a passing interest in Naugatuck history, having served as the first executive director of the Naugatuck Historical Society Museum during 2002 and 2003.

Gagliardi is the historian of Cheshire High School and the town historian of Cheshire. He is also the public educator and archivist for the New England Carousel Museum and the assistant director of the Barker Character, Comic and Cartoon Museum. He has recently been named director of the Lock Twelve Museum at the Farmington Canal in Cheshire. He is a member of the Naugatuck Historical Society and is a lifetime member of the Cheshire Historical Society, where he serves on the board of directors. He has also served in numerous community civic groups and is currently the honorary town crier in his hometown. He is a retired elementary school art teacher with 30 years of experience and continues to teach in numerous art programs in the Cheshire area. He has lived in Cheshire with his wife, Diane, since 1972. They have two grown children, Gina DaLan and Jeff.

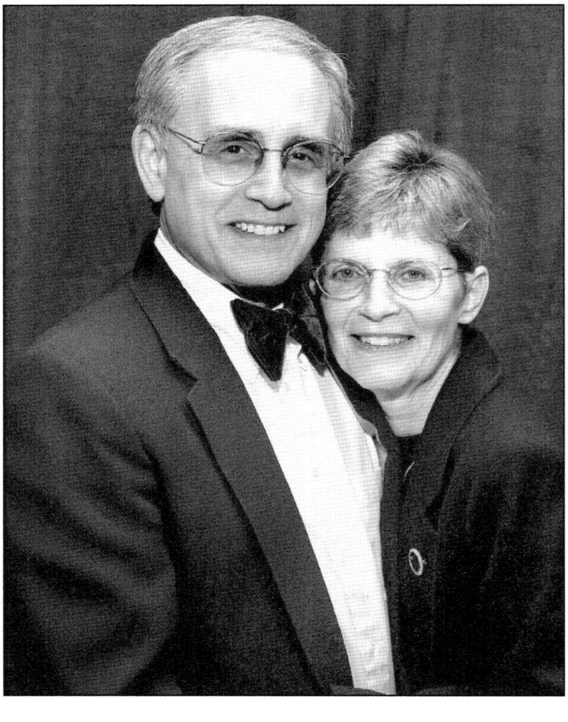

THE HAPPY COUPLE. Ron Gagliardi with his wife of 35 years, Diane, are ready to celebrate the birth of *Naugatuck Revisited*. (Photograph by Anthony Esposito.)